Cooking, Cuisine and Class

Themes in the Social Sciences

Editors: Jack Goody & Geoffrey Hawthorn

The aim of this series is to publish books which will focus on topics of general and interdisciplinary interest in the social sciences. They will be concerned with non-European cultures and with developing countries, as well as with industrial societies. The emphasis will be on comparative sociology and, initially, on sociological, anthropological and demographic topics. These books are intended for undergraduate teaching, but not as basic introductions to the subjects they cover. Authors have been asked to write on central aspects of current interest which have a wide appeal to teachers and research students, as well as to undergraduates.

Other books in the series

Edmund Leach: *Culture and Communication: The logic by which symbols are connected: an introduction to the use of structuralist analysis in social anthropology*

Anthony Heath: *Rational Choice and Social Exchange: A critique of exchange theory*

P. Abrams and A. McCulloch: *Communes, Sociology and Society*

Jack Goody: *The Domestication of the Savage Mind*

Jean-Louis Flandrin: *Families in Former Times: Kinship, household and sexuality*

John Dunn: *Western Political Theory in the Face of the Future*

David Thomas: *Naturalism and Social Science: A post-empiricist philosophy of social science*

Claude Meillassoux: *Maidens, Meal and Money: Capitalism and the domestic community*

David Lane: *Leninism: A sociological interpretation*

Anthony D. Smith: *The Ethnic Revival*

For a list of other books by Jack Goody see p. 253

Cooking, Cuisine and Class

A Study in Comparative Sociology

JACK GOODY

CAMBRIDGE UNIVERSITY PRESS

Cambridge

London   New York   New Rochelle
Melbourne   Sydney

Published by the Press Syndicate of the University of Cambridge
The Pitt Building, Trumpington Street, Cambridge CB2 1RP
32 East 57th Street, New York, NY 10022, USA
296 Beaconsfield Parade, Middle Park, Melbourne 3206, Australia

First published 1982

Printed in Great Britain at
the University Press, Cambridge

Library of Congress catalogue card number: 81–17035

British Library Cataloguing in Publication Data
Goody, Jack
Cooking, cuisine and class.—(Themes in social sciences)
1. Cookery—Social aspect
I. Title II. Series
641.5   TX651

ISBN 0–521–24455–2
ISBN 0–521–28696–4 Pbk

Contents

Illustrations

Preface

Most prefaces are postscripts, and this is no different. On reading what I have written, I need to call attention to the three points which should be made at the beginning rather than the end. First, I have used the terms 'hierarchic' and 'hieratic' to refer to those states with developed, stratified sub-cultures and those without (the crude difference, I argue, between most Eurasian and African states). Secondly, I have employed the word 'cuisine' in three distinct ways: in the general sense of the products of the kitchen, more specifically (as in the title to the book) for a culturally differentiated cuisine – the high and the low – and finally in the special-ised sense of those highly elaborated forms of cooking found in only a few societies such as China, the Middle East and post-Renaissance France. The third point is more general and arises out of a visit to Australia and South-East Asia. For the same contrast that I note between the cooking and cookbooks on Africa and Asia is found between those of New Guinea and Indonesia, for example, in Anne Mac Gregor's *Papua New Guinea Cookbook* (Milton, Queensland, 1972) and Rosemary Brissenden's *South East Asian Food* (London, 1969). The inhabitants of New Guinea, like the original inhabitants of Australia, are adopting the foods characteristic of the earlier industrial cuisine of Europe – corned beef, tinned pilchards in tomato sauce (or Japanese mackerel), heavily sweetened tea, and bread. In Indonesia the elaborate cuisine of earlier times remains largely intact, though there was an important division between the cooking of the interior 'tribes', that of the kingdoms based on intensive rice cultivation, and, as in West Africa, that of the merchant communities of the ports. In Bali the elaborate apreparation and decoration of traditional foods at temple festivals is directed at attracting the gods and their followers to come down and join in the worship. Later on the congregation retrieves their gifts, taking home the leavings of the god's table, which they call, literally, 'what is asked back'.

A visit to Australia inevitably provokes an interest in the kind of 'de-evolution' that occurs in frontier situations, in the outback, on the homestead, out west, since the search for history involves the resurrection of recipes on how to bake your own damper and instructions on how to build your own dunny. But that theme, like many other such topics, must await a future occasion.

I am conscious that while I have given notes for my written sources, I have not acknowledged my oral ones. Since this book was half-intended to be an inaugural lecture, I should begin by expressing my thanks to my colleagues at Cambridge, first to my earlier ones, especially to Audrey Richards, Meyer Fortes and Edmund Leach, and secondly to my present ones, especially to Gilbert Lewis and Stephen Hugh-Jones who have provided references and comments. Martha Mundy, Asha Sarabhai, David McMullen and John Iliffe, among others, have saved me from a number of errors. Kum Gandah and Suhrid Sarabhai have made field trips pleasurable and stimulating experiences. Cathie Roth, Anne Robson, Jane Moon, Norman Buck of St John's College Library, the librarians of the Haddon Library and the Center for Advanced Studies in the Behavioral Sciences, among others, have helped with the production. Esther Goody participated in the fieldwork, developed some of the ideas, read an earlier version and made many valuable comments. And I am especially in debt to Patricia Williams and Geoffrey Hawthorn who rightly insisted on the need for more work than I had intended.

Cambridge, November 1981   JACK GOODY

TO MY MITHER,

who like many good Scots, and to the greater benefit of her children, showed more interest in other things. However she learnt some cooking from one of her many older sisters, Edith Rankine, whose recipe book was the outcome of a course in nursing and records with startling clarity the imprint of empire on British tastes. It begins with Skink Soup, and goes on to Girdle Scones, Pitcaithly Bannocks, Curry of Cold Meat, American Dough Nuts, Imperial Biscuits, English Stew, Welsh Cheese Cakes, Fish Kedgeree, Russian Fish Pie,...

AND TO MY DAUGHTERS,

Joanna and Jane, whose various concerns with food, professional and spiritual, have been deeply affected by the imperial past and the international present.

1

Intentions and remarks

This essay started life as an inaugural lecture, at least in contemplation. That is to say, while I had little intention of delivering such a discourse, I did have a general audience in mind, one that would not only want to hear the details of a distant culture in which I had worked over many years, but would wish to know something of the general trends of recent work, including my own, and how these discussions took their place in the wider field of social anthropology and the social sciences. I took as my topic one that was receiving attention from a variety of scholars and approaches, that of food, mainly the cooked but also the raw. The subject linked up with the broad contrast between the domestic economies of Europe and Asia on the one hand and Africa on the other, which I had previously tried to examine in terms of the relationships between family systems and modes of production, as well as between oral and literate cultures, that is, in terms of modes of communication. I have tried to present this contrast in as direct a way as I can, perhaps over-simply. Today so much writing in the humanities and social sciences consists in unnecessary obfuscation that is often a way of disguising intellectual problems rather than illuminating them. Subtlety is not a function of obscurity.

The question behind the present essay can be stated in a few words. Why are traditional African cultures largely lacking a differentiated cuisine, even in great states with differentiated political structures? What are the conditions for the emergence of a high and a low cuisine? These questions are neither frivolous nor yet of purely historical interest. The answer bears upon the differences between African and Eurasian societies today and upon the strategies to be used to change or to preserve them.

The form this essay takes can be seen as an expression of anthropological experience, both my own and that of others. It begins with a discussion of general approaches to the subject, those that have dominated the area of interest and have shaped my own enquiry. Here I argue for the contextualisation of social theory, which needs to be linked more closely with the methods and the ends of the enquiry; the potential contribution of apparently alternative approaches has to be assessed in terms of the analysis in hand. Then I look at cooking in two African societies in which I myself have lived and worked, since my understanding of those cultures provides the point of departure for the empirical questioning. It was dissatisfaction with one formal account of the 'African cuisine' that led me to realise the need, first, to analyse cooking in the context of the total process of production, preparation and consumption of food, and, secondly, to set this analysis within a comparative perspective. Contextualisation is especially important in looking at the African cuisine comparatively, because it raises the question of hierarchical, regional and temporal variations. But, comparative analysis apart, these considerations are relevant even in understanding the meaning of a mode of cooking to the people concerned, since at one level its characterisation involves 'placing' oneself in relation to others, as the English do in referring to 'mother's cooking', to 'Yorkshire recipes' and to the 'English cuisine'; for the actor's context itself is not limited to the set of internal relations of a particular culture, even where that culture can be considered as relatively undifferentiated. The smaller the group, the greater the boundary problems and the less one can ignore the cuisine of one's neighbours. In any case, even in Africa, ingredients have been imported and exported for centuries, especially low-volume, high-priced items like salt, spices and medicines of various kinds. And over the last hundred years the food of that continent has influenced and been influenced by the modes of consumption in industrialised countries. From Ghana cocoa is imported into Europe, America and the Soviet Union; in turn French cube sugar, Portuguese sardines, Italian tomato paste, American corn, are virtually 'staples' of the Ghanaian urban diet, while Yugoslav tractors, Bulgarian wine, Chinese bicycles and Polish conserves have been prominent elements in the recent repertoire of imported consumer goods.

After looking at the wider context of the consumption in northern Ghana, I turn for comparison and contrast to some major Eurasian societies. Here, I narrow down the enquiry to one aspect of the phase of consumption, that is, the cuisine itself. In doing so I try to bring out the relevance of the nature of the system of stratification, its link with the productive processes and the role of the means of communication in formulating and formalising a cuisine. The central contrast is between a social system, even a state (a hieratic one), with minimal cultural differentiation, and one comprising a hierarchy of estates, castes or classes, with differences in styles of life of such significance as to produce sub-cultures.

In the two following chapters I outline the development of the industrial production of food that now bears so forcefully upon the Third World both as producers of the raw materials and as receivers of the finished product. In advanced countries the industrial process and its related modes of communication, such as mass newspapers, radio and, especially, television, have almost erased many of the external boundaries defining areas of food consumption, as well as rubbing out some of the internal differences between classes and regions. The large-scale importation of foreign produce enables the masses of today to enjoy the luxuries of yesterday's rich. These products are the fruits of the labour of individuals located in poorer countries, and the internal differences in the living standards of the inhabitants of industrial countries have decreased, at least in the initial phases, at the expense of the growth of the gap in consumption between regions and nations, and within those of the Third World. This gap is now beginning to make its appearance even in northern Ghana. For here too the local rich are shifting to international standards while the bulk of the people live at a quite different level of existence, certainly more adequate than in pre-colonial times but far removed from that of their better-off compatriots. Up to the present such differences have not greatly affected the daily meal, even though the social environment of eating varies very greatly.

I look at these contemporary problems before returning to the general question of the differences in cuisine in pre-colonial times, by which I mean the period covering the expansion of Europe over the last five hundred years. The progression is important. For I do not see anthropology as concerned only with the pre-literate or with pre-industrial societies, either by design or by default. For me it is the comparative study of socio-cultural systems in which Nottingham is as relevant as the Nuer. Even confining the field to 'other cultures', we would still no longer be dealing with pre-industrial societies when we are carrying out observational studies. Communities of human beings are not like groups of monkeys; there are no societies in the world today that remain uninfluenced by the world system, that is, by the industrial economy and by the political developments of colonial empires and the independent or quasi-independent nations that succeeded them. If we want to observe or experience the 'simpler societies', we have to study the Third World, whether we like it or not. A scholar who undertakes a field study, even in the most remote area and among the most exotic peoples, needs to acquire some knowledge of how the local relationships articulate with the wider network if he is to understand his data.

On the other hand, in order to understand pre-industrial societies, as distinct from (though the distinction is never absolute) the non-industrial segments of the larger world that we now tend to observe, it is becoming increasingly necessary to turn to evidence of a different kind. You cannot do fieldwork in the past; and 'oral history' needs to be weighed against documentary, archaeological and linguistic research. Immersion in fieldwork becomes of less immediate relevance for the reconstruction of earlier social systems, whether of the Inca, the Ashanti or the Rajputs, though, as Marc Bloch insisted, the walk over the fields should always remain part of the work of the social historian, even the historian of the distant past.

I do not see these various kinds of enquiry, traditional or modern, past or present, documentary or observational, as radical alternatives. After all, they are fields or methods of enquiry rather than modes of understanding. Nor do I see either fields or methods as attached in any exclusive way to particular academic disciplines. Social anthropology is committed to a combination of intensive and extensive approaches. Extensive, because to understand any particular society, one needs to have some understanding of the social structure of that type of society in general. But there is also a direct benefit to be derived from intensive sociological experience of a society other than one's own, and even enquiry into past structures (the dying if not the dead) needs to be comparative and analytic, an undertaking that involves the study of 'other cultures'. But the contemporary situation, here or in Africa, is also the proper subject of our study, one that may need to be pursued by extensive as well as intensive methods. Once again such an enquiry needs to be set within a comparative framework, both of a spatial and a temporal kind, a task that social anthropology should be one of the most qualified of the social sciences to undertake.

If the form of this essay retraces the life experiences of many anthropologists, from the general studies of the university student, to the particularities of fieldwork as a graduate, to the subsequent effort at a wider synthesis, the general approach reflects my understanding of social anthropology as a branch of comparative sociology. Hence the significance of the title I gave, not only to this 'lecture' but much earlier to my first dissertation at Oxford, 'The sociology of the Lobi'. To put the point in another way, I regard both sociology and social anthropology as falling under the heading of comparative sociology. Few of my colleagues, here or elsewhere, would agree. The Americans among them often see themselves as studying 'culture' rather than 'society', a forced choice that I see as either 'polemical' or else irrelevant, but certainly not as substantive.[1] The British among them often regard their field as 'other cultures' or 'other societies', especially 'simple', 'tribal', 'rural' ones. The French, who regard most Anglo-Saxon endeavours as overly 'empiricist' and insufficiently 'theoretical', avoid a direct confrontation with this particular issue, having at their backs the range and the depth of the *Année Sociologique* and the School of Durkheim.

The widespread idea that the field of social anthropology lies in the study of *other* cultures is bolstered by various practical considerations, such as the myopia that often accompanies an enquiry into one's own kind, a myopia that derives from self-identification, the constraints of one's linguistic concepts, and the reluctance to undertake intensive fieldwork ('we know it already'). But such talk may also conceal a plain love of the exotic, the different, even though the exploration of the other is in some sense an exploration of self, cultural and individual, through an investigation of alternative possibilities, the functional equivalents in human living; in another way, of course, it can also be a flight from the realities into which one was born and raised. Whatever gains this particular process of understanding may provide, and useful as many find the technique of participant observation, neither the limitation to one set of societies nor to one set of techniques seems to be an adequate way of defining a specific field of study. This is especially true of today's world. The logical extension of these limitations would mean modes of enquiry different in essence (not just in particulars) for each nation or for each continent. For we Europeans are what Africans see as 'other cultures', their exotic societies; we are (from one viewpoint) their 'primitives', their 'ethnics'. Nor does an attachment to the technique of intensive research, in a world of increasing differentiation, offer any solution in the long term. The problem is not one for anthropology alone but for all those fields of study (theology, history, literature and the like) whose roots lay in the period when the world system was marked by the intellectual as well as the politico-economic domination of the West. The rationale for sociology's field of interest is equally in doubt, a function of its western past and its indecisive present.

It may be that the separation of sociology from anthropology will continue to exist in those western countries where the pre-industrial components were either totally annihilated (as was effectively the case with hunters and simple agriculturalists in America and Australia) or else thoroughly incorporated at a much earlier period (as with 'peasants' in England and the Low Countries). It seems unlikely that this dissociation of academic sensibility will become established in Africa or Asia, and it seems unhealthy that it should exist at all. While we can profit from specialisation, there can hardly be different *logoi* (logics) for societies of the same (human) species – as if we had different psychologies or anatomies for blacks and for whites, or for developed and underdeveloped, for men and for women.

It is true that another possible line of differentiation exists, based not upon the 'relativity' of the 'other cultures' view but upon the 'absolute' character of long-term development. In the USSR, anthropology (or rather ethnology) was defined as the study of pre-capitalist social formations.[2] And it is a view, phrased in terms of pre-industrial societies,

5

that is commonly held elsewhere. But a *purely* 'historical' definition is unlikely to find much favour with those who see themselves primarily as social scientists involved in a process of enquiry based upon fieldwork, a process that includes the observation, analysis and explanation of behaviour. Even those who see the study of past societies as an essential part of anthropo-sociology would be unhappy at the idea of the subject as a kind of generalising, comparative history (whether this be 'ethnohistory' or 'graphohistory'), without any direct observational component. In some areas of enquiry the concentration on secondary, written sources (what the historian refers to as 'primary sources' or the sociologist 'questionnaires') is a poor substitute for watching, participating and asking. Moreover this 'ethological' experience (with the linguistic and participant supplements that turn it into an 'ethnological' one) is valuable in making judgements even about quite different societies, in getting a sense of the 'social system', of the nature of 'social relations', quite apart from any more specific advantages it may have.

The ability to place abstract concepts in a particular empirical context, to offer a non-western perspective, to formulate an initial hypothesis linking this with that – these are useful (if not essential) attributes to bring to any study with wider comparative implications. At the same time such studies cannot be restricted to a specific range of 'dead' societies because some problems inevitably point in another direction and require the collection of data in the field. For a comparative sociology we need to consider both the present and the past, and to elaborate appropriate hypotheses, concepts and techniques for their study. These must obviously vary according to the problem in hand, so that we cannot be satisfied with any approach that attempts to limit the range of the society or technique at our disposal. We must reject definitions that predetermine the scope of the analysis by placing societies in simplistic binary categories, whether of European and 'other' cultures, savage and advanced, simple and complex, traditional and modern, industrial and pre-industrial, anthropological and sociological. And we must reject a definition that prevents us from combining intensive, extensive, historical and comparative techniques of research in the investigation of a single problem.

With these preliminary remarks in mind I want briefly to review some aspects of the sociology of cooking as a way of sketching certain developments that have taken place in social anthropology over the last half-century, developments that in Britain are sometimes seen in terms of a movement from the functionalism of Malinowski through to the structuralism (1) (or functional-structuralism) of Radcliffe-Brown to the structuralism (2) of Lévi-Strauss.[3]

Intentions and remarks

Let us briefly consider how we should view these particular lexemes, these 'isms', these single words offered as descriptions of approaches to the social sciences and which are taken by some as denoting 'theories'. The prospectus for a recent journal on 'theory' in the social sciences expresses the founders' hopes

> to present the vital front of sociological theory, across the range of dialectical and critical sociologies, neo-Marxism and conflict theory, social phenomenology and ethnomethodology, linguistic sociology, historical sociology, structuralism, mathematical and positivistic sociology, and the new departures that continually appear.

It is difficult to see these terms as designating 'theories' in the more usual sense in which this word is employed. We are dealing with general orientations (or even with topics of study) which require some more inclusive description than the word 'theory', so often used only for its prestigious associations. 'Approaches', perhaps, might be a more accurate designation, since we are not dealing with any testable assertions, nor even general paradigms, but rather with a variety of modes of attack which each have their gains and their costs but which rarely constitute analytic alternatives. Gellner's comment on functionalism is appropriate here: '"Functionalism" is only a theory in a very loose sense, of a formal rather than a substantive paradigm.' And again: 'the importance of functionalism lay not in its doctrine, which was quite unspecific in its failure to locate that mysterious mid-point, but in summarising and conveying a certain state of mind and research strategy – *look for* the way in which institutions reinforce each other and favour stability!' (Gellner 1974: 1166–7). At this level a new theory often takes the general shape of an earlier one. Gestalt theory appears in a different garb as systems theory; aspects of Marxist theory re-emerge once more in various forms of neo-Marxism; evolutionary theory goes out with structural–functionalism and comes back in the framework of comparative analysis. There is indeed a feeling of *déjà-vu,* a perception in the field of ideology (or theory) of the cycles that were distinguished by the philosopher Spengler and the historian Toynbee among the great civilisations, by the anthropologists Leach and Gluckman among the Kachin hills of Burma and the flood plains of the Zambesi, and by Fortes and others among humbler domestic groups throughout the world. The continuous creation of 'theories' implied in the prospectus displays some of the characteristics of a merry-go-round, defining 'new directions' more precisely than 'new achievements'.

Cycles are by definition non–cumulative, except in a purely quantitative sense. Are we right to observe a lack of theoretical progression? On the most inclusive level the answer is probably that little cumulative

7

advance can be perceived, only change, a revolving world of non-revolutionary movement. It is on a less general level that advances have been made. To take a restricted area, no one familiar with the development of the study of, say, kin groups, prescriptive marriage or the development cycle would deny that advances had been made over the past thirty years, whatever detailed criticism they may have of the present state of play. Such advances have been associated with individuals identified in their turn as functionalists or structuralists. But the relationship between the general 'theory' on the one hand and more substantive interest or specific hypothesis on the other is rarely clear; especially since a new approach is almost invariably stated (and if not stated, seen) in terms of its opposition to previous ones. That of course is understandable; a new path has to branch off an existing track, and by doing so proclaims its independence or its individuality.

The fact that one element in the emergence of new sociological theory consists of the statement of opposition to the present establishment, and that this process is often cyclical, 'repetitive' in Max Gluckman's characterisation of rebellions contrasted with revolutions (1955: 46), suggests a rather different function for such theory than the paradigmatic changes or gestalt shifts discussed by the historian of science Thomas Kuhn in his book, *The Structure of Scientific Revolutions* (1962). Instead of the revolutions of natural science, we find the rebellions of the social sciences. Rather than crystallising existing knowledge and offering a model for future experimental and intellectual work, such changes indicate a shift of emphasis between possibilities that lie permanently embedded in the analysis of sociological material, e.g. between the actor's or observer's point of view,[4] between qualitative and quantitative methods,[5] between synchronic and diachronic analysis, between the study of surface and deep structure, and so forth. In other words, these polemical shifts may serve to redirect research energy into neglected channels, but in very different ways from the paradigm shifts discussed by Kuhn (as indeed he himself recognises). For they affect 'normal science' in a highly generalised way; they act as signposts, often pointing out a vague direction, rather than serving as a constraining model, a map for new discoveries, a reformulation of past knowledge.

We could, then, easily reduce recent developments in social anthropology to an absurd caricature by thinking of three dominant paradigms as functionalist, structuralist and Marxist. Numerous qualifications would need to be made. There are after all structural-functionalists, post-structuralists, structural-Marxists, as well as 'Marxisant' functionalists and cultural materialists. But while Kuhn's notion of the predominant paradigm is hardly satisfactory for discussing the social sciences, one can point to modes of analysis and explanation that are *influenced* by these three main approaches, even though at the level of theoretical practice there are many continuities. These trends are discernable in the sociology of cooking as well as in the larger fields of the sociology of food and of modes of consumption, and it is to a discussion of the specific contributions to this topic that I now turn.

2

State of play

The intention of this chapter is not to provide a synopsis of anthropological thought but to sketch out the kinds of attention that anthropologists have given to the study of 'food' over the years, partly as a guide to the general reader, partly to spell out the background to my own interest. After looking briefly at the contributions of nineteenth-century scholars I comment upon work done in the functionalist and structural-functional traditions of British anthropology. But it is the work of the structuralists, and particularly of Lévi-Strauss, that demands more detailed attention, since notions of the 'cooked' and the 'raw' play such a central part in his analysis; more generally the domain of cooking itself has been used to demonstrate the validity of an approach modelled on linguistic binarism.

THE PRECURSORS

In the nineteenth century anthropological interest in food centred largely upon questions of taboo, totemism, sacrifice and communion, that is, essentially on religious aspects of the process of consumption. Typical of this concern was the work of that famous Cambridge figure, Sir James Frazer (1854–1941), who was induced to write articles on taboo and totemism for the ninth edition of *Encyclopaedia Britannica* when its distinguished editor, Robertson Smith, joined him at Trinity High Table after his career in Scotland had been cut short by the appearance of his notorious article under the heading 'Bible'. In 1907, following the successful publication of *The Golden Bough* in 1890, Frazer's desire to produce more reliable evidence for his comparative purposes led him to issue a little pamphlet (based on an earlier document that had been privately circulated) which he entitled *Questions on the Customs, Beliefs and Languages of Savages,* and of which at least three editions were printed by Cambridge University Press. The section on Food begins with the questions 'Do they eat everything edible? Or are certain foods forbidden?' The catechism continues, though on a mundane level, until we reach section 138. 'Is cannibalism practised? Do they eat their enemies or their friends?' The theme has never lost its interest, especially for those studying the Highlands of New Guinea[1] and for those with psychoanalytic inclinations.[2]

Similar interests marked the work of Ernest Crawley (1869–1924) in *The Mystic Rose* (1902), a book that stressed the close relationship between sex and food. Crawley was mainly concerned with the religious aspects (and specifically the spiritual dangers) of sexual relations, symbolised by the Maiden-Mother, the Mystical Rose, whose figure 'enshrines many elemental conceptions of man and woman' (1927: ii, 261). He also includes a long section on Commensual Relations, which attempts to answer the question, put after the fashion of Plutarch, 'Why, according to a very general custom, are husbands and wives, brothers and sisters, required to avoid each other in one or more ways, and why, in particular may they not eat together?' The answer, of course, is framed in terms of the mystery of sex. While the organisation of the table clearly relates to the economy, to the polity and to the wider domestic domain, these activities hold little interest for him. The processes of production and reproduction are neglected in favour of consumption, that is of food and sex, and interpreted largely in mystical, or at least 'symbolic' terms.

In 1929 and 1931, Crawley published two further 'studies in social anthropology', the first of which was called *Studies of Savages and Sex,* a snappy title that bears a close kinship to that of Malinowski's famous volume *The Sexual Life of Savages,* also published in 1929. Two years later this volume was followed by *Dress, Drinks, and Drums: Further Studies of Savages and Sex.* In the case of both Crawley and Malinowski an important part of their discussion, with its emphasis on the taboos of sex, clearly derives from Freud's analysis of such prohibitions in *Totem und Taboo* (1913). That influential volume has been a continuing focus of interest in the work of Meyer Fortes (1959, 1961, 1967, 1974, 1980), which forms part of the important dialogue between anthropology, psychology, psychiatry and psychoanalysis.

Another favourite topic of these earlier discussions was sacrifice, the offering that feeds both the living and the dead (as well as the divine). The feeding of the departed is linked in very definite ways with the domestic relationships existing among the living, and especially, as Cicero argued long ago, with the obligation of the heir to make offerings to those from whom he has inherited (Goody 1962). Outside the sphere of ancestor worship anthropological enquiry has been directed to examining the links between the offering of food to supernatural agencies and other aspects of social organisation. The solidary effects on the community, the moral dimension of the distribution of sacred food, often in a sacrificial but at least in a ritual context, lay at the heart of the well-known study of sacrifice by Robertson Smith (1846–94):

11

The ethical significance which thus appertains to the sacrificial meal, viewed as a social act, received particular emphasis from certain ancient customs and ideas connected with eating and drinking. According to antique ideas those who eat and drink together are by this very act tied to one another by a bond of friendship and mutual obligation. Hence when we find that in ancient religions all the ordinary functions of worship are summed up in the sacrificial meal, and that the ordinary intercourse between gods and men has no other form, we are to remember that the act of eating and drinking together is the solemn and stated expression of the fact that all those who share the meal are brethren, and that all the duties of friendship and brotherhood are implicitly acknowledged in their common act. By admitting man to his table the god admits his friendship; but this favour is extended to no man in his mere private capacity; he is received as one of a community, to eat and drink along with his fellows, and in the same measure as the act of worship cements the bond between him and his god, it cements also the bond between him and his brethren in the common faith. (1889: 247–8)

Commensalism was seen as the great promoter of solidarity, of community; the communion of brethren establishes and reinforces common ties.

The attention of these early anthropologists, many of whom were continuously wrestling with their own religious practices and beliefs, was directed towards the ritual and supernatural aspects of consumption. Taboos, totemism, sacrifice – these were the rejects from Christianity and other world religions which nevertheless bore traces of just such practices in times past. All were found distributed across a wide range of human societies and turned up in a diluted form even in their own cultures of nineteenth-century Europe. It was a rational explanation of these surviving elements in the light of the evolution of social institutions that such authors were searching for.

Their contribution was far from negligible, despite the rejection of 'evolution', of 'pseudo-history', of the 'comparative method', by their immediate successors. For they isolated certain widespread features of human behaviour that set the terms of much later enquiry. That enquiry took a radically different turn with the development of a tradition of field observation which involved the immersion of the observer in a particular society and hence encouraged the search for relations between different aspects of the total culture. The isolates became recontextualised, ritual acts and beliefs being set within the wider social processes. It was the doctrinal aspect of this research activity that became known as functionalism.

THE FUNCTIONAL APPROACH

Robertson Smith's insistence upon the role of commensalism in establishing and maintaining social relations came very close to one of the central themes pursued by those writers who had been influenced on the theoretical side by the approach of French sociology (and particularly by the the work of Emile Durkheim) and on the methodological side by the new stress on the direct collection of data and the experiencing of other cultures by living in them, in other words by participant fieldwork. The most important figures in these early developments were A.R. Radcliffe-Brown (1881–1955) and Bronislaw Malinowski (1884–1942).

Radcliffe-Brown's discussion closely follows the approach of Robertson Smith and Durkheim. He emphasises that among the Andaman Islanders of the Bay of Bengal 'by far the most important social activity is the getting of food' (1922: 227), and it is around food, he says, that 'the social sentiments are most frequently called into action'. These sentiments are implanted in man by a series of initiation ceremonies which at the same time impress upon him his dependence on society. During these performances the growing boy or girl has to give up certain relished foods, a prohibition (or taboo) from which they are later released in the course of the rites. By this means the 'social value' of food is brought home to the individual at his most impressionable age, a form of moral education that is carried out not by one person but 'by the whole society backed by the whole force of tradition'.

Stress is placed on the social function of food in bringing out sentiments that help to socialise an individual as a member of his community. The function is the maintenance of the system; the explanation is social rather than purely religious. While a measure of circularity is present in the argument, it is not without merits, especially when we shift from the macrofunctional (societal) level of the statements we have drawn from Radcliffe-Brown to the microfunctional analyses that he, but mainly the fieldworkers who followed, carried out on the institutional level. For example, some elements of his analysis of the prohibitions on food in the initiation ceremonies have a wider significance. In various parts of the world, whether in first-fruit ceremonies or in entrance rites of the kind we find in the Bagre performances of the LoDagaa of northern Ghana, rituals appear to treat items of food, at times consciously, in a way very similar to that described above. But one continuing limitation in this analysis lay in the emphasis on the 'symbolic' aspects of food, partly because of the neglect of other levels of meaning and partly because of uncertainty about the status of the symbolic relationship.

When anthropologists working in the 'functionalist' tradition discussed the 'symbolism of cooked food', as Audrey Richards did in *Land, Labour and Diet in Northern Rhodesia* (1939: 127), they referred to the way a transaction in food acted as an indicator of social relations. Of a

13

particular feature of marriage transfers, she writes: 'the giving and receiving of cooked food has become symbolic of the legal or economic relationship which entails it' (p. 127); and again, 'the preparation of porridge...is the woman's most usual way of *expressing* the correct kinship sentiment towards her different male relatives' [my italics]. As Radcliffe-Brown had maintained, in this way one can explain less explicable forms of human behaviour, see the logic in the illogical, the reason behind the non-rational: 'Customs that seem at first sight meaningless or ridiculous have been shown to fulfil most important functions in the social economy' (1922: 330). Strange habits were now explored not in terms of the evolution of human beliefs about this world and the next, but in terms of the part they played in a particular society.

The claim has been made that such 'objectivist' forms of explanation, which are the currency of much sociology, overlook the meaning of the actions to the actor and apply a scheme of interpretation of his actions that falls outside his awareness, even potentially. To him his action may be anything but 'meaningless or ridiculous'.

For some types of enquiry the objection has some force if it means that the actor's exegesis of his actions is neither sought nor considered. In the present case, however, the objection has less validity since actors are often aware of the advantages of solidarity, in some form or other of that elusive notion. For example, '*aṣabīya*, often translated as 'solidarity', is seen by Ibn Khaldūn as a critical concept among the Bedouin (Issawi 1950: 10) where it certainly has more than observer status.

In any case, the consciousness of the actor cannot be the sole source of explanatory concepts or ideas in the social sciences. Dumont has rightly stressed that the social anthropologist looks at his data both 'from within and from without' (1966: 22), a 'positive-cum-subjective' view that he sees 'as lying at the core of serious social anthropology, and particularly in its British form'. The comment is just, since this approach derives from the combination of sociological intent with fieldwork methods; the former inclines towards the elucidation of 'real' or 'objective' signi-ficance, while the practice of participant observation, carried out in the language of the actors, tends to stress 'perceived' or 'subjective' meaning.

The more serious criticisms of functional explanations, and indeed structural ones as well, are threefold. First, there is the Popperian problem of validation and acceptability; secondly, there is the ease with which relations and sentiments are posited: thus symbols express social structure, eating together expresses a relationship; thirdly, there is the absence both of a historical dimension and of a non-functional (or dysfunctional) component. Function is seen as giving meaning to the 'meaningless', the preparation of food 'symbolises' a jural or economic relationship. These claims for functional analysis play on the multiple

14

uses of 'meaning', 'symbol', 'expression', and the enquiry itself gains little by the introduction of such broad-ranging terms. On the contrary, it loses concreteness and, to some extent, credibility. The attribution of kinship sentiments follows from the observation, description or analysis of a woman preparing porridge and engaging in a range of other activities; the characterisation of the jural relationship emerges from the giving of food and similar acts, verbal and non-verbal. The existence of the relations and sentiments is thereby posited on the basis of a series of observed acts. Such notions therefore constitute generalising but not explanatory ones. Nor can they be regarded as symbolised or expressed in actual behaviour except as the result of tautological assumptions. One cannot invest a set of functional principles or structural forms with powers of this kind simply on the basis of evidence derived from their supposed manifestations. That would be to commit, once again, the error of misplaced concreteness.

It would be a mistake to see these anthropologists as only interested in the expressive significance of food. Malinowski himself was more concerned with the processes of production than with the symbolic aspects of food, and his work had a direct bearing upon some of the outstanding contributions to this field made by Audrey Richards. Her first essay on the subject was entitled *Hunger and Work in a Savage Tribe* (1932) and its subtitle ran 'A functional study of nutrition among the Southern Bantu'. In his introduction Malinowski describes the book as 'the first collection of facts on the cultural aspects of food and eating' (p. ix), and as laying 'the foundations for a sociological theory of nutrition' (p.x). Eating was placed in direct competition with sex. 'Nutrition as a biological process', declared Richards, 'is more fundamental than sex.' 'The individual man can exist without sexual gratification, but he must inevitably die without food.' But sex came second, not only for physiological reasons. It is 'necessarily a disruptive force in any human society, and one which must be checked and regulated to some extent if the community is to survive', while 'man's food-seeking activities not only necessitate co-operation but definitely foster it'. This declaration closely echoed Malinowski's feeling that, because of Freud, 'modern psychology has been too much dominated by an exclusive, one-sided and unsound interest in sex', an interest which he himself had done much to stimulate in *The Sexual Life of Savages* (1929) and other works.

Richards goes even further, at least in retrospect, for she later regarded her first monograph as an attempt 'to prove that hunger was the chief determinant of human relationships, initially within the family, but later in wider social groups, the village, age-grade, or political states' (1939: ix).

Being first concerned with problems of nutrition, Richards's primary orientation was towards the process of consumption itself, to the *nutritional system* which is parallel to the reproductive system; it has its primary extension from the household to kin group, with an emphasis on sharing and distribution, and its secondary extension to the wider food-producing system of clan or tribe (1932: 213). The physiological basis of human life was clearly an appropriate area for the application of the kind of biologically based functionalism, the satisfaction of human needs, characteristic of some of Malinowski's general statements. Audrey Richards herself had been trained in the natural sciences and later worked with a nutritionist, E.M. Widdowson, in a project which formed part of a wider scheme, promoted by a special committee of the International African Institute, appointed in 1934 'to consider the possibilities of co-operation between anthropologists and nutrition experts in the study of native diet' (1937: 3). But even in this earlier study Richards was not concerned with nutrition alone. While it concentrated on consumption, as a self-declared functional analysis it touched upon the social and psychological context of food, its production, preparation and consumption, and the way these processes were linked to the life-cycle, to interpersonal relationships and to the structure of social groups as well as the problem of 'food as a symbol'. She concluded by stressing the 'sociological significance of food' and the value of 'the study of eating customs' (1932: 214). Subsequently the programme of the International African Institute enabled her to follow up this analysis based on secondary sources with her notable field study on the Bemba entitled *Land, Labour and Diet in Northern Rhodesia* (1939), which placed patterns of consumption more firmly and more specifically in the context of the whole process of productive activity. The author had been asked to write 'a short book...describing in the case of one particular tribe, the different sociological factors which directly determined the food supply' (1939: ix). So, continuing to tread the borderline between the biological and social sciences, she wrote a monograph, no longer short, describing 'the whole economic life of the tribe', the value of which lay in 'its comprehensive treatment of the subject'. The range and detail of the material is a remarkable feature of this outstanding study in which we find not only description but analysis of a number of topics, such as the organisation of labour in relation to notions of time. Throughout there is an insistence on the 'sociological aspects' of diet and the 'cultural determinants of food and feeding' (p. 405).

Richards acknowledges the influence of Malinowski's magisterial study of productive processes in the Trobriands, *Coral Gardens and their Magic* (2 vols., 1935). More directly related to our enquiry was the other work arising from the same survey on nutrition in Africa, especially the article by Meyer and Sonia Fortes entitled 'Food in the domestic economy of the Tallensi' (1936), which also dealt with aspects of production and consumption at the domestic level. In his more extensive studies of the Tallensi of northern Ghana, Fortes took up themes from earlier anthropologists, those I have called 'the precursors'. Although he examined the processes of production and consumption especially in relation to domestic organisation, he paid particular attention to those aspects of the consumption of food that were clearly connected with religion and with the wider distribution of food outside the household, especially in sacrifice, which he treated as an important mechanism of group solidarity from various angles. The role of the production and distribution of food in the domestic group, the significance of sacrifice for humanity as well as divinity, the meaning of prohibitions on the consumption of food, especially the flesh of domestic animals (totem and taboo) – these have remained important themes in the work of anthropologists in many societies, particularly those characterised by the simpler forms of agriculture.

THE STRUCTURAL APPROACH

In recent years the analysis of cooking has been associated with the name of Claude Lévi-Strauss, whose work displays a very different focus of interest. Lévi-Strauss has declared himself to be an inconstant disciple of Durkheim, much influenced by Mauss. But whereas these authors were mainly looking for links between modes of thought and other features of the social system, Lévi-Strauss, who worked initially within the same tradition, attempts to look at the structure of human thought itself, even of the human mind, *l'esprit humain*. In simple terms, he attempts to look inwards to the 'deep structure' rather than sideways to other aspects of the surface structure. Or rather, he looks at other aspects in order to elicit homologous patterns, which are then referred to the deep structure. Phrased in this way the undertaking is not so very different from the approach of those scholars who attempt to find common 'principles' or 'themes' in the analysis of a particular society (though the nature of the elements differs). While the main thrust of the functional approach was to examine the interlocking nature of social institutions, its practitioners were often engaged in this very search for underlying principles. However the structural approach of Lévi-Strauss came to assume an affinity, a homology, perhaps an identity between the deep structures of the human mind and of human society, or at least between the unconscious attitudes of individuals and the social structure of a particular group, which even implies at times a causal relationship. To achieve this aim, Lévi-Strauss himself considers a number of problems to do with universals and with the evolution of humanity, problems that had attracted the nineteenth-century precursors but which had been largely set aside in favour of the intensive observational studies that have absorbed the interests of most anthropologists in recent decades.

These concerns are clear in Lévi-Strauss's first major work, which took an established theme, that of 'incest', used a comparative and even developmental framework but applied a set of abstracting and formalising analytic procedures to the material. While he made his mark in the analysis of the institutions that surround sex (incest, marriage, kinship), he then turned his attention to that other basic element in human affairs, food, or rather cooking. The shift of emphasis is clearly seen in the change of titles from *Les Structures élémentaires de la parenté* (1949), with its Durkheimian resonances, to the first three volumes of his major work on myth, *Mythologiques*, entitled *Le Cru et le cuit* (1964), *Du Miel aux cendres* (1966) and *L'Origine des manières de table* (1968). Only the title of the final volume of *Mythologiques*, *L'Homme nu* (1971), lacks the direct reference to food, though the equation 'naked' = 'raw' is ever present. His specific theoretical interest in the subject of cooking was first laid out in chapter 5 of his collected essays entitled *Structural Anthropology* (1958 [1963]), and it is developed with both brevity and clarity in 'Le triangle culinaire', an article that appeared in *L'Arc* (1965).

In his work on myth, Lévi-Strauss had turned his attention to the role of fire in transforming food from the raw to the cooked state, a process he sees as marking the emergence of humanity, just as he had earlier pointed to the incest taboo as the critical factor separating 'nature' from 'culture': the transformations of sex and food by (or into) culture are treated lineally (as homologous) rather than laterally (as interacting). Of course the role of fire, especially the ritual role, had been stressed in many earlier works, in the study of fire festivals, in sacrifice (burnt-offerings), in domestic cults, 'in continuing the incense smoke', to use the phrase of Francis Hsu describing ancestor worship among the Chinese (1949: 76). But Lévi-Strauss made it a dominant component in his discussion of the transformation of food not only in the narratives of myth but also in the terms for the processes by which it is prepared. However his first attempt at a general analysis of 'cooking' was directed to the distinctive features of a cuisine to which he gave the name 'gustemes'.

Given his earlier interest in structural linguistics, in the work of Saussure, Jakobson and others, it was natural that he should apply some elements of a linguistic approach to cooking as a way of eliciting and assessing the distinctive features. One result is the recourse, following Jakobson, to binary divisions of the marked/unmarked type, whose presence or absence is recorded by means of plus and minus signs. A table based upon binary categories appeared in Lévi-Strauss's first incursion into the sociology of cooking, that is, in the comments in *Anthropologie structurale* (1963: 86) upon the difference between French and English cuisine. His intention is clearly comparative at an abstract level, using selected features to make the contrast which is presented in the following terms:-

	English cuisine	French cuisine
endogenous/exogenous	+	−
central/peripheral	+	−
marked/not marked	−	+

In other words [he writes, and words are needed both to explain the oppositions and to fill out the corresponding signs], in English cuisine the main dishes of a meal are made from endogenous ingredients, prepared in a relatively bland fashion, and surrounded with more exotic accompaniments, in which all the differential values are strongly marked (for example, tea, fruitcake, orange marmalade, port wine). Conversely, in French cuisine the opposition endogenous/exogenous becomes very weak or disappears, and equally marked gustemes are combined together in a central as well as in a peripheral position.

Can this scheme also be applied to Chinese cooking? he asks. 'Yes, if we restrict ourselves to the preceding oppositions; no, if others are introduced (such as sweet/sour) which are mutually exclusive in French cuisine, in contrast to Chinese (or German)' (p. 86). Abstract these structures of oppositions, see if they are found in other spheres of the same society, and if they are, 'we have the right to conclude that we have reached a significant knowledge of the unconscious attitudes of the society or societies under consideration' (p. 87). The analysis of English or French cooking that results from these procedures excludes the concrete consideration of social and physical factors. What class, what period, are we studying? Is olive oil endogenous to the Ile de France? How relevant is overseas trade or regional difference? Is a binary framework the best way of handling these variables?

Since the binary mode is used so widely in contemporary anthropology, we need to look carefully at its logical basis. To this end it is worth turning to a review of the role of binarism in phonology by Latraverse (1975). The author points out the difference between the logical opposition of contradictory terms involved in the cybernetic model (1/0) and based upon computer technology, and the kind of oppositions found in phonology, which may be of two types, either 'polar' (as in the contrast grave/acute) or else 'absolute' (as in voiced/unvoiced). In anthropological analyses these various forms are all subsumed under the signs +/−, in the same way that Lévi-Strauss had earlier tried to characterise the relationship between close kin as 'positive' or 'negative'

(1945).[3] A measure of formalisation is essential to any comparative work of the kind the author is undertaking. Our doubts are firstly whether in these particular cases the signs are not too inclusive (Goody 1969 [1959] : 45) and whether such contrasts can reasonably form the basis of any model either of the relations between social institutions or of a common deep structure. In any case, at one level there is a confusion between, or at least a merging of opposites and absence, between types of contrast.

The technique of making a linguistic analysis of this kind involves isolating the phonemic contrasts of a language and then entering them on a classificatory matrix, with the 'distinctive features', the traits, as the coordinates. The result is a catalogue or verification list (Halle) or a codebook (Cherry). This procedure is the kind envisaged and practised by Lévi-Strauss in his analysis of cooking as well as in the earlier work on kinship. While Latraverse rejects some of the criticisms of binarism, his paper gives little encouragement to the attempt to turn a simplifying analytic procedure into an instrument for discovering any important psychological or sociological verities about the structure of the human mind. On the other hand, the procedure possesses more mundane virtues, which are brought out in the author's later contributions and the discussion to which they gave rise.

The next stage in Lévi-Strauss's analysis of cooking, which appeared in *L'Arc* (1965), makes use of formalisation and the linguistic model in a rather different way. In the first place the units on which it is based are no longer 'gustemes', units of taste, but the basic types of operation ('technemes'?) for transferring food from raw to cooked. There is a shift from consumption (cuisine) to preparation (cooking). The change holds out more promise if only because the elements are capable of a more careful specification and seem less arbitrary, less liable to internal variation. Like language, he maintains, cooking is universal in human societies. Just as we have the vowel triangle,

a

u   i

and a consonantal triangle,

k

p   t

which represent the common, simple basis of the complex opposition of phonemes, so we have a culinary triangle. His version is constructed from 'semantic' rather than phonetic elements and takes the following form:

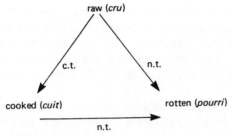

c.t. = cultural transformation

n.t. = natural transformation

Fig. 1 *The culinary triangle* (after Lévi-Strauss 1965)

Underlying the structure of this particular model there is a double opposition of distinctive features, first, between elaborated and non-elaborated, and, secondly, between culture and nature. The cooked is a cultural transformation (or elaboration) of the raw, while the rotten (or spoilt) is a natural transformation of both. Referring back to the earlier comments on binarity, the first of these oppositions is seen to be of the presence/absence kind, the second polar.

As the author himself insists, this approach takes its stand on the utility of the linguistic model for the analysis of other cultural data, and for constructing a common deep structure. For him the relation between culture and language is not only an analogy or a model; he maintains in the earlier article that we can interpret 'society as a whole in terms of a theory of communication', an interpretation, he declares, that leads to a Copernican revolution (1963: 83). Lévi-Strauss rejects the suggestion, made among others by Haudricourt and Granai (1955), that he has *reduced* society or culture to language. However he does argue that not only cooking but 'marriage regulations and kinship systems can profitably be treated as a kind of language, a set of processes permitting the establishment, between individuals and groups, of a certain type of communication' (1963: 61). Language is therefore the model for the analysis of socio-cultural phenomena, which are interpreted in terms of communication, that is to say, of exchange. Women are like words in language systems and goods in economic systems, objects of circulation: 'The rules of marriage serve to ensure the circulation of women between groups, just as economic rules serve to ensure the circulation of goods and services, and linguistic rules the circulation of messages' (p.83).

Note the macrofunctionalist tone of the argument, reinforced by subsequent references to surmounting disequilibrium.[4] It is only rarely that the so-called functionalists resort to statements of this kind, for they are working on a more concrete level of microfunctional analysis rather than on flows through the total system. Note secondly the constant stress on distribution and the absence of any extended consideration of production and reproduction (that is, of filiation as distinct from affinity).

The aim of Lévi-Strauss's analysis is very different from the comprehensive (or 'thick') description of Richards's account of the Bemba. He does not attempt to provide 'an exhaustive knowledge of societies' but 'to derive constants which are found at various times from an empirical richness and diversity that will always transcend our efforts at observation and description' (1963: 82–3). The constants derived from studying various 'sub-systems' display homologies. To put it another way, the examination of kinship systems, political ideologies, mythologies, ritual, art or codes of etiquette produces 'a certain number of structures' which may display common properties, homologies, which as we have seen represent 'unconscious attitudes of the society or societies under consideration' (p. 87). Indeed they represent aspects of that 'uninvited guest, the human mind'.

Some abstraction is clearly necessary for any general treatment of the kind undertaken by Lévi-Strauss, and linguistics offers a precedent not only for the isolation of distinctive features on a binary basis but also for the use of the triangular model for vowels and certain consonants. However, his study of cooking goes on to produce a more complicated figure than the simple culinary triangle with which it began and which

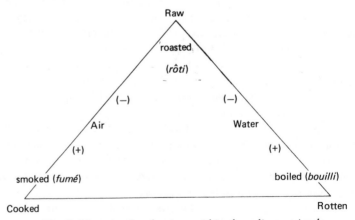

Fig. 2 *The triangle of recipes within the culinary triangle*
(after Lévi-Strauss 1965)

only allowed for the transformation of the raw into the cooked and the rotten. Now he introduces other aspects of the preparation of food for consumption, including the processes of 'smoking' and 'boiling'. To the culinary triangle is now added the 'triangle of recipes', that is, of operations where the first, smoking, is set apart from roasting by the mediation of air, and boiling by the intervention of water. While the author writes of this as semantically based, he is not analysing terms but rather techniques, as is clear not only from the logic behind his introduction of 'smoking' as the third element but also in his references to 'means' and 'results' (p. 28).

This triangle, once again, is seen as resting on the overriding opposition between nature and culture. But the relationship is much more complex: 'With regard to means, roasting and smoking are on the side of nature, boiling on that of culture. With regard to results, smoking is on the side of culture, roasting and boiling on the side of nature.' By the first sentence we are to understand that as compared with boiling, roasting requires no utensils, and, while smoking (among a certain South American tribe to which he refers) does use a rack (*boucan*), the support is 'voluntarily' destroyed after every operation, so it is as if it did not exist at all. The second sentence means that roasting changes the meat hardly at all, but smoking turns it into a durable commodity. Meanwhile, the boiled is close to the rotten (i.e. natural), partly because a number of cultures assert this to be so. Note that the boiled is made 'natural' because of the language used, that is by metaphor; while the 'smoked' is made natural by the destruction of the cultural instrument that created it, a transformation of the metonymic kind since it consists in acting as if the effect stood for the cause.

This opposition leads Lévi-Strauss into a passage that bears the imprint of Hegelian metaphysics and which I quote partly because of the light it sheds on his view of myth:

As a consequence, even when the structure transforms or completes itself in order to overcome a disequilibrium, this is only at the price of setting up a new disequilibrium which is manifest on another level. To this ineluctable dissymetry the structure owes its ability to engender myth, which is nothing other than an effort to correct or hide its constituent dissymetry. (1965: 28)

One might remark that, whether or not myth acts in this macrofunctional way, to claim that it does nothing else is hardly acceptable. But so perhaps is the claim itself, for is it really possible that this ineluctable dissymetry, produced at times by a figure of speech, a metaphor, is based on some kind of basic opposition or contradiction that threatens society to the extent that it has to be disguised or corrected? And if this were so, are there not simpler ways of dealing with a metaphor, or even with a contrast that might after all have been drawn in the wrong place? Are there not more immediate, more concrete, perhaps more fundamental, causes of disequilibrium which cannot be neglected in the analysis of cooking and which relate to the internal and external strains in society and manifest themselves over time?

The triangle of 'recipes' is further complicated by the introduction of added operations. In a culinary system where the category of roast (*rôti*) is divided into roast and grilled (*grillé*), the last should be placed at the hierarchy of the triangle of recipes because it places the least distance between fire and meat. 'Roast' now takes its place between grilled and smoked. Where there is a distinction between boiling and steaming (*cuisson à la vapeur*), this would be placed midway between boiled and smoked. With the category 'fried', a more complicated 'transformation' is necessary, finally turning the triangle of recipes into a tetrahedron that includes oil as well as air and water among the intervening agents through which active agents such as fire operate on the raw food by means of the set of cultural utensils. This addition allows of the distinction between roast in the oven with fat and roast on the fire (*à la broche*) without any intermediary. Indeed the final elaboration (1965: 29) moves beyond the scope of any simple geometrical representation, including as it does 'oppositions' between animal and vegetable, cereal and legume, which would require listing in some kind of matrix using the binary values, plus and minus.

In this way the author hopes to be able to elaborate a schema that includes all the characteristics of a specific culinary system. No doubt, he adds in parenthesis and very much to the point, there are other characteristics of interest to 'diachronic analysis', as well as those features that concern the order, presentation and behaviour at meals. But it is on the operations he concentrates, and when they have been isolated one can apply the procedure outlined before. Find the most economical way of orienting the elements in a grid, then superimpose these other contrasts, of a sociological, economic, aesthetic or religious kind: men and women, family and society, village and bush, husbandry and prodigality, noble and commoner, sacred and profane, etc. One can then hope to discover, for each particular case, the way in which the cuisine of a society is a language in which it unconsciously translates its structure, although Lévi-Strauss notes that it may resign itself, also unconsciously, 'to unveil its contradictions' (1965: 29). The structure then speaks in the language of culture (or in that of an aspect of culture, like cooking) and reveals its totality when the grid of oppositions and correlations derived from any one sub-set is superimposed upon the grid from other sub-sets (e.g. the economic system).

The method requires the abandonment of any idea that one sub-set is privileged as against any other, that one sector is more significant, more influential (in a vectorial sense) than any other, an objection that has been raised against various forms of functional and structural-functional analysis. At the same time it depends upon the initial selection of a specific sub-set (or sector) for analytical purposes, the choice of which is bound to influence the subsequent operations. Relationships between the component sub-structures are established not at the 'surface' level, where we might expect to be able to assess causal inference, functional dependency or simply tendencies to influence, but at a 'deeper' level of 'structural causality', of homologous relations or of formal similarity, where any causal networks are much more difficult to evaluate. This means that in approaching the sociology of cooking we have first to set aside other 'contrasts' or variables of an economic or religious kind, in order to establish on the basis of a limited set of data a grid for later comparison, which in practice turns out to be a comparison of a visual or formulaic kind. While the isolation of domains is critical to many types of analysis, the value of postponing a consideration of the links between cooking and the economy or the family to the 'unconscious level' seems doubtful, certainly if it excludes an explanation of such interrelations closer to the surface. Such doubts exist even when we are dealing with semantics where field theory or componential analysis have often proceeded on the basis of the formal isolation of sets of terms (Lehrer 1974); the value of these procedures is more open to doubt in the wider behavioural contexts in which such category systems emerge (the lived-in rather than the thought-of to use a popular but deceptive dichotomy). Indeed there is a tendency to spirit away the more concrete aspects of human life, even food, sex and sacrifice, by locating their interpretation *only* at the 'deeper' level, which is largely a matter of privileging the 'symbolic' at the expense of the more immediately communicable dimensions of social action. The opposition, or assumed opposition, between the definitions of structure of Radcliffe-Brown and Lévi-Strauss (see de Heusch 1971 [1965]: 14), which is more often manipulated to make a polemical point than to advance the study of human behaviour, should not lead to a neglect of the 'surface' in favour of the 'depths', especially in areas as closely tied to the whole domestic domain as that of cooking. Without the consideration of such related areas, comparison and contrast within and between cuisines lacks an essential dimension.

Other factors too suggest a modification of the linguistic model used in the seminal work of Lévi-Strauss, apart from the limitations of binarism. In the first place, he argues that the language of cuisine, unlike the language of ordinary life, 'translates' *unconsciously*; it is not used to communicate between men as much as to *express* a structure. Here the link with the idea that the cooking of food expresses sentiments of kinship is close. Secondly, the analogy of the vowel triangle, which derives in part from the nature of human vocalisation, is dropped when the pattern becomes more complex; triangle becomes tetrahedron and more. Thirdly, while the representations (of whatever shape) are presented in an abstract, universal form, the arguments by which the triangle of recipes is attached to the culinary triangle sometimes derive from features of the cooking operations of particular societies, as for example, in the destruction of the rack for smoking meat by a group of South American Indians.

The utilisation of a notion of a particular people for the construction of a general model raises in acute form the problem of objectivism and subjectivism that impinges upon so much sociological analysis. In the present instance the author seems to skip from one analytical level to another. But it raises a related problem of whether we are employing as analytical concepts ones located within the actor frame of reference (e.g. lexemes, the units of some linguistic studies of this kind) or objectively defined operations such as roasting, the elements of which are closer to phonemes. In the latter case we have to be especially careful about the danger of defining the units on the basis of our own cultural experience as actors, as speakers of the language in which we are trying to perform the enquiry. It might seem that the omission of the distinct notion of 'baking', except as *cuire au four*, parallel to roasting (in the oven as distinct from on the spit), *rôtir au four*, stemmed from the particular nature of French categories rather than from a more objective assessment of alternative techniques and alternative lexemes.

We are faced here with the consequences of the obvious fact that sociological analyses, unlike mathematics, are carried out in the language of the sociologist. One can invent, elaborate, or borrow technical terms to describe the 'family' in other societies and so try and avoid importing concepts and ideas based upon our own kinship structures. Translation is not the issue since one needs to recognise difference as well as similarity. It is a process in which we are only too liable to give our folk-concepts or metaphors a universal significance, for example when the phrase *pot pourri* is taken to indicate rapprochement of the boiled to the rotten (Lévi-Strauss 1965: 22).

The lexemic analysis of *cooking terms* is of course an enquiry in its own right, but different from that either of gustemes or of technemes (operations, practices). Moreover the same kind of comparative study can be undertaken, as Berlin and Kay (1969) have carried out with 'basic colour terms'. An attempt to analyse comparatively a set of 'basic culinary terms' has been made by the linguist Adrianne Lehrer, a more extended account of whose work is given in the Appendix. Her data come from eight societies and do little to confirm associations such as raw/roasted, that are central features of the link between the triangle of recipes and the culinary triangle. However on the level of operations she agrees that it is possible to say something general about cooking across human societies. This leads her to offer a modified form of the culinary tetrahedron (Fig. 3) which serves as a neat guide for operations but not for categorisations (1972: 169). It is critical to note that she recognises this generality as arising from common techniques, that is from the world outside rather than the structure beneath. Indeed it would be surprising to find that the terminology of cooking did not vary systematically both within and between societies, just as the activities and products of the fields, the kitchen and the table differ from society to society. And not only from society to society but from class to class. For even when the 'structural' approach does not tend to stress the unity of mankind, it tends to overestimate the unity of 'cultures'. Not only are culinary terms themselves more variable than is suggested by the model, but a richer variety of meaning and operations emerges in the interchange of daily life which a formal analysis confined to the terms themselves cannot fully explore. Such a paring down of meaning involves both a cost and a gain. The benefits have often been spelled out; the limitations became clear to me in considering an attempt to apply the culinary triangle to African rather than to European or South American cooking, an attempt that constitutes a test as well as an exemplar of the approach.

Lehrer's analysis exemplifies the need and value of submitting such general theories to a critical examination from both the logical and empirical points of view. While all theories obviously require a testing of some kind, the nature of functional and structural hypotheses, with their assumptions of fit and homology combined with the initial plausibility of suggestions that give an all embracing unity to the diversity of experience, place them in a special position. The dangers can perhaps be gauged by the ease with which this type of analysis can be parodied. The structuralist analysis of cooking has had its fair share, culminating in that remarkable volume produced by the 'pataphysicians', Asger Jorn and Noel Arnaud, and entitled *La Langue verte et la cuite: étude gastrophonique sur la marmythologie musiculinaire* (1968).[5] This attempt to apply the approach is a parody, which in itself offers no grounds for rejection. But a liability to such treatment may highlight the softer parts of a theory.

Thomas's attempt to apply this type of analysis to Africa (1960) was a more serious undertaking, but one which, I suggest, reveals important lacunae in the theory. Starting from the remarks on the differences between English, French and Chinese cooking, Thomas tries to isolate similar 'constitutive elements' in the cooking of the Diola of the Casamance in Senegal. The 'constitutive elements' or gustemes that

Thomas regards as significant are patterned upon the structures of opposition and correlation defined by Lévi-Strauss, items (i) and (iii) having appeared in the original article.

   (i) endogenous/exogenous
  (ii) luxurious dish/poor dish
      (satisfying/non-satisfying)
 (iii) central/peripheral

It is possible, of course, to describe Diola cooking in terms of such 'pairs', though once again the oppositions display the ambiguities seen in much binary analysis, for some are polar oppositions (A/B) and others marked by presence/absence (A/−A); the latter, as in (ii) above, can be seen as a unity rather than a duality. From Lehrer's study and other attempts to assess the structural approach to cognitive categories and operations in a wider context (for instance, Thomas *et al.* 1976), the gains of a formal analysis of lexemes and even operations are seen to be more limited than some of the original claims might suggest. With gustemes, the problem is yet more complex. In the present case, the process of isolating the 'constitutive elements' seems more like an application of imported analytic categories, the justification for which is rather weak. For their rationale appears to derive from a prior commitment to 'oppositions and correlations', that is, to multiple rows and binary columns, which is presented as part of the structure of the human mind but which could be considered to be a product of the reduction of speech to writing, of the shift from utterance to text.

Let us leave aside such considerations and accept, for the sake of the argument, the utility of these particular gustemes as descriptive tools, interpreting them as coordinates of the same kind used in componential analysis. Starting from here, we still have to recognise the possible limitations of an approach that overlooks internal differences in an attempt to draw out the general features of, say, English cooking, set them against the cuisine of the French and finally to use the same set of elements to analyse food in an African or Chinese context. By concentrating upon the behavioural unity of specific groups, tribes or nations at a cultural level, one may neglect those important aspects of that culture which are linked with social or individual differences.

Comparison is also made more difficult by the exclusion of certain closely related processes that have been defined out of the analytic system, a procedure that is seen by Piaget as one of the advantages of structuralism, but in this case emerges as a distinct hindrance. I refer here to the relation between consumption, production and the social-economic order. The neglect of these processes is seen, first, in the absence of any consideration of hierarchical (or indeed regional) factors in the references to French and English cooking, and secondly in the failure to give sufficient weight to the biological, climatological and other external factors that act as constraints on social action. This absence is occasioned not by space or forgetfulness; it derives from a theoretical stance. At one point, for example, Thomas makes the following comment upon the subjects of his essay: 'With his realistic peasant mentality, the Diola sees in the meal above all a means of suppressing hunger and regaining his strength.' A note to this passage states that 'In fact this attitude is frequent in Black Africa' (p. 338). One wonders if the author, lost in the more recondite significances of food, can really be so little prepared to acknowledge its more immediate meaning. Not that such an attitude should come altogether as a surprise, since anthropologists are only too prepared to examine marriage with equally little regard for sex. The attempt to define biological factors out of the explanation of social action, the least satisfactory part of the legacy of Durkheim, is as inadequate as the opposite tendency in the writings of some sociobiologists. Neither of these extreme 'theoretical' positions have much to recommend them to the social scientist, and both are carefully eschewed by those who, like Richards and the historians of the *Annales* school, have made the most substantial contributions to this field. They have seen no need to proclaim the complete autonomy of the cultural.

CULTURAL APPROACHES

There have been other more recent theoretical accounts of cooking, but to present these in every detail would lead away from the main purpose of this chapter, which is to sketch out the general background of anthropological contributions to the topic of this essay. Let me however refer briefly to two recent studies that represent varieties of what one might call the 'cultural approach', though certainly no more weight should be placed on this term than on 'functional' or 'structural' in a similar context. These are all terms of art that are used to break up the continuities of theoretical and empirical enquiry in ways that are often more necessary as crutches for the commentator than as guides for the practitioner.

Mary Douglas's general interest in processes of consumption led to the writing of a book with Baron Isherwood entitled *The World of Goods* (1979). But she had earlier directed her attention more specifically to cooking and, following the work of the linguist Michael Halliday, to 'the analysis of the meal'. Her general orientation derives from the functionalisms and structuralisms of both Oxford and Paris. While she sees food as linked to biological as well as to social facts, it is the latter

29

aspect that interests her, particularly when she attempts to 'decipher a meal'. In this context, food becomes a 'code'; 'the message it encodes will be found in the pattern of social relations being expressed' (1971: 61). Once again, food is 'symbolic' of social relationship; there is 'a correspondence between a given social structure and the structure of symbols by which it is expressed' (p. 66), phrases that are very reminiscent of Audrey Richards. As Douglas explains in the introduction to *Purity and Danger* (1966: viii), her structural approach is derived from Evans-Pritchard; the concept of social structure goes back in slightly different forms to Radcliffe-Brown, Durkheim and Spencer, and tends to equate social structure with the aggregate of social relations between 'persons', that is, human beings considered as filling social roles. In fact Evans-Pritchard uses the phrase in two senses, a more restricted concrete one, which refers to 'groups and the relations between groups', and a more analytical one, as a 'system of separate but interrelated structures' (1940: 263) which included the political system.[6]

The use of the term 'code', like that of symbol and metaphor, is associated with the idea that it provides a means of 'expressing' social structure or social relations, an idea we have found common among anthropologists, whether functionalist, structural-functionalist or structuralist. The terms themselves are often used in a highly generalised way that makes them somewhat ambiguous. On a more specific level we understand what the words mean; that is to say, we understand what constitutes a telegraphic 'code', what the bread and wine 'symbolise' in the Mass, what is 'metaphorical' about the sentence, 'The room was flooded with people.' In each case two languages, objects, words (or concepts) that are logically and perceptually separate are brought together and interpreted in relation to one another by operations of a graphic, ritual or linguistic kind.

But when we speak of food – or a ritual (see Leach 1954, Gluckman 1962, Fortes 1962, and any other anthropological text) – as expressing social relations or symbolising social structure, what is brought together in a similar way? Do social relations and social structure stand in the same relationship to the bread and the wine as the body and blood of Christ,[7] or as a naval cipher does to open speech? The assumption is unacceptable, partly because it pushes the cart before the horse. Whether we understand our enquiry as perceiving existing social relations and social structure, or as constructing them in any of a variety of possible ways, in practice the notions make sense only as abstractions from or constructions of the acts of individuals. Neither social relations nor social structure 'express' or 'symbolise' the acts of individuals because the former are necessarily derived from and totally encompass the latter. It would be preferable to claim that what we have here is metonymy rather than metaphor, but the recourse to rhetoric, the utilisation of figures of speech, does little to improve the logical clarity of the analysis.

There is somewhat more logical justification for using verbs like 'express' and terms like 'code' when we are dealing with ideas of 'deep structure'. For such notions are endowed with generative implications, and it is conceivable that a deep structure derived from surface elements could be used to 'predict' a hitherto unknown surface structure. But in practice there is no adequate way in which this programme could be carried out. Therefore, because the deep structure is derived from surface elements alone and is unknowable without them, it is meaningless to discuss one as expressing the other, except in a circular, Pickwickian sense.

Mary Douglas asks that we consider the meal not simply as an assemblage of binary oppositions (which takes us only part of the way along the path towards a satisfactory understanding) but that we place it in the context of other meals consumed in the course of the day, of the week and of the year, thus extending the restricted analytic field that Lévi-Strauss deliberately adopts on the basis of the linguistic model. The 'meaning of a meal' is found in a system of repeated analogies (or repeated metonyms). This approach is strongly reminiscent of Radcliffe-Brown's attempt to extract meaning by examining similar 'ritual' acts in dissimilar social contexts.[8] The procedure is far from standardised but an indication of similarity is given by the words, images and acts of the actors, including their own exegesis of the events themselves. The recognition of repetitive idioms is a common feature of field experience,[9] and the examination of the variety of contexts in which they appear must necessarily constitute one level of any interpretation. The same is true of any semantic analysis, for example, the study of the imagery ('symbolism' or metaphor) of a particular poem, play, novel or even author.[10] One usage modifies another. So for Mary Douglas: 'Each meal carries something of the meaning of other meals; each meal is a structured social event which structures others in its own image.' But the structuring is not simply repetition and reinforcement; following the lines of contextual analysis, we must also see the elements as reacting to the different situations in which they occur (1971: 69). In addition, she suggests, the symbolic structure must be seen to fit squarely with some demonstrable social considerations; otherwise the analysis has only begun (p. 63). For the fit between the medium's symbolic boundaries and the boundaries between categories of people is its only possible validation. The fit may be at different levels, but without being able to show some such matching, 'the analysis of symbols remains arbitrary and subjective' (pp. 68–9).

The formal analysis of the meal, suggested by Halliday (1961) and elaborated by Douglas, is of value quite apart from the question of the relation of the 'structure' of the meal to the structure of other repetitive clusters of human behaviour. For while we accept the need to search for meaningful relations, the problem lies in evaluating what we find. In the end the interlocking nature of these relations must be a matter for empirical validation within a framework of theoretical assumption. The danger of functional and structural analysis lies in unchecked and uncheckable speculation. The burden of proof always rests with the proposer, and the 'fit' must be demonstrated, or at any rate supported, rather than simply assumed. Otherwise the intellectual enterprise becomes a matter of mere assertion.

The contextual analysis of the meal, like the study of repetitive idioms, takes us part of the way along the road and adds another dimension to our understanding. Its strengths and its weaknesses derive from the tendency to limit the search for relations to an abstraction called a 'cultural system', a tendency that contains the same kind of danger surrounding the efforts of Durkheim and Parsons to establish the autonomy of social factors or, more widely, of the social system. In some social and intellectual contexts this conceptual isolation is associated with the desire to set up 'anthropology' and 'sociology' as independent fields of study and units of academic organisation. Whatever its origins, the isolationism of the 'cultural' approach tends to give material and hierarchical factors less weight than they deserve while the concern for continuity often leads to the neglect of change and that for holism to the neglect of difference. Phrases like 'deciphering a code' suggest a defined and objectively determined locus and content of 'meaning'.[11] Given that other writers, for example those in the tradition of Parisian structuralism, carry out their 'decoding' in different terms and with different assumptions, the existence of any such objectively determinable relations seems somewhat doubtful.

The autonomy of the cultural is much more of an issue in the second study we have in mind, the work by Marshall Sahlins entitled *Culture and Practical Reason* (1976) which consists of an extended debate against the idea of praxis theory that 'human cultures are formulated out of practical activity and...utilitarian interest' (p. vii). Rather, they are created by symbolic, meaningful or cultural reason which structures utility. Indeed, he claims 'that the contest between the practical and the meaningful is the fateful issue of modern social thought' (p. ix). The object of anthropology is to concern itself with culture, 'collective tradition', with meaningful orders of persons and things, orders that are not free inventions of the mind but are essentially (though this is not stated in the Preface from which I quote) 'symbolic orders'.

The cultural system here has its own 'cultural logic'. Only by reference to such a calculus can we explain the eating habits of, say, the Americans, who reject the flesh of horse and dog on grounds that cannot be explained by any variety of utilitarian theory. The problems arise mainly because of Sahlins's relentless binary approach to social theory. He is unwilling to allow explanations that derive from the interaction of social and biological phenomena in the manner adopted by Audrey Richards and others. Like Parsons he would see this as the biologising of social theory and of cultural reality. The result is an approach that, whatever its other merits, tends to assume a cultural unity that inhibits reference to internal differentiations, to external socio-cultural influences, to historical factors and to material elements.

CHANGING WORLDS

Despite the framework of opposition given to or assumed by the various approaches I have discussed in the context of the sociology of cooking, it is clear that they are not so much alternatives as complementary, at least in some of their aspects; a concern with 'meaning' (at whatever level) does not exclude a concern with the social role of food, which some see as an important kind of meaning. Indeed much of the disagreement lies not at the level of theoretical practice but of theoretical assertion. One example we have taken is the use of the idea that social action 'expresses' or 'symbolises' another order of being, that is, a relational or structural order. Indeed the notions of relationships and structure are themselves used in more similar ways than polemical or ideological frames, such as 'rationalism' versus 'empiricism', allow for.

However one dimension that all these various approaches play down is time – and to a lesser degree space. The importance of the developmental cycle in the domestic economy was raised by the work of Fortes, Richards and others, and it is a theme taken up in the following chapter. What is absent is a consolidation not of the 'cyclical' aspects of time but of the longer-term, developmental, ones. Its absence arises partly from the objections of Malinowski and Radcliffe-Brown to any confusion between history and anthropology, between diachrony and synchrony.[12] It is understandable that in the course of intensive observational studies that their energies and explanations should be directed elsewhere. Besides which many of the 'pseudo-historical' speculations of their evolutionist precursors left much to be desired, both from the standpoint of evidence as well as intellectually. Even where they do not object to history, they do not use it in any precise way. Lévi-Strauss does put forward some hypotheses of a developmental kind, but makes little effort to give them flesh; for him, history consists in a vague recourse to transformations is the 'unconscious elements of social life' from the

33

study of which anthropology is said to draw its 'originality' (1963: 18,23).

A similar vagueness, even hostility, marks their view of the comparative approach, which was also based on the supposed shortcomings of their predecessors. The formal objections of these writers to comparative analysis over time and space are well-known; Lévi-Strauss appears to support Boas's criticism of that method and comments adversely on Malinowski's use of comparative sociology. Evans-Pritchard, Leach and others have expressed grave doubts about the enterprise. Yet at the same time, all these writers, each in their own fashion, have undertaken comparisons, often very valuable, and mostly of the rather unsystematic kind to which we all succumb.

The blatant contradiction between 'theory' and practice requires a more satisfactory resolution. History and comparison, or more precisely the use of historical and comparative data, need to be brought back into the forefront of the study of society, not as slogans but as ways of developing and testing more substantive theories and more fleshy hypotheses.

The reintroduction of the historical and comparative dimension into anthropology is often associated with the influence of Marx, though he has been used to justify other trends. Some have seen Marx as the first structuralist. Lévi-Strauss has spoken of his own 'endeavours to reintegrate the anthropological knowledge acquired during the last fifty years into the Marxian tradition' (1963: 343), and some of his colleagues have tried to create a structural Marxist approach in anthropology stimulated by the writings of Althusser. The influence of Marx has also strongly affected analyses of the domestic domain carried out by a number of other French scholars, in particular by Meillassoux (1975). In the work of a number of American and British anthropologists, for example, White and his students, as well as Gluckman, Gough, Worsley and others, the influence has been less explicit but nonetheless present. It has helped to keep alive an interest in placing the results of particular synchronic studies in the wider context of 'la longue durée', in the setting of the major changes that human societies have undergone in the course of their development.

There are important reasons of a theoretical and empirical kind for paying more attention to the time dimension. When anthropologists talk about the culture of food, they tend to see this as a continuing normative structure that, in the words of one recent writer on the subject, 'absorbs or rejects foreign imports according to their structural or stylistic compatability' (Chang 1977: 7). One can view the work of writers like Lévi-Strauss, Douglas and Sahlins as attempts to specify the structure of the culture that exercises this selective supervision and that is often specified by isolating sets of linked lexemes, 'classificatory systems', 'distinctive features' or 'constitutive elements'. These are certainly not the only ways of characterising a culture. But however it is done, there is little evidence, except of a purely *post hoc* kind, on which to base the claim that the decisive element in the selection of alternative possibilities, whether these are created by external contrast or by internal change, is solely or even mainly the voice of this abstract structure, which is homologous with what Khare calls 'ideology' and others 'a classificatory schema' or deep structural paradigm.

The related assumption that continuity occurs at the underlying level while only the surface changes seems open to question, partly because of the mainly retrospective character of the evidence. But as we have argued earlier it is equally possible for the 'trivial' to survive over time, at least in a literate culture, simply because it is not closely entailed with the more central features of the social system; the more peripheral a feature, the greater the possible autonomy. The alternative assumption tends to place conflict and contradiction on the surface, the boundary, the periphery, rather than at the centre, especially insofar as they lead to structural change. It is not surprising, therefore, to find so-called 'conflict' theory, which owes a general and diffuse debt to Marx, standing in opposition to much cultural and societal analysis that favours a more integrated, a more 'fitting' representation of social action. For it tends to concentrate on the role of internal and external contradictions over time, the opposition between individual groups and sub-cultures, and the external conflicts that are not simply part of the repetitive structure but alter the control over resources, the locus of domination or even the nature of the socio-cultural system itself.

Neither approach holds the monopoly on truth; nor are they alternatives in any real sense. Elements of social behaviour continue over time, others change. The idea that even revolution alters all is as naive as the view that the Chinese are just as they were before the victory of the Communist forces. As the Hsus point out (1977), the Revolution may not have altered Chinese cooking itself, but it did significantly modify the enormous meals and banquets of earlier times. The reason for this change, which was certainly not superficial, lies in the nature of earlier Chinese society, with its far-reaching differences in styles of life that were so marked in the restaurant culture of banqueting. We find that the contradictions inherent in the internal differentiation of cooking emerge more clearly in the work of those writers who modify the holistic assumption of much socio-cultural theorising. For the different forms of consumption in hierarchical societies are not simply transformations of a timeless cultural pattern that continues unaffected by a changing social system. They are in conflict with one another not only at the formal level

35

but in action too. They may generate conflict and conflict may generate change.

Change in the cuisine also comes about as the result of the introduction of ingredients and techniques from outside. While the domain of cooking is in many ways highly conservative – for reasons that will be discussed later – there have also been surprising changes. The advent of the potato in Irish diets, the appearance of the tomato in America, the land of ketchup, of maize and cassava in Africa, are all relatively recent. Since the sixteenth century, the cuisines of both Africa and Europe were transformed through the introduction of numerous cultigens from America, though both the potato (the 'Irish' potato) and the tomato (the 'love apple') were only taken up much later in the United States itself. It is difficult to conceive of Italian food without pasta and tomato paste. But the use of pasta may have arrived from China via Germany only in the fifteenth century.[13]

The study of change necessarily requires historical sources and methods. Some of the most interesting studies of food have been carried out by the contributors of that great journal of social and economic history, *Annales E.S.C.*, founded by Marc Bloch and Lucien Febvre. The leading figure has been Braudel whose *Capitalism and Material Life, 1400–1800* (1967 [1973]) contains a substantial section on food in Europe, the consumption of which he links directly with the processes of production. In 1961 *Annales* launched an appeal for more historical work not only on the study of nutrition but on food in general, eliciting a statement by Roland Barthes (1961 [1979]) on the 'psychosociology' of contemporary food consumption as well as a series of more specific studies.[14] The most important of these is an exhaustive book by Louis Stouff, *Ravitaillement et alimentation en Provence aux XIVe et XVe siècles* (1970) that also provides a useful bibliography for the France of that period. Stouff concludes by denying that there was an original Provençal cuisine in the late Middle Ages. The general elements of its food were found all around the Mediterranean. That outstanding feature of 'traditional' Provençal cooking of the nineteenth and twentieth centuries, olive oil, was used only for eggs, fish and frying beans. Otherwise it was the fat of salted pork, used particularly to flavour the soup of peas, beans and above all cabbage. This was the basic food, he claims, of the ordinary folk of Provence, just as it was in the rest of Europe at that time. The aristocracy also enjoyed a cosmopolitan menu but of a different kind (1970: 261–2). 'Traditional Provençal cooking', like many other folk-ways, only emerged in recent times, a salutary thought for those attached either to the holistic or to the timeless view of culture.

Work on the social history of food has not of course been confined to France, nor yet to Western Europe. The series of studies edited by K.C.

Chang on *Food in Chinese Culture* (1977) combines both historical and anthropological perspectives. Theoretically more important is that wide-ranging essay by Mintz on 'Time, sugar and sweetness' (1979). In this paper the author examines the political and economic forces behind the availability of sugar, the increasing sweetness of the European diet and its relation with slavery, indentured labour and the production of primary commodities in the Third World. The concentration on 'meaning' in a specific cultural context, he argues – and it is essentially the same argument as my own – has tended to push aside studies of longterm change. Even if one is trying to analyse meaning, symbolic structures cannot be treated as timeless; the meaning of sugar for the Lancashire mill worker is not determined in the metropolitan heartland alone. It is embedded in a world economy.

My own discussion of cooking takes place not so much in terms of the dichotomously based structures of gustemes, lexemes or even tech-nemes, but of the more diversified structures of household and class. Food and sex must both be related to the central human process of production and reproduction.[15] Since the former is linked to the mode of production of material goods, the analysis of cooking has to be related to the distribution of power and authority in the economic sphere, that is, to the system of class or stratification and to its political ramifications.

More specifically, the study of the process of providing and transforming food covers four main areas, that of growing, allocating, cooking and eating, which represent the phases of production, distribution, preparation and consumption:

Processes	Phases	Locus
Growing	Production	Farm
Allocating/storing	Distribution	Granary/market
Cooking	Preparation	Kitchen
Eating	Consumption	Table

To which should be added a fifth phase, often forgotten:

Clearing up	Disposal	Scullery

It is in the first of these phases that economic factors most clearly dominate,[16] since it is linked to aspects of primary production, the work organisation and the technology of producing and storing food, leading to the distribution of what is produced. The process of allocation is the most overtly political phase, because it is here that demands for rent, tribute and tax intervene, as well as the internal divisions within the domestic unit for conservation as seed, for sale in the market and above all for consumption until the next harvest. In the third phase, the

37

preparation of food, we shift from the field and the granary (or market-place) to the kitchen, to the arts of cooking and the cuisine. This is the arena usually allocated to women rather than men, and to servants rather than mistresses, where the system of division and stratification of domestic or patrimonial labour is made explicit. The fourth phase is that of the table, the consuming of prepared food, both the cooked and the raw, where the identity and differentiation of the group is brought out in the practice of eating together or separately, as well as in the content of what is eaten by different collectivities; this is the arena of feasts and fasts, of prohibitions and preferences, of communal and domestic meals, of table manners and modes of serving and service.

The boundaries that we adopt for any particular study are largely arbitrary – do we choose a set of cooking terms, a set of operations, a set of recipes? My own predilection is to try to link the nature of different cuisines to the ways in which food is produced, and to relate the system of agricultural production to the question of 'manners', 'cuisine' and more generally to the sub-cultures and social strata that are differentiated by their styles of life. It is possible to express some of these features in binary form. But I am more interested in seeing the endogenous/exogenous contrast in terms of the development of trade and other modes of exchange, and in seeing the presence of a concept of 'baking' as related to the adoption of the oven. Above all I am concerned with the existence and emergence of internally differentiated cuisines, which I see as related to the contrast between the 'food-ways' of Africa and Eurasia – to use Simoons's term for 'the modes of feeling, thinking, and behaving about food that are common to a cultural group' (1967: 3). In this context 'Africa' and 'Eurasia' have more than a geographical significance. Certain of these internal and external differences in 'food-ways' or 'nutritional systems' are related to the wider socio-economic situations that mark those continents. At the same time it is important to stress the similarities between various socio-cultural systems (manifestations of the total human situation, rather than the human mind *per se*) as well as the internal similarities that may crystallise around a common tradition. One has to aim at a balance between the acceptance of the dogma of cultural unity on the one hand (whether on the surface level of meaning to the actor or on the underlying one of homologous structures) and the recognition and explanation of diversity on the other. Methodologically, the investigation of concomitant variation still provides a fertile bed in which to cast the seed of a comparative sociology.

Like other social sciences, social anthropology does not produce sudden discoveries to parallel the decoding of Linear B by Ventris, nor does the idea of a revolution by paradigm shift have much relevance.

Certainly shifts of the kind from functionalism to structural functionalism can hardly be said to reorganise a body of theory and data in the way that Kuhn suggested for the natural sciences. Our frames are more general, and the problem for the anthropologist should not be the discarding of one in favour of another so much as trying to make a conjunction between them, in the interest not only of his own analysis but of the study of human society more generally. It is in the realm of theories of the middle range, to use Merton's phrase, that the intellectual struggle should take place. For it is at this level that we can seriously engage in integrating social theory and social enquiry. Moreover, the attempt to incorporate the most insightful elements should not be limited to the propositional frames current in one's own field alone. Those findings should relate to the broader context of the study of human society by historians, economists, political scientists and others; one cannot dissociate oneself from their work by taking refuge in parochial formulations of theory and practice; the world will catch on and catch up.

In the following chapter I look at the processes of production and consumption in two societies in northern Ghana with which I worked – one a former kingdom, the other a 'tribal' people. I do this partly in order to compare and contrast the two, with a view to making a further contrast with the major societies of Asia and Europe. But I also try to set the cuisine within the total context of the productive process, since this contributes an important element to my explanation of the more general contrast. At the same time I want to give some idea of the changing situation, of the links between northern Ghana and the wider world system, largely as I have experienced them, since the nature of the socio-cultural changes that are now taking place bears directly upon my general theme.

3

Production and consumption among the LoDagaa and Gonja of northern Ghana

One way, then, of looking at cooking and the sociology of cooking somewhat differently from those we have outlined, is to examine the link with the processes of production, distribution and consumption of food, not only in a particular society but also in a comparative perspective. This approach in no way negates attempts to elicit universal or even widespread features of the verbal concepts and expressions, or of the actual practices of cooking.[1] However, it must affect the nature of the general patterns we seek, whether these are assumed to originate in the human mind or in some more proximate source, just as it certainly modifies our understanding of the differences. That is to say, certain differences between French and English cooking have to be related at some point to differences in the local crops (such as the virtual absence of the vine and the olive in England), in the organisation of production (for example, the early death of the 'peasantry' in England, some would say its total absence[2]), just as certain broad differences in African and Eurasian cooking need to take into account the nature of hierarchy and the means of communication. Not that all important differences and similarities can be accounted for in this way, but nor do cultural explanations in terms of underlying homologies, nor yet a universalising account of the same kind, make much sense until the other aspects have been adequately explored and adequately comprehended. This is what I understand the linguists Lehrer and Rosch to be saying, and social scientists ought to be saying it a good deal louder.

To develop this point further I turn to two societies in West Africa in which I worked, both located in the savannah zone of northern Ghana. The dangers of generalising about Africa, even West Africa, on the basis of such limited studies are self-apparent; particularly at the level of production and the consumption of food, there are great differences between the people of the savannah and the people of the forest, between those living on cereals and those living on roots and fruits (especially bananas),[3] between pastoralists, hunters and agriculturalists, between the areas of Middle Eastern influence (especially through Islam) and of 'pagan' peoples, between the states of the great lakes (e.g. Ruanda) and other kingdoms, between the trading communities on the coast and in the hinterland, and the inhabitants of farming villages and dispersed settlements. To some of these differences I will refer later, but my two examples are chosen not merely because of personal knowledge over a number of years, but because they represent a contrast in terms of their political organisation.

The complication of dealing with the situation in northern Ghana, as in most of Africa, is that during the short period of an individual's allotted span of three score years and ten there has been a general shift from pre-colonial regimes through colonial rule to national governments. These political transformations have gone hand in hand with socio-economic changes that have affected the processes of production, distribution and consumption, as well as the nature of the divisions between social groups and between individuals. Such changes, which provide support for my general thesis, are in a sense incorporated in the present, which has not simply dismissed the past out of hand. Where relevant, I have tried to distinguish the different periods to which my comments refer. But the procedures of a field anthropologist should always be borne in mind when assessing his remarks. My primary data come from intensive work among the LoDagaa in 1949–51, and in Gonja in 1956–7, and again in 1964–6. I have revisited these regions many times, the last occasion that I stayed in the village of Birifu being the Christmas period of 1978–9, so that my own observations cover a thirty year period. For the pre-colonial regimes I rely upon what historical documents exist, works of travellers like Binger (1892), early administrative records, and Arabic documents. But perhaps most importantly I depend on a careful assessment not only of the recollections of old men but of socio-cultural continuities and discontinuities, an assessment that is not necessarily the less valuable simply because it is personal. In other words, an anthropologist has to make the maximal use of documents for reconstructing recent social history but places more reliance not so much on the impersonal collection of 'oral traditions' but on active participation in a cultural setting in which he remains a stranger but not always an outsider. The most important clues to the social organisation of the recent but poorly documented past lie in the present, if only because in reconstructing that past one has to reconstruct, in reverse, the process of change. If these procedures lead me at times to delve into what may seem excessive ethnographic detail, that is because there are so few alternative ways of supporting a hypothesis, of giving substance to one's theories.

The LoDagaa were a 'tribal' people before the British conquered northern

41

Villages, towns and peoples in Ghana

Ghana at the beginning of the present century. They had no system of chiefship, though leaders might arise in special situations. The social organisation was based on a network of 'parishes', areas under the supernatural control of a particular Earth shrine, which placed sanctions on its congregation, especially upon shedding the blood of any other inhabitant. Each parish was divided into areas that were identified with a group of shallow lineages belonging to one patriclan which contributed the bulk of the residents; other members of these clans would be living in other parishes, distributed near and far. In addition to being a member of a patriclan, every individual also belonged to a named matriclan through his mother, a clan that in one section of the LoDagaa (which I call the LoDagaba, as distinct from the LoWili) was important in the transmission of moveable property. The property so transferred included the objects of production, the contents of the granary, the animals that had been bought with the cowries got from selling any extra grain that remained over at the end of the year, indeed all livestock, cowries, and other forms of wealth, leaving the sons with only the house, the land and the main instrument of production, the hoe.

Politically, Gonja was quite different. Covering a large though very thinly populated area of northern Ghana, it formed an independent kingdom before the coming of the British, one which had remained under the rule of a group claiming descent from the horsed invaders, under the leadership of Jakpa, who had conquered the territory, probably at the end of the sixteenth century. These foreign conquerors from the Niger Bend were accompanied by Muslim men of learning who provided assistance in their conquests and whose descendants have held a privileged position ever since. The state was thus made up of the ruling estate, Muslims and commoners, together with a considerable number of slaves. Whereas the LoDagaa were an agricultural people, the Gonja were also horsed warriors (the ruling estate) and traders (largely the Muslim estate), while among the commoners there were some craftsmen, such as weavers, and throughout a greater use of slave labour.

In order to compare and contrast cooking among the LoDagaa and the Gonja, we need to see the process of preparing materials for human consumption as the end point of that major activity of humankind (reproduction apart), that is, the production of food. And to do this we must examine, as a 'set', a whole, a unity, the phases of the production, distribution, preparation and consumption of food.

THE PHASES OF PRODUCTION (P/P)

The main phases of the process of production are:

plants	*animals*
a. preparation of field, tools, labour	preparation of byre, feed, herders
b. planting	breeding
c. cultivating	herding
d. harvesting	slaughtering
e. conservation (including seed)	husbandry

In pre-agricultural, pre-pastoral societies, indeed in hunting and gathering activity in general, the second phase is left to nature, requiring no direct human input. Of course husbandry is necessary even for wild resources, and religion is a major means by which this is ensured. I have suggested elsewhere that one aspect of the phenomenon that goes under the name of totemism is precisely this husbanding, this protection, of natural resources, which means both protecting the resources for man's future use and protecting man from the consequences of their destruction (Goody 1962: 117ff.). And while wild animals and plants do not have to be weeded or herded, they do have to be searched for. The hunt for animals is especially complicated, since their location is more directly a reaction to earlier human activity; to find their whereabouts men employ not only the techniques of the tracker but also those of divination, which, it has been claimed, can make a useful contribution by 'randomising' man's actions with regard to his prey. In contrast to the deliberate and time-taking search that is characteristic of most hunting and gathering before the plant is picked or the animal killed, the essence of the Neolithic way of life is the process of domestication whereby plants and animals are brought in from the wilds once and for all, then installed in the vicinity of the house (the *domus*).

THE ASPECTS OF PRODUCTION (P/A)

In addition to the phases of production we need to consider its main aspects under the following heads:

a. items of production
b. the labour force (and the division of labour)
c. the productive resources, land, water and fertilizing agents
d. the technology and techniques of production
e. the quantities and quality produced, which relates to famine and plenty, to the viability of the unit of production and to the disposal of any surplus.

Aside from the division of labour, the first four items are aspects of the forces of production; the relations of production are considered in the wider context of the total social organisation. Among the Gonja and LoDagaa the means of production were very similar; farming was carried out by the hoe, there was little pressure on land (more among the 'tribal' LoDagaa), but with much on labour at the critical periods of clearing, weeding and harvesting. Here slave labour, in the fields as well as in the house, in trade as in the workshop, played a greater part among the Gonja.

THE PHASE OF DISTRIBUTION

The phase of food distribution is affected in straightforward ways by the nature of the produce. In the simpler societies located in the warmer climates, it is difficult to conserve meat and fish, though smoking is sometimes resorted to. The flesh of the larger animals is therefore distributed over a short period of time, creating specific relations of exchange; hence the importance of its wide distribution in hunting bands, who cannot control the moment of slaughter, as agricultural and pastoral communities do, waiting either for the advent of the market or for the moment of sacrifice (Goody 1981). More importantly, the phase of food distribution is affected by the location of 'essential' products, the level of productivity, the nature of the system of transport, the division of labour, the level of tax or tribute, the presence of a market, in other words by central features of the socio-economic system.

The framework for the analysis of modes of distribution has been made in terms of types of transaction, rather than phases, though it must be insisted these types do not refer to a society's total transactions but to specific sets of relations within societies. Even in systems dominated by market exchange, gift-giving and reciprocal exchange occur; one of the main problems of economic anthropology, and more generally of political economy, has been the tendency towards the exclusive identification of types of transaction or indeed modes of appropriation with particular types of social system. The relationships are more complex in character.

TYPES OF TRANSACTION (D/T)

a. allocation within the unit of production (e.g. to the different wives in a polygynous family)
b. gift, without expectation of return
c. 'reciprocal' exchange
d. the market

e. obligatory transfer, centric or non-centric, up or down
f. destruction

Market exchanges are clearly most developed in fully-fledged market economies, while obligatory centric transfers largely depend upon the ability of a state to collect, consume and possibly redistribute the items under the ultimate threat of force. But the latter also includes exactions made by freebooters and other raiders. The phrase 'centric transfer' is derived from Pryor (1977), for whom transfers differ from exchange transactions in lacking a balanced counterflow; they can be arranged along a continuum according to the 'centricity' of focus, i.e. in terms of how far they centre upon an institution or individual having a society-wide role. I have, however, excluded gifts, 'voluntary' transfers, from this category, since it seems important to distinguish them from tax, tribute and transfers of similar kinds, whether 'accumulative' or 'redistributive' in character.

THE ASPECTS OF DISTRIBUTION (D/A)

The aspects of the distributive process consist not only of (a) the nature of transactions within the group, but also those outside the unit of production (b):

a. the nature of transactions within
b. and without
c. the equality of distribution within
d. the technology of storage
e. the technology of transport
f. the periodicity of distribution.

Within the unit of production, distribution varies in its periodicity (which may clearly depend upon the product), in the system of allocation, e.g. whether *per capita* or *per stirpes*, by head or by stock, and in the equality of shares (especially of prized foods) among seniors and juniors, among men and women, among masters and servants. The quantities and kinds of food distributed will vary according to the season, which may result in an alternation between times of plenty (usually after the harvest) and times of dearth (usually after the planting). It is this seasonal variation that plays an important role in determining what menus are appropriate or possible for the time of year, the availability of different foods depending upon their intrinsic conservability, the existing techniques of storage, on the length of the harvest season.

The result of Pryor's elaborate analysis, which he calls *The Origins of the Economy*, is summarised in his concluding chapter:

Societies at very low levels of economic development seem to rely on reciprocal exchange of goods and labour and the noncentric transfer of goods as their primary modes of distribution, while societies at higher levels of economic development seem to rely primarily on the market exchange of goods and labour and the centric transfers of goods and labour (1977: 314).

The conclusion seems obvious enough but each term in this statement is carefully defined and it can be argued that we need to demonstrate in a reasonably definitive manner what we assume to be true on other grounds. Many authors have expressed the view that systems of transaction, including those in food, vary in accordance with politico-economic factors. I want to make a similar point, at somewhat lesser length, about aspects of the consumption of food, centring upon the kitchen and the table, partly in order to emphasise certain general differences between the traditional hierarchies in Africa on the one hand and in Europe and Asia on the other. For without appreciating such differences one cannot begin to explain the nature of the cuisine, nor yet the nature of the hierarchy.

THE PHASE OF PREPARATION

A characteristic feature of pre-industrial societies is the close link between the processes of production, distribution, preparation and consumption, processes that are often carried out within a set of closely related domestic groups (Fortes 1949a; Goody 1958; E. Goody 1973). A rough paradigm for the analysis of consumption requires a further breakdown of these processes into the preparation of food ('in the kitchen') and the consumption of food ('on the table').

The *preparation* of food comprises three phases (Pr/P):

a. preliminary work, the butchering of meat, the shelling of nuts, the husking, winnowing and grinding of cereals
b. cooking, the application of heat, or other transforming agents (cold, vinegar, salt, etc.)
c. the dishing up

while the aspects (Pr/A) we need to consider are:

a. who cooks, with whom (the cooking group) and for whom (the consumption group)
b. the technology of cooking (hearth, containers, instruments, oven, spit and fuels).

THE PHASE OF CONSUMPTION

The *consumption* of food consists of the following phases (C/P):
a. the assembling of the participants

b. the serving or distribution of the cooked food
c. eating the food
d. clearing away,
while the following aspects (C/A) require comment:
  a. the distribution in time (daily meals, feasting, fasting, etc.)
  b. the structure of the meal
  c. ways of eating (sacralisation, 'table manners', cleansing, service)
  d. the technology of eating (table, containers, instruments, etc.)
  e. who eats with whom (the eating group)
  f. the differentiation of the cuisine.

Finally, there is the question of the disposal of the left-overs, of great importance in sacred meals but of considerable significance in secular ones too.

PRODUCTION

The central items of the diet of the LoDagaa fall in broad categories that are essentially similar (at an analytic level) to those found among the majority of the human race and that resemble closely (at an emic level) those found throughout the savannah region.

The major types of food are: cereals, root crops, meat, vegetables, condiments, oil. The cereals (guinea-corn, bullrush millet and maize), sometimes root crops (yams, sweet potatoes, ground-nuts, bambara beans, frafra potatoes) and occasionally beans, provide the bulk of the diet, the solid carbohydrate base. Vegetables and meat, both wild and domesticated, provide the soup or relish which, seasoned by condiments, mainly salt and pepper, accompanies the main dish. And the oil is occasionally used for frying.

The oil was provided from wild sources, mainly from the shea nut, but nowadays ground nut oil is increasingly used, though it is purchased in the local market rather than prepared in the house, largely because of the advantages of milling devices that are not available to everybody. Like other wild vegetable products, shea nuts are collected almost exclusively by women. Men's contribution from the wild consisted of game animals and occasionally honey. It is women too who collect firewood for cooking, an arduous activity in densely cultivated areas since they have to travel so far to get the wood. But men are responsible for chopping down the larger trees used for building houses, for making dug-out canoes, for carving ancestral figures and for heating the house on special occasions.

It is men too who look after domestic livestock, though women sometimes own smaller animals. Like most agricultural peoples in Africa the LoDagaa do not milk their animals, except to give to dogs, so that women are not involved in that aspect of pastoral care. Sometimes a LoDagaa or Gonja will place his cattle in charge of a Fulani family, who has come to settle, temporarily at any rate, in the area. In these Fulani families the women milk the animals and sell the products, including butter.

There are some differences in the cultivated crops that affect the diets of the LoDagaa and Gonja. Gonja is situated some 100 to 200 miles nearer the rain forest, and yams are much more plentiful. Among the LoDagaa, yams were not grown on any scale; young men would be permitted to cultivate their own small patch under a tree in the evenings, but the yams were often sold in the market, given as gifts or used to provide food for honoured guests. In Gonja yams are much more plentiful and form a major part of the diet, as well as being exported. Nowadays many LoDagaa have migrated into western Gonja and more recently into northern Ashanti (Brong-Ahafo) in order to plant much larger areas on a commercial basis. These they sell to traders for transporting to the markets of the south, where they are a staple food. In eastern Gonja a mass migration of Konkomba for similar purposes (Crellin 1979) extends into the Volta Region. In effect there is a kind of pincer movement of these active agriculturalists, 'tribal' peoples who have adapted to the new market conditions and whose settlements meet in central Gonja. Both in the west and the east, the new migrants, sometimes in collaboration with the non-Gonja speaking commoners, have upset the political balance by exercising their right to vote against the ruling estate and its allies, now in the minority, who have held a virtual monopoly of power at the national as well as the local level ever since the first elections in 1951.

It is of course the advent of lorry transport that enabled the LoDagaa and Konkomba to turn to commercial yam farming on this scale, although the initial migration of members of these groups was undertaken for other reasons, for refuge and expansion in the first case, and for farm work and expansion in the second. In this way rural migration helped to meet part of the demand for food created by the movement into towns not only of their own tribesmen but also of the inhabitants of the former kingdoms of the north and south where agricultural labour was less well regarded. However, a large part of this demand has to be met by the importation of food from outside the country, using scarce foreign exchange but producing lower food prices.

The importance of the commercial farming of yams has grown recently with the wild inflation of the last few years. On a recent visit (from December 1978 to January 1979) to the LoDagaa settlement of Birifu (Chaa) where I first worked, I found that at least one male from each of 24 houses (I went round 27 in all) had left to farm yams and maize in the neighbourhood of Techiman in Brong-Ahafo. The returns were considerable, for under the particular conditions of inflation, these farmers, who made few demands on the market, accumulated a large surplus of cash, some of which was invested in the improvement of houses in their original settlement. The continuing density of population in that settlement was made possible by these migrant farmers who sent cash and food back to their natal homes, just as other areas of northern Ghana were actively assisted by their urban migrants.

Despite the contribution of the LoDagaa to their production, yams do not play the same part in their diet as they do for the Gonja. Indeed, as with the kola nut among the Ashanti to the south, the abstinence of the producers (or at least their low demand) increases the surplus available for export. But among the Gonja, yams are the preferred food, eaten either boiled or pounded into a starchy ball, that is, in the form of the dish known in Ashanti as *fufu*. The other major crop found in Gonja but not further north is cassava (*manihot esculenta*) which, mixed with flour made from millet (*pennisetum*) or guinea-corn (*sorghum*), forms the basis of the porridge (*kude*) that is eaten all the year round, especially when yams are not available, and is also the major food distributed at festivals.

There are some differences in livestock, too, though few that influence the diet or the cuisine. Being nearer the forest, Gonja is less hospitable to cattle, mainly because of the tsetse fly. The ruling estate had to import their horses since foals did not survive; indeed the horses themselves were very susceptible, and one chief told me he had bought some twenty horses in all during his lifetime, simply to have an animal always on display. Nowadays there are very few horses, though every major chief has to have one; in January 1979 the paramount chief, Yagbumwura Mahama, had his horse tethered in front of the house he was using as a temporary 'palace' in Damongo, and it was perhaps the most visible sign of his occupancy. But horses never formed any part of the diet of the Gonja; nor did the donkey that was used for the transport of goods to the market towns of the northern savannahs (in contrast to horses which carried only humans), and that is now extremely rare, though it is making a comeback in the neighbouring territory of Upper Volta, where it is used to pull small metal carts. The increase in oil prices and the difficulty of obtaining lorries argue for the extension of such intermediate technology to Ghana, an aim that is being encouraged by a current project for the development of the region.[4]

Camels, which were occasionally seen as far south as Salaga, did not form any part of the Gonja diet either. But cows did, though unlike the other animals these were and are scarcer in Gonja than among the LoDagaa. Even in pre-colonial times, cattle, sheep and goats were imported, especially from the Mossi Kingdoms, just as were the transport animals, a fact that is clear from the report of the French traveller, Louis Binger (1892). In early colonial times, before the advent of mechanical transport, the trade in livestock developed vigorously; Salaga was a major market-place, though its main role was as the operational centre for Muslim traders who had the cattle driven down from the north by nomadic Fulani, fattened them up in the tsetse-free environs of the town and dispatched them to Kumasi for sale at a substantial profit. Another major track went from the Mamprusi town of Yagaba, down through Daboya and Gbuipe to Kintampo and Kumasi, but this route through the bush gradually diminished in importance with the coming of motor transport. Even those moving cattle on the hoof preferred to drive them down by the side of the motor road built some fifty miles to the east rather than through the less accessible countryside.

Thus Gonja found itself in the midst of a market economy in livestock, with a strong demand for meat from the forest areas to the south. Part of this demand was met by dispatching domestic livestock, part by the sale of the smoked meat of wild animals, often fetched by southern traders themselves. But the town had always known market activity, and its existence was largely dependent upon the control of trade routes leading to and from Ashanti. Even the LoDagaa were involved in some market exchange of a long-distance kind, quite apart from the vigorous activity of local markets. So it is certainly a mistake to see the members of these societies as unaware of 'the market principle'. Otherwise it becomes impossible to explain how readily they have engaged in such activity so soon after the coming of colonial rule; in earlier times Salaga merchants often travelled very widely in search of goods, and today the LoDagaa have quickly taken to commercial farming. The question is not the presence or absence of an abstract 'market principle' (and here it seems that the writings of some substantivists and some Marxists are misleading), but rather the extent to which this so-called principle is applicable in a given social system, the range of social action over which it operates, differences in which are much more important than formalists like Hopkins, the leading economic historian of West Africa, would allow.[5] The point is not simply a matter of finding some uneasy compromise; the ranges of market activity clearly do vary systematically under different forms of social organisation; it is not a matter of a loosely structured, loosely perceived continuum beloved by 'empiricists', or rather by atomists, but of ordered links within certain types of socio-economic system.

In Gonja there was a market in meat, of which the elaborate hierarchy of butchers in Salaga provides ample evidence; in the few major towns of the kingdom we find professional butchers, often reputed to be of Hausa origin, as distinct from the simple sacrificers of rural life. But little of this meat found its way to Gonja bellies. In eastern Gonja the divisional chief of Kpembe did benefit, since his representative, the Leppowura, received a portion of every animal killed in the nearby commercial centre of Salaga, the twin-town of the capital. But otherwise it was on the flesh of wild animals that they relied. The Gonja had not only more open land than the LoDagaa but also more effective weapons, including some guns even in the pre-colonial era. These had to be brought along the northern trade routes, or later up the Volta valley, because Ashanti refused to allow guns or gunpowder to pass through its own territory to its vassals or dependent neighbours.[6] With regard to game the chief also benefited from every kill, at least in principle, for he received one leg of each wild animal slaughtered.

The greater dependence of the Gonja on the flesh of wild animals derived, then, partly from the thinner population, partly from the relative absence of cattle, and partly from their martial activities, both in warfare and the chase: the killing of men and of game always make close neighbours. But they were also able to exploit other wild resources to a greater extent; fish from the many rivers were used in soup, sometimes supplied by the professional ferrymen (*ntere*) who manned every river crossing, though nowadays handed over by Hausa and Ewe fishermen who have migrated up every river and who catch for export more than for local consumption. In this climate fresh fish keeps for no time at all, so it is usually smoked or dried for conservation as well as for flavour. Other wild produce to which the Gonja have greater access include the shea nut, the source of the 'butter' which was sometimes exported to Ashanti as a pomade, as well as the numerous wild fruits and vegetables that are eaten raw, go into the soup, or are used not for meals as such, but for healing men of their maladies. Medicine (L.D. *tíi*), whether good or bad ('poison'), is closely related to food (L.D. *bundiri*, edibles, sometimes excluding 'meat', *nen*), although the first is generally 'drunk' or sometimes 'swallowed'.

One resource stands out as providing a refreshment unknown to the LoDagaa, namely palm wine. Here and there, in the thicker vegetation by the river banks in the southern part of Gonja, one finds clumps of palms which are tapped (or rather beheaded) to provide a deliciously sweet drink that soon ferments and becomes more vinegary. In principle the chief is entitled to a proportion of this wild resource (as is the case with fish), and in the evening farmers coming back from distant plots sometimes arrive at his house with a bottle-gourd full of the frothy sap. It is some years ago that the Gonja acquired the technique of distilling from the Ashanti, who in their turn had acquired it from the Europeans;

there had previously been no distillation in Africa, only the brewing of beer. In forest clearings, far removed from the main tracks, tar barrels were set up to serve as stills which turned the palm wine into *akpetassi*, 'local gin'. Until Independence in 1957, distilling was illegal; indeed no spirits were on sale in the north, both of which facts were sources of conflict with the government authorities. After Independence, the restrictions were lifted, and local distillation was allowed providing the product was sold to the national distillery for further treatment. Within a short time, many pools or dams near a road saw the growth of little encampments, inhabited mainly by Ashanti, who used the water to mix with imported sugar and imported yeast (delivered by lorry) to make into a cheap gin. The palm-wine base was by-passed, and so too was the injunction to sell to the state. The use of gin, already a part of many ceremonies (as in Ashanti), became much more popular among members of the ruling estate and the commoners, and its consumption may even have affected the productivity of labour, a subject to which I shall return.

In any case, it seems probable that Gonja agriculture has been less productive than that of the LoDagaa for some time past, a contrast that applies to other savannah states in comparison with the tribal areas. In the first place, Gonja has more specialists, blacksmiths, weavers and others, who, while they farm, do not depend upon their plots alone; secondly, the soil is poorer; but thirdly, and most importantly, neither the Muslims nor the chiefs regarded farming as their major activity – indeed it was one which in earlier times they had gladly left to slaves. In 1957 the Gbuipewura proudly declared to us that he had never gone farming in his life. And while his boast is not necessarily to be taken literally, it does indicate a general attitude to farming, and one which was in some ways easier to sustain in pre-colonial times than in the period since 1900. Among the LoDagaa, such an attitude would be considered outrageous (except among the 'educated') and even the very old play their part in farming. Moreover, farmers work a good deal harder than among the Gonja, whose plots are situated at a considerable distance from the settlement, so that much time is spent walking to and fro, and there is little incentive for a spell of evening work when the sun is cooler.

When the Gonja possessed slaves, who had to be constantly replenished by raids, the aversion to farming could be fully expressed; though the surplus derived from servile labour must have been low, it was sufficient to live frugally. With the disappearance of slavery, they have had to pay more attention to farming, or else to make money in some other way so that they can buy food from the immigrant farmers, some of whom have built their houses on the old slave settlements, which were situated near towns and were therefore convenient for the market.[7] Gonja certainly gives the impression of having a less plentiful food supply, partly because one sees less, as the fields are far away and the harvested product kept in the fields. In contrast, the LoDagaa house is built around the swelling granary which plays such an important part in social life, especially its ritual aspects, which in itself indicates the greater dependence on cereals, since cassava and yams may be stored in the ground or in other ways. But the difference is not simply a matter of external appearances.

The greater specialisation in Gonja was, as we have seen, a function not only of the division into 'rulers'–'warriors', Muslim–traders, commoners (who were farmers and hunters, and sometimes craftsmen or gunmen as well) and slaves (largely agricultural, though involved in transport, trade and probably in craft-production as well), but also of the various clusters of specialist tasks, weaving and dyeing, smithying and butchering, barbering and, for women, the making of pots. The extent to which such groups were also involved in the production of food in pre-colonial times remains difficult to assess. Binger notes that his host in Salaga, an important Muslim trader, possessed a farm at a slave village north of the town, where his brother was living at the time of his visit (1888) and apparently supervising the agricultural work. Judging by the relationship of present members of the ruling estate with descendants of former slaves, the same kind of close association existed then too, suggesting that even those performing other roles and not actually hoeing themselves did run their own farms, cultivated by servile labour but managed by a member of the immediate family. Indeed male slaves not only undertook farming but also carried water and collected firewood, tasks otherwise undertaken by women; a sketch by Binger shows this very clearly for Salaga, where the large number of dry season traders placed heavy demands on such supplies. However, elsewhere too the fetching of water was often a burdensome task in the dry season, for water generally lies deeper than in the region occupied by the LoDagaa and in some parts it can only be found in the permanent rivers. Binger (1906: 27) speaks of women sleeping by the well in the dry season to be next in line. The sale of water and firewood were both profitable enterprises in Salaga at that time.[8]

While there are some advantages in living close to such rivers, because of the availability of fish to eat and of water for dry season gardening (especially tobacco), they are unhealthy places and recognised as such. They formed the breeding grounds of the mosquito, the simulium fly and the tsetse which were in their turn causes of the major diseases, malaria, river blindness and sleeping sickness. Ferrymen were deliberately stationed at river-crossings to provide the necessary transport for official and trading purposes, but free men preferred to keep their distance. And in the absence of alternative sources of water, women (or slaves, male and female) might have to travel a long way to fill a pot for domestic purposes. The LoDagaa, on the other hand, had fewer problems with water, living as they do near the Black Volta with its various tributaries and springs; on the other hand, because of the greater density of population there was more of a problem with firewood, whose collection was again the task of women.

The division of labour occurs within units of production as well as between them. Apart from the division between the free and the slaves which was much more relevant in pre-colonial Gonja than among the LoDagaa, there were also the divisions between elders (*ainés*) and juniors (*cadets*), and between men and women, which some recent writers have attempted to assimilate to a division between classes.

I do not myself find this way of looking at the division between generations very helpful in the analysis of the data from northern Ghana. Here as elsewhere the senior generation exercises a good measure of control over the activities of the younger members of the group and it is true that where bridewealth is high, as among the LoDagaa and the other tribal peoples (J. and E. Goody 1967), the ability of a man to marry depends upon his kin releasing the goods required. But such goods cannot simply be considered as the product of the labour of young unmarried men. In the first place they are generally produced by the marriage of a sister. In the second, we have to consider the developmental cycle. Over the first twenty years of a man's lifetime, he can hardly be said to produce much more than he consumes, given the limited contribution he makes over the first ten or even fifteen years. It is only at adolescence that he really begins to add to the family's larder. Today this stage is often further postponed, indefinitely so in the case of most of those who have received a school education, and temporarily so for those who take this time as their one opportunity to push off south and work in an urban, or, more usually, a rural context, as wage-labourers.

Labour migration of this kind is more frequent among the LoDagaa (Fiéloux 1980) than the Gonja, but in earlier times the latter were less constrained, partly because bridewealth was low (as in the other savannah states) and provided no obstacle to marriage, while some youngsters were encouraged to leave their homes, either being sent as foster-children (E. Goody 1981) or setting off on a kind of walk-about to explore their field of kin connections, and at the same time their kingdom (E. Goody 1973).

The division of labour by sex dominates the productive process, and it is very early that boys and girls are socialised into their respective adult roles. We have seen that as far as wild produce is concerned (*wie*, bush, or *mwo puo*, in the grass, is how the LoDagaa would describe this sector of their universe), it is men who take part in hunting, either *en masse* with bows and arrows among the LoDagaa, or individually but with more sophisticated equipment among the Gonja.[9] On the other hand, it is women who do the collecting or gathering of wood, water, shea nuts, baobab pods and leaves, dawa dawa fruit and leaves, that make up a significant portion of the diet, while members of both sexes collect the leaves that are used for their respective medicines.

In the fields, it is men who play the major part in food production, a situation that distinguishes the savannah belt of West Africa from the forest region nearer the coast, as well as from much of East Africa (Boserup 1970; Goody 1973). This does not mean to say that women have no role in productive activities; the collecting of fuel and water is quite as essential to the domestic economy as the production of the raw produce itself, because these are the items required to make the ingredients into a meal, as well as to transform guinea-corn into beer, to wash and to warm oneself in the cooler season or when sickness strikes.

While it is men who cultivate the fields, women plant cereals and assist in harvesting grain and ground-nuts, although men cut off the heads and dig out the yams and other root crops. More importantly, women grow the vegetables needed for the soup (okra, squash, tomatoes, garden eggs, pepper, etc.) – among the LoDagaa in the fertile patch of garden land (*semaan*) that surrounds the compound and in Gonja on their husbands' more distant farms.

The apparently smaller role of women in primary productive activities in comparison with their counterparts elsewhere in Africa is difficult to explain. It is true that farming itself is more arduous here than in the forest region, where the major effort lies in clearing the ground, a male task. Moreover, the provision of fuel and water can be much more time-consuming than in the well-wooded, well-watered parts. Certainly, if we take the balance of work involved in the activities seen as necessary to run the domestic groups, there is no obvious inequality in the contribution of the sexes, perceived or felt, as between the savannah and forest regions. On the other hand, the allocation of key roles in the production of vegetable food in the south gives women a more central role in the running of the household, even if the total workload is roughly similar to that in the savannah. And just as they are more closely linked to central parts of the domestic economy, so they play more role in the market too. Of course in most parts of West Africa, it is women who retail food in the market, whether cooked or uncooked, though men deal in the larger quantities that the advent of lorries now makes possible to distribute to the urban markets. But it is in the south that 'market mammies' have come into their own in a big way, where they form a significant part of the total retail network and play a correspondingly important role in politics. In the north, too, women enter vigorously into trade, especially now that the existence of a *kalabule* (or 'black market') economy in Ghana combined with very rapid inflation, means that all non-producers have to trade in some goods in order to survive. But they do not dominate the market place in quite the same way as their counterparts in the south.

I have touched upon the nature of the major productive resources, that is, land and water. Land is plentiful in Gonja and nowadays, as is shown by the influx of immigrant farmers, strangers have few problems in getting land to farm, although in pre-colonial times states did not have the same attraction for 'tribal' peoples, who were reluctant to barter their freedom for land. The greater density of the LoDagaa, as against the Gonja, is typical of tribes and states respectively in this area, a situation that runs counter to many assumptions about the relations between political centralisation and population density. But greater density was to some extent the result of the slave-raids made by states upon these uncontrolled, 'acephalous' peoples (tribes without rulers), driving them into less accessible areas, and partly a deliberate reaction against their continual depradations, engendered by a policy of clustering together in scattered dwellings so as to offer more effective resistance. For such raids were needed in order to pay the tribute demanded by their southern neighbours, the Ashanti, whose control of guns and powder meant a perpetual superiority in weaponry as against the Gonja, who were dependent largely on the horse, the sword and the spear, though with some gunmen of their own. But they needed slaves not only to pay off the Ashanti and to purchase horses from the north, but also for their own internal purposes, that is, for males to undertake work in the fields as farm-hands and carriers, for women to work in the house as wives or concubines.

The control of water throughout the region is very elementary; favourable circumstances, such as exist in Chaa (Birifu), allow for simple irrigation by gravity drainage along crude channels. But without the pulley or the wheel there is otherwise no way of drawing water for anything except limited household purposes. Even then the water sources, where they exist, are of a primitive kind, despite the evidence of more complex cisterns in earlier times and the presence today in Salaga of many simple wells. So the dry season is often a time of shortage when the little water that remains in pools becomes thick with mud. At this time cattle are driven near the banks of rivers, many of which are impermanent, in order to get what water and grass is available. At the same time, some water is carried up in pots from the few permanently flowing rivers to sprinkle on the dry season gardens. But certainly the supply of water was and remains one of the major problems of the region, and particularly of the Gonja.

Among the LoDagaa the cattle wander over the home fields after the harvest has been gathered in and provide some fertiliser additional to the domestic waste that gets scattered over the women's vegetable patch. But in Gonja the fields are some miles from the village (as are the bush farms of the LoDagaa), and the cattle are usually kept near at hand. The fertility of the soil comes from the natural processes of regeneration – for farms are moved every few years – as well as from the ashes of the trees, bushes and grass that are burnt when the ground is cleared. The greater degree of permanent cultivation among the LoDagaa (combined with a limited use of manure) is certainly related to their greater density.

As far as technology is concerned, the hoe was the major instrument of production, the plough (like the wheel) never having been adopted in Africa south of the Sahara. In northern Ghana, attempts were made to introduce bullock farming during the colonial period, but for the newly independent government of Nkrumah, encouraged by the advice of foreign experts of Eastern and Western powers, all keen to export their mechanised products and development ideologies, the animal-drawn plough was backward-looking as compared with the petrol-driven tractor. While the majority of the farming population continued, as they still do, to use the hoe, governmental schemes such as the large-scale project of the Gonja Development Corporation,[10] the State Farms, the Builders Brigade, in all their various transformations, attempted to introduce mechanised agriculture, at considerable costs and minimal returns, at least as far as the production of crops was concerned. Only recently, with a tardy realisation of the cost of mechanised farming, has animal traction begun to enjoy a modest success.[11] At the same time, the development of high-yielding varieties of crops and the subsidising of farm inputs and equipment through an overvalued currency has led private individuals to invest in the large-scale tractor farming of rice and maize, a development that is having far-reaching consequences for land-holding and stratification in the rural areas. But the bulk of the population still farm by the iron hoe, as they have always done in the past.

I suggested that with the disappearance of slavery less food was available in Gonja than among the LoDagaa, although this lack has probably been made up by the labour of 'tribal' immigrants who have moved into the empty spaces and who are now exporting food to the south. It is clear that in pre-colonial times hunger, even famine, was more prevalent than today, despite the dramatic droughts of the Sahel region and the rapid growth of population in recent times. An entry in the Gonja Chronicle for 1745/6 reads: 'Then came a sickness which killed many people in the country of Gonja; there also came a famine and there was no food. The people were about to fly the country and a measure of corn was sold for one hundred and fifty cowries' (Goody 1954). Other references speak of a plague of locusts in the same year, and the constant wars were clearly no help to those engaged in the productive process, for even if these took place in the dry season, the contents of the granaries were likely to be plundered or destroyed.

Epidemics, pests and wars might restrict farming; the lack of rain, always a subject of concern in the Sahel and the savannah, was another problem, and in the past recurrent droughts have driven pastoralists and agriculturalists southwards towards the forest regions as they did in drought of 1974. Even when the crop had reached maturity, there was the danger of a plague of locusts descending on the cereal crops. And even without these special problems, people had difficulty in growing enough food for their families, especially where the population was dense, given the limitations of hoe agriculture and the low yields of the crops. It was this recurrent shortage that gave rise among the Tallensi to what Fortes called 'the hungry period', a period that came at the end of the agricultural year when people needed their full strength to hoe the fields and enough in the granary to provide the food and beer for those who come to help. The regularity of this phenomenon among the Tallensi was no doubt related to their higher density, but no population enjoyed a large surplus and all were subject to occasional famine.[12]

Famine often brings its own cuisine, based upon a selection of foods that are not ordinarily consumed. In towns, animals such as cats and rats enter into the repertoire from which in normal times they are excluded. The most extreme instances include the flesh of horses and men. In the country people have more direct access to the bounty of nature and often revert to 'wild' foods, even formerly domesticated species that played a more important part in the diet of earlier times. In wartime Europe of the 1940s, many country dwellers went about collecting chestnuts and berries, using them for a far greater range of cooking than happens today; now the large chestnut plantations of France and Italy have fallen on hard times, mainly due to the labour involved in their collection when alternative 'commercial' foods are available. In China the peasant knows of a whole range of 'famine plants' which are not ordinarily used but knowledge of which is handed down from one generation to the next (Chang 1977: 9). A similar situation was found in Europe (Stouff 1970). Some such knowledge exists in northern Ghana. Binger (1892: ii, 49) writes of a wild tuber, *Tacca involucrata*, that appears to have been used in times of hunger. Knowledge of such plants is less close to the surface than in the pre-colonial period when Binger was travelling in the area. Nevertheless some of this lore has been preserved not only by hunters, whose sources of food are closer to nature, but also by those responsible for collecting and compounding 'medicines' which give preference to natural constituents, especially those that have a firm link with the past. Just as there are ceremonies in which individuals abandon the modern invention of matches and resort to the earlier technology of the flint blade or the 'tinder box', so too in other ritual contexts they tend to keep alive the knowledge of abandoned or alternative sources of food.

What has changed the situation of occasional but recurrent local famines, despite the rapid growth of population? What indeed has allowed this growth to occur? One cannot say that increased medical facilities have played a very large part, since in most of the rural areas today, hospitals and doctors are few and far between. Moreover, measures of public health, seen as an important factor in the growth of the European population, have hardly made so great in impact over this period. In towns the conditions are often worse than in the country except in 'residential' areas designed for the middle class. There has of course been effective control of certain epidemics, such as cerebral spinal meningitis, smallpox, cholera, as well as an important programme of biological control of the vectors of sleeping sickness and more recently of river blindness. But medical factors do not in general appear to have had sufficient influence over the population as a whole to have produced such a rapid growth.

The cessation of wars and slave-raiding has undoubtedly led to more favourable conditions for the production and preservation of both children and food. But the food supply appears to have increased for other reasons. In many parts of West Africa there has been little change in the techniques of production, in the varieties of crop, in control over water. What then has created a larger food supply? Improved transport has played its part. The famines caused by lack of rain were often very localised so that the advent of motor vehicles in the early 1920s enabled crops to be moved quickly to affected areas. On a much wider scale, it was the coming of the steamship (and on land, the railway) that not only permitted the export from West Africa of bulky crops such as rubber, palm-oil, and cocoa, but also allowed the import of cheap foodstuffs from abroad. Control over locusts and the cessation of local wars have also been important in increasing productivity. But perhaps the single most important factor has been the availability of cheap iron imported from Europe. In the pre-colonial period iron was manufactured locally over a very wide area, though there were parts where production was more specialised, for example, in the country around Kong visited by Binger where the high chimneys of the furnaces dotted the whole countryside (1892: i, 261). But it was an expensive process; the ore was lowgrade, the furnaces crude and the charcoal difficult to make. Hence the basic tool of production, the hoe blade, was expensive. I have been told that it could cost the equivalent of a cow, and I have heard of families without the resources to buy blades for all their sons who had to take turns at working for an energetic spell with a single tool. The impact of lowcost blades must have been enormous, for the local industry collapsed almost overnight. I have never seen iron smelted in the region (though there is an extended description in the Myth of the Bagre), yet the remains of workings are everywhere. When I was in the region at the end of 1978 and beginning of 1979, imported blades were no longer getting to the markets. The worn remnants of old blades were on sale, as they must have been in pre-colonial times; and there was a certain amount of local production from scrap metal. But one could see the enormous extent to which the whole process of production now depended on the importation of cheap iron. The import of cheap iron and the cessation of local wars and raids were the most significant factors in improving the food supply and in increasing the size of the population. Both were related to the advent of bulk trade with Europe and *de facto* with the coming of colonial rule.

DISTRIBUTION

Given the limited means of transport, most produce was consumed where it was grown, so that the crops and livestock corresponded to the major elements of the diet; what was grown was largely consumed within the locality, and much of it within the group of people who produced it. There were few 'exotics', apart from salt, kola nuts and meat coming in and shea-butter going out.

The transport of goods was largely limited to head-loading by humans, often slaves, which inhibited the bulk movement of foodstuffs; the tsetse has made animal transport impossible in the forest, where chiefs and white men had to be carried in hammocks or palanquins. In the savannah regions, donkeys were used but their capacity was small. Horses carried only humans, though in the Sahelian regions on the desert borders, camels were employed as carriers of both men and goods. But the major restriction was the failure to adapt the wheel for local use.

The food items of high value carried along the trade routes of West Africa in pre-colonial times were animals, driven from north to south, some for consumption (cattle, sheep and goats), some for transport (horses, donkeys, camels and ostriches). The stimulant kola nut, coming from the forest zone, played an important part in trade (Lovejoy 1973), being chewed over a wide area of the savannah and entering into numerous ceremonials, especially in areas influenced by Islam where the usual liquid accompaniments of offerings to supernatural agencies, that is, gin or palm wine in the forest and millet beer in the savannahs, were

61

discouraged because of their alcoholic content. Some shea-butter travelled from the north, where it was used for cooking oil, to the south where it was used as a pomade or skin cream. But the major feature of the long-distance trade in ingestibles was certainly salt, that most widespread of human trade goods.[13] While the LoDagaa are able to make an alkaline equivalent out of burnt ashes, salt constituted their only major food import from outside the region, paralleling the role of cloth in the non-food goods; cowries, used as 'shell-money', as decoration and as ritual, fall in another more general category, but were of course imported from even further afield. The singular importance of salt as an import is illustrated in the Myth of the Bagre, where a standardised tale tells how a salt-trader had lost his way. Following the noise of the music at the Bagre Dance, he came across the settlement where it was being performed and sold its inhabitants the salt they needed for the meal being prepared for the new initiates and for their seniors.

Other items for the ceremony also had to be bought in the local market – some meat, some grain, some oil – but these are all local products and, had it not been for the amount required, they could have been provided from the resources of the house itself. Nevertheless it should be insisted that local markets in food were characteristic of this part of Africa, and these are well described by Binger in his travels through the area in 1888–9. Markets were essential not only to the many travellers but also as a supplement to the resources of individuals in the settlements themselves. If one was called upon to make an offering or a sacrifice, to entertain a stranger, to brew beer or carry out a ceremony, one did not necessarily have sufficient of the right food available at the right moment. Market exchange of foodstuffs supplemented subsistence production in this way, although it is clearly more important today when many individuals are withdrawn from the process of food production in order to fill other jobs such as teacher, policeman, administrator, and so on.

The consumption of food, then, was essentially the consumption of the crops grown in the immediate vicinity. In times of shortage people would sometimes go to collect grain from the family of their mother (*mamine* or *madebmine*, 'mother's brother'), but the reaction to famine was often the movement of people rather than the movement of food. Meat, especially game, had a somewhat wider radius than other foods. Among the LoDagaa the search for wild animals often led outside the normal boundaries of community activity; the density of human population was obviously correlated with the density of wild animals. In Gonja, where the population was very thin (a total of 118,000 even in 1960, giving a density of 8.2 per sq. mile), there was much more activity, especially by individual hunters, some of whom did little else in the dry season. At Gbuipe in 1956–7 the meat was often dried and sold to Ashanti traders (among whom the most important was a woman) who then had it head-loaded to the nearest road junction where it was taken by lorry to Kumasi, the capital of Ashanti (population 260,000 in 1970). The extent of these exports is certainly new; livestock are trucked down in lorries and the yams, maize and ground-nuts form part of the bulk trade in foodstuffs from north to south. But even in pre-colonial times, meat travelled from the north, and the ruler of Ashanti had snails brought to him from the forests of Ahafo (Dunn and Robertson 1973: 31). These latter of course were delicacies, like the imported tea and sugar Binger found in the market of Salaga in 1888, which were the counterparts of the kola nut then being imported into Europe to flavour wine and biscuits, and valued because of its medicinal properties as it had been by the Arabs for at least seven centuries.[14] But meat was in itself a delicacy; hence its importance in Gonja political relations, where it was transferred between subject and ruler outside the immediate locality, at least up to the divisional chief who received a portion of the proceeds of hunting expeditions, the left front leg of each animal killed, as well as part of each catch of fish, while a tusk of each elephant went in principle to the paramount himself.

Even among the tribal peoples such as the LoDagaa, local markets in food were important features of pre-colonial life. While the markets in Gonja came under political control, these were generally under the religious aegis of the Master of the Earth. Here beer was drunk, chickens were purchased, small quantities of grain were bought (especially by women who wanted to brew beer), cooked food was on sale; here too one could buy pots for cooking, vats for making beer, calabashes for the kitchen, hoes and hoe handles for the farm. Goods of all kinds were purchased for cowries, a form of shell-money. In Gonja, on the other hand, the markets were fewer but more varied; the items on sale included larger animals, goods from Ashanti and beyond, slaves, and gold which acted both as a commodity and as a medium of exchange, as salt did in the Sahelian region. As far as food was concerned, even in the market towns most inhabitants had their own farms on which slave labour played its part. But large caravans of strangers, especially those engaged in the kola trade with Hausaland, required feeding, so that the market had to cater either to their needs directly, or more usually to the needs of the landlords whose responsibility they were. It has been reckoned that during the dry season the population of Salaga sometimes doubled as the result of the arrival of caravans.

The markets among the Gonja and LoDagaa were formerly very different. The Gonja market of Salaga was essentially an export as well as a local market, carrying on a vigorous entrepôt trade, with goods and merchants travelling between Ashanti in the south and from Hausaland and other territories, to the north. The local basis of all the markets in foodstuffs was similar (and is so today), the great difference being the active trade in cloth among the Gonja, in and out of the market-place, a commodity for which the LoDagaa, like most of the acephalous tribal peoples, had little use.

While there was a market in foodstuffs and in human beings, there was none in land; that was *extra commercium* as indeed was the labour of free men,[15] for there is no record or recollection of wage labour. The 'market principle' was certainly in evidence but its application was restricted partly because most food was produced and consumed within the unit of consumption so that there was little external distribution.

It would be difficult to detail the role of gift-giving in the distribution of food without going into a lengthy analysis of the social organisation. Among the LóDagaa, prestations of raw produce, as distinct from cooked food, are made not only to sustain the important initiation ceremonies of the Bagre association but also at every funeral, where the chief mourner has to distribute a basket of grain to some of those who have attended (Goody 1962: 161). Livestock are also part of the funeral transfers, but even more important in this respect are the enormously valuable bridewealth transactions in cattle made in the course of a marriage. In Gonja, such prestations are perhaps no less frequent but lower in value; the funeral distribution is one of cooked food, and marriage payments are low. The part played by food in accumulation by chiefs was not large, as we have seen, but there is another category of transfers, which partake of the character both of gifts and of centric transfers. Among Muslims in Gonja, the Arabic term *saddaqa* is widely used for a gift, even for marriage prestations. But its more usual meaning refers to gifts made in God's name. These can be charitable gifts to help build a mosque. Nowadays the old-style Sudanese mosques are sometimes felt to be inadequate monuments to God, and a rich trader, grown wealthy on modern developments, may give funds to build a concrete construction, as has happened recently in Bole. But every year at 'Ashūrā (the fire festival), the leading Muslims of a town pray to God that the chief will be generous to them during the coming year, making them presents worthy of God's servants. Such requests are made at the time when the Book of Years is read out, the book that prophesies what will happen during the course of the next twelve moons. The requests are extravagant; today, Muslim traders are more likely to provide financial support for the indigent chief, in expectation of reciprocal help of a different kind, rather than vice versa. But Muslims themselves do make gifts in the name of God, which in intention though not in scope vie with the munificent gifts that built up the great complexes of hospitals, schools and markets surrounding the splendid mosques of Istanbul. Every Friday, a neighbour of ours in Kpembe bought some bean cakes from a woman in the town, took them back to his compound, where he offered prayers to God, and then called out, '*Yara, yara, yara*'. In a few minutes he was surrounded by young children come to collect the cakes. Giving in God's name to the poor or to little children is an act which brings religious grace. Giving alms is a peripheral part of Muslim life in Gonja, substituting in one context for the blood sacrifices and offerings that, if not forbidden, are at least downgraded in Islam. As with Christianity, one of the effects of the universalistic, written religion is the tendency to shift the direction of material offerings, which are less likely to be buried with the dead or offered on an altar, but more likely to be used for the glory of God, either to be accumulated by his trained servants or else distributed as alms to the poor.

Other forms of gift-giving do exist in Gonja. The 'greeting' of chiefs and elders, as described by Esther Goody (1972), involves the transfer of kola (often used as the general word for such gifts), drink (used in a similar way among the LoDagaa) and meat. The same kinds of gifts are offered when a man is seeking a wife, a chiefly office or favour, or the reparation of a broken relationship. Cooked food is provided at all *rites de passage,* and the preparation of large quantities of porridge for distribution to those attending is a conspicuous feature of the ceremonies centred upon the life-cycle.

The storage of food was quite efficient, though among the LoDagaa shortages did develop towards the beginning of the next harvest, so that an effort had to be made to distribute the food evenly over the year, after separating off next year's seed. The problem was less severe in Gonja, as the yams mature earlier than the grain, and so spread the harvesting over a longer part of the year. The LoDagaa kept their grain in specially-built granaries at the end of the long room, the main room of the house. These large granaries were carefully cleaned to prevent pests from eating the grain, and a fire was sometimes built at their base, which had the effect of keeping the contents dry. Only the head of the household had access to the main granary, though he could ask a small boy to climb down to get out the grain needed either for daily use or for some special ceremony. The head would then call his wives, his sons' wives, that is, all those entitled to a portion, and allocate a similar amount to each one, *per stirpes.* The regularity of the distribution varied according to the season. After the harvest it might be every three days, but later on every six. With this ration, and any supplements they might themselves be able to provide, the women would prepare the meals, although the husband remained responsible for providing salt and meat in addition.

Among the Gonja, at least today, things are not very different except that crops are normally stored in the fields, i.e. at some distance from the village; it is from there that the head of the household distributes his yams or his grain, while cassava is normally dug up when required.

Gonja, however, was a centralised state, with its courts, officials, chiefs, some of whom did not do much by way of farming. In the states of Europe and Asia, farmers were made to contribute part of their product as taxes to the central authority, as rent to local landowners, or both. As in the rest of Africa, there was no rent for land in Gonja. Nor was a man expected regularly to contribute part of his produce either to a political or to a religious authority. Of course, men gave both food and livestock for religious purposes, but not as a tithe. Moreover 'centric transfers' to chiefs were of a limited kind, apart from the produce provided by their own households. It is true that in many commoner villages Gonja chiefs enjoyed the right to receive a portion of the palm wine collected, the fish caught, a leg of the wild animals killed and of the domestic animals sacrificed. They might also receive food (and perhaps some farm labour) from their subjects, and would attempt to extract larger amounts if they were asked to make judicial decisions. But this tribute was limited in quantity and sometimes appeared to be more a token of political hierarchy than an economic privilege. While it could become exploitative, such tribute was more often recognised as a proper measure of support for an individual who had to entertain strangers and look after the affairs of the village. Even if the chief had accumulated a large amount of foodstuffs as the result of his command of force, given the means of transport available and the nature of the demand, he could not dispatch this surplus to the market unless it was close at hand. The opportunities for sale as distinct from redistribution were few. In any case most market towns were 'agro-towns' producing what they required by means of their own labour and that of their slaves.[16]

One type of transaction, much emphasised in the accounts of pre-industrial states, is 'redistribution' of which we need to distinguish two forms. There is the immediate redistribution characteristic of feasts and gift-giving, whereby what is received is at once handed out, where the chief or central institution serves as a focus for accumulation and then for dispersal. And there is the delayed redistribution that Joseph carried out for Pharaoh by accumulating grain in years of plenty in order to redistribute it in the lean years. This latter form of redistribution is not a notable feature of present-day Gonja, though it doubtless occurred in earlier times. But it featured prominently in some of the colonial developments in the less centralised 'tribal' societies.

In such societies the degree of political centralisation was by definition low; leaders arose in the context of specific activities, better-off men sometimes wielded greater influence, but there was no chiefship of the kind found in the neighbouring states, vested in a ruling group who controlled the means of coercion, the means of destruction. The advent of colonial government brought these independent peoples within the orbit of a larger state which needed local representatives to assist in the administration. Chiefs and headmen became essential instruments of colonial overrule, and were appointed, elected or emerged in every settlement.

Since there was no model for this new role inside the community, both government and appointees looked outside. In some areas the new chiefs asked their subjects for help, since they were assisting their fellows in dealing with the invaders. The help consisted in carrying out the same kind of services to which chiefs has long been entitled in the states, namely work on their farm, corvée labour, some tribute in kind. In this way not only was the new chief able to maintain a large household, but he could use part of the produce he had acquired to sell in the market since transport had now created the possibility of shipping larger quantities of foodstuffs to urban areas. The rest was stored in his granaries against a future emergency, or simply to help those villagers who were in need. This is what happened in Birifu; men were asked to come and farm for the chief (a practice long since abandoned, except on a minute scale), and in return he offered them not only beer, but help in dealing with the Europeans as well as providing them with a reserve against hunger and starvation. Potentially his granary served the whole village. Just the same reasons were given to me this past year by a well-off and educated chief when he was defending the immense acreage of rice which he had now brought under mechanised cultivation; his own household alone required 300 bags of rice a year, quite apart from the needs of the poor.

Thus some 'acephalous' societies suddenly achieved a degree of centric accumulation from the labour of the farmers, and in some cases this seems to have been greater than in the states themselves. It enabled chiefs of relatively small settlements to marry many wives; I counted 33 at the funeral of Chief Gandaa in Birifu, and Chiefs Kayanni of Tugu and Karbo of Lawra were equally well endowed; they were much better provided for than anyone in Gonja, including the paramount himself. It enabled them to influence the course of events and to produce huge families – the Chief of Birifu had at least 200 children, the educated among whom are now important figures in the elite of the region. But there was not at this stage any tendency to develop different styles of life; from the domestic standpoint the new chiefs lived just like everyone else, but with more of everything.

It had earlier been the same in the older, traditional states. None of the traditional chiefs had very different styles of life from other members of the state, at least as far as cuisine was concerned. While they had more food, it was of the same kind. Only with regard to meat was there some difference in distribution, here as among the LoDagaa. Chiefs, like lineage elders in the tribes, were entitled to special portions of the animal killed, and while not all of this was intended for the named recipient who had to display the generosity that seniority requires, he certainly obtained the major part. Since sacrifice and killing were male tasks, there was also a considerable difference in the distribution between the sexes. The same disparity exists today. Even when the meat does get into the common soup, I have known educated women wait until the men had taken their portion before helping themselves, though men also jokingly claim that if women do not help themselves beforehand, they are fools. More usually, women of both societies distribute the cooked meat in bowls, giving the larger portions to the men. Children are little affected by any such discrimination, at least while they eat with their mother; only when boys join the male eating group does this difference impinge directly on their lives.

While women feed young children irrespective of sex, they may not necessarily feed them equally, at least after they are weaned. In societies where preference is given to sons rather than daughters, women may themselves be the instruments of their own subordination by giving larger portions of choice foods to their male offspring. Other parts of the world provide definite evidence of differential treatment of children by sex which is reflected in comparative figures on mortality. Data from India and from China show that the trend of infant mortality ran against the general experience of human populations where the male, though more numerous at birth, is more subject to disease in the early years of life. In India and China (Taiwan), on the contrary, it is the female children who are most vulnerable, just as in earlier times they sometimes were liable to infanticide (Barclay 1954). It is in keeping with our general hypothesis, suggested in a number of other publications (Goody 1976; Goody *et al.* 1977, 1981a, 1981b) that differential treatment of children is not a significant feature of African society; we did not find any evidence of sex preference in the distribution of offspring of a large sample of 9, 293 Ghanaian mothers (Addo and Goody 1974), nor is there any evidence of differential treatment of young children on the medical side, a difference that might take the form of the willingness of a parent to go further to get medical attention for a son than for a daughter. In this significant feature Africa differed from Asia, in a way that directly relates to the respective systems of stratification.

PREPARATION

The main focus of the sociology of cooking and of eating is plainly the processes of preparation and consumption. If we have spent some time on the two previous phases, it is because we see them not only as intimately linked but as explaining certain general features of African cooking, which we shall place in a very broad contrast to the cuisines of the major Eurasian societies.

The preparation of the meal, in Africa as elsewhere, is often a long and time-consuming process.[17] I refer here not so much to the male task of cutting up the meat but to the more complicated female ones of processing shea nuts to make oil, or turning the dangerous cassava into a safe food. While cereals are stored as grain (and without being threshed), other foods are dried to make them last; the fruit of the okra, pepper and soup leaves are all laid out on the roofs in the sun before being packed away in pots and baskets for the empty season.

Among the LoDagaa, grain is sometimes stored in its malted form to be used for brewing beer at a later date. Once again the whole process is in the hands of women, who buy the grain, process it in the complicated way required to make the beer which they sell either in the market-place or more often in their own homes. Some women nowadays make malted grain for sale to others who run permanent beer bars in the market or in administrative settlements.

The preparation of a meal normally takes a long time because the produce has to be transformed directly from its natural state. In the case of guinea-corn or millet, the grain has to be removed from the head, husked and winnowed, then ground in a mortar or on a stone slab to produce flour. The grinding is especially hard, and women sometimes try to lighten their work by singing songs and chatting amongst themselves. Neither here nor in drawing water, nor yet in making pots, did they have the help of the wheel. It is perhaps small wonder that the most conspicuous new feature of many villages, apart from the bicycle and the occasional gun, is the grinding mill, established by some enterprising trader and run by means of a diesel motor. Here women queue up to have their grain ground into flour, preferring to try and earn a little extra money in the market or by brewing beer, rather than undertake the heavy work of grinding by hand. It is easy to see what a dominant position the ownership of a mill gave to a landlord, or other investor, in the European Middle Ages, quite apart from the monopoly he claimed. The application of wind or water power for the processing of grain would have an immediate attraction, even for women who had the advantage of the rotary quern. The mill is a labour-saving device of great significance, for which women themselves are prepared to pay by additional work of a less demanding (but possibly more time-taking) kind.

The technology of food preparation, then, is complex, even in the simplest agricultural societies, and it lies largely in the hands of women; it is they who have the knowledge (*nooro be nooro*, 'working their wonders', as it is called in the Myth of the Bagre) to undertake these tasks, the making of soap, the extraction of oil, the brewing of beer, the preparation of cassava, and indeed the whole process of applying heat to the raw products in order to turn them into a meal, the process of cooking.

I do not know of any LoDagaa tales about the origin of fire. Certainly it plays no part so far in the Myth of the Bagre, where virtually all other techniques of human life are accounted for. In the Black Bagre (I), the beings of the wild show mankind how to grow grain and cook porridge, but in contrast to many societies of Europe, Asia and of South America, the invention of fire is passed over in virtual silence. The maintenance of fire is in the hands of women; they fetch the firewood, get a light to start it, and keep it going for as long as they need. Nowadays, they can start from scratch using matches. Formerly if a light was not available, they would have to call a male to make fire using a stone, a piece of iron and some kapok, a procedure that is still occasionally used for ritual purposes. As far as I know there was no ritual attached to the lighting of the fire itself. Like yeast, fire was one of those marvels passed down from hand to hand, the embodiment of communal living, difficult to start, easy to keep going, especially if one has kin and neighbours on whom to rely. And in certain respects, the women's world is more immediately dependent upon such cooperative activities than the man's.

The hearth generally consists of three stones on top of which the pots are balanced, a separate hearth for each pot. Virtually all the food cooked by women is boiled. Since there are no ovens (except for new bread ovens in market towns), baking is difficult. Fish and meat are occasionally smoked above the fire for preservation. Some frying is done, more often in the market where delicacies such as bean cakes are offered for sale. Corn cobs are sometimes roasted, but roasting is a form of cooking that does not require a hearth, and which is more usually carried out by men. They will roast special portions of the meat after a sacrifice, while young boys may put a cob of maize over a fire or roast some of the smaller animals they catch as part of their 'play'. But while roasting is an important adjunct to ritual, it plays little part in domestic cooking *per se* which falls determinedly in the woman's domain, as in all other pre-industrial cultures.

In his cross-cultural survey of the status of women, Whyte notes that of all the 'economic' variables considered, it is only in the area of housekeeping that there is a definite bias towards one sex (i.e. the female one); 'while work outside the home tends to vary very widely from one culture to another throughout the world work within the home tends to be predominantly done by women' (1978: 68). We can add a comment on the relation between cooking and gender as well as between cooking and sex. In human societies generally cooking is seen as part of women's role. That is not to deny that men may carry out other functions in the preparation of food. They are generally the killers of other animals (and of other men) as well as the butchers of domestic meat. Moreover they often play a part in the roasting as distinct from the boiling of meat, in cooking in the fields or forest as distinct from the house, and in ritual as distinct from profane cooking. All these aspects can be illustrated from an initiatory ceremony for a diviner that I attended recently in Birifu (January 1979). On the previous day a number of chickens, a goat and a dog had been sacrificed by the participants, who consisted only of men. On the second day, more chickens were killed, the feathers removed, and the flesh roasted by one of the younger men on a fire built outside the compound; this meat was immediately eaten by those of us sitting round. The rest of the raw flesh of the animals was divided up among those present, some portions being set aside for the pot. Another fire was made, this time at a hearth of stones, and cooking pots were filled with water. When the skin of the animals had been removed, the innards and parts of the flesh were boiled up in the water. On another fireplace, porridge (*saab*) was prepared, initially by the men but later assisted by one woman. Into one eating bowl porridge was ladled out, into another the boiled meat, each pair of pots being shared between two men; the same portions were given to the few women who had helped, though they did not, I think, receive any meat of the dog which is normally forbidden to women. The dog is associated with the exclusively male activity of hunting, whose exclusivity is emphasised by the prohibitions on sexual contact with women before the hunt, for fear of displaying non-manly qualities in the face of danger. It is in the context of the hunt and in war that the opposition to the domestic work of women is most intense. The division of labour is not so heavily reinforced in agriculture where women play a part that varies between societies. The major contrast lies between men killing and women bearing, nurturing and cooking.

CONSUMPTION

The LoDagaa bury their dead resting on their sides, men facing the east and women towards the west, that is, towards the setting sun. One accompanying 'explanation' runs: the man leaves for the fields when the sun rises, whereas the woman gets the meal ready when he returns. In fact men usually return from farming long before, but it is at dusk that the main meal is served. In the morning a man will take little to eat before going off, some ground-nuts or a portion of last night's food. And it is rare that he will have any cooked food in the middle of the day, especially if he is working in the bush farms, though special farming parties will sometimes have food brought to them in the fields. Most of the year, of course, a man is around the compound or at least nearby in the settlement, and it is easier for him to get back to eat. But in most households, it is the evening meal that counts, though the children are fed more often.

During the course of the day a man will eat snacks, and among the LoDagaa he will often drink beer when he returns from the farm at one of the compounds where it is available that day. It is impossible to treat of the sociology of cooking without discussing drink. By and large, drinking and eating are seen as separate activities, not ones that take place concurrently (as when drinking wine with a meal) nor even in the same place. For example, the palm wine of Ashanti was drunk when the men came back from the forest.

Outside the forest belt, where, since the coming of the European, palm wine was often distilled into spirits, it was beer that constituted the main beverage, other of course than water. In different parts of the grassland of West and East Africa, beer is made from a whole range of cereal products, sorghum, maize, as well as from bananas. It also varies greatly in density and in sweetness. In Ruanda, honey is added, making a brew of heavy consistency. Among the LoDagaa, it is lighter and sharper, more like cider than mead. In both cases the process is similar to that used in the making of European ale.[18] But for the LoDagaa, at least, beer is 'food'. That is to say, the LoDagaa often apply the same term to beer as they do to the basic cereal element of the meal, porridge, namely the word *bundire*, derived from *bun*, thing and *dire*, eating. Interestingly, this word is not applied to meat (*nen*), which is chewed (*ɔɔr*) rather than eaten (*di*). The reason is not very far to seek, since beer and porridge are made from the same basic ingredient, namely sorghum.

The phrase 'beer is food', *dāā ni bundire*, was once used by the headman of Tom, Nibe, when he was explaining to me the difficulties of his domestic life. For some reason, probably to do with sex, his wife had refused to cook for him, and he told me that he had been subsisting for many days on beer alone (though this was not altogether true). Beer that has not been imprisoned in bottles and impregnated with gas does not keep long, for it is still alive. It contains many of the nutritive elements present in the cereal, supplemented by the vitamin B of the yeast. It is in fact as adequate a food as porridge.

As in the case with other peoples influenced by Islam, the Gonja rarely drink beer, for which on ritual occasions they substitute the kola nut. But it is produced for some ceremonial occasions, especially at offerings to the Earth shrine, since it is known to please the ancestors of the autochthones. For similar reasons it is used by the commoner diviners (*lejipo*) in their various ceremonies. And while it is sold in some of the bigger market towns, the producers are generally strangers.

The LoDagaa also pour libations of beer at ceremonies, and no major sacrifice, funeral or performance of the Bagre would be complete without it. Beer is essential for every occasion when one invites friends or affines to come and farm, or to help build a house. Even those operating in the new economy – teachers, migrants, administrators – rarely offer any recompense other than beer to those who work on their houses or farms. You do not pay for the labour of free men. You offer them beer (and food, if they are affines) and expect help in return, but you also are expected to reciprocate on a similar occasion. It is the reciprocity that is lacking in many of the modern situations, so that it becomes increasingly difficult for non-farmers to get labour, unless they make it very clear that a substantial return will be forthcoming. Individuals are increasingly reluctant to engage in a one-way flow of labour services in return for food and drink, when this benefits not the local chief but a distant kinsman already earning good wages. I have known of 'fortunes' built up by employing labour in this way. And while the balance of favours is rarely clear cut, a perception of continuing inequality (implicit in the process of development) leads to a reluctance to follow the same path.

Apart from ceremonies, LoDagaa drink beer in the ordinary course of life, especially during the farming season. The beer may be brewed by one's own wife, in which case it is paid for as anywhere else, because it has been with *her* grain, grain that she was given by kin whom she helped at harvest time, that she has saved in bits and pieces, or that she has purchased in the market-place, often travelling to distant settlements to buy more cheaply. Women walk a long way to save quite small amounts of money, partly for the adventure of attending other market places, always the scene of plenty of activity. The distance they travel has doubtless increased since the pre-colonial period, since it is now safer and easier to move; but the fact that the days of the week are named, as elsewhere in West Africa, after a set of neighbouring markets (six in the LoDagaa case, some of them long since disappeared) is evidence enough of earlier circulation. Weekly time is market time.

Beer can be purchased in any of the LoDagaa markets; indeed some very simple ones, the evening markets (*zaanuora daa*), seem to exist only for the sale of beer and cooked food – the market of Birifu (known as Wa *daa*) remains of this kind despite the efforts of successive chiefs to try and stimulate activity. But while markets are held weekly and often lie at some distance, beer is brewed every day at some house in the lineage or section area. Women themselves disperse their days of sale over the six-day week, so that everyone knows that today Brumo will be brewing, that tomorrow it will be Popla (White Woman), and so forth. When a man comes back from the fields, he may send his wife to one of these houses to buy a pot, or more likely he will walk across himself, partly for the company, partly because he will pay by the calabash. The sequence of events is well illustrated in the section of the Myth of the Bagre which tells how a man and his son went off to look for termite mounds to bring back to feed to their chicks. Without realising it, one of them scoops up a ripe shea fruit (the nut used for oil is surrounded by a tasty fruit) which is the sign that the time to start Bagre has arrived. On reaching the house, his wife comes out to collect the basket he has been carrying. The Myth continues:

> The knowledgeable father
> lay down there
> under the big tree,
> and when they came back,
> the knowledgeable mother
> took his load
> and hurried back
> to the big tree
> and put it on the ground.
> There and then,
> the knowledgeable father, ,
> he it was
> who asked the wife
> to go in the room
> and fetch some water
> for them to drink.
> The thoughtful one
> heard all that,
> and then she said,
> Your lover's beer
> is on sale today.
> He said to her,
> Go in the room
> and take five cowries
> and bring them to me.
> You heard that,

74

and turning round
(she) entered the room,
took out five cowries,
brought them out,
put them in his bag
and came out with it.
At the beer house
they had put aside the beer.
Now their thirst
was killing them
and they left
for his lover's house.[19]

The woman comes out to greet her husband, who sits down and is brought some water to drink, the treatment more typically shown to a stranger. Water is the first 'greeting' made to a stranger, unless beer is immediately available; and often it is water into which a little flour has been mixed. 'Now that we have drunk, let us greet,' is a frequently heard remark, indicating that the verbal exchange of greetings and information should attend this act of hospitality, an act that turns the alien individual into 'a stranger' to whom obligations attach, the principal of which is to provide him with food for a limited period. 'After three days', runs a Sierra Leonean proverb, 'you give him the hoe,' so that he becomes a producer as well as a consumer.

Among the Bedouin, a host's obligations to his guest continued as long as the salt of the meal remained in his belly. Among the LoDagaa, too, the consumption of the produce of a particular parish, the ritual area whose inhabitants are forbidden to shed each other's blood on pain of heavy sacrifice to avoid the inevitable retribution of supernatural agencies, places the alien within the jurisdiction of the Earth shrine. Indeed one does not even need to consume food. My friend Bonyiri once told me that if I was visiting another parish where the people seemed hostile, I should bend down, take up a pinch of earth, and put it in my mouth in full view of everyone. In this way I placed myself under the protection of the local shrine and people would be afraid to harm me.

The term 'lover' in the Bagre account is my translation of the LoDagaa *sen*, which does not always carry the sexual implications of that word; on the other hand it has a somewhat stronger sense than the Yorkshire 'love' as a term of address. In the context of drinking beer, it means a woman who puts aside a pot for you on the days she is selling. For men have regular places they will go, meet their friends and talk about this and that. This beer house may be anyone's house, and it is the resident woman rather than the man who is important in this context. When people collect together, it inevitably becomes the place where you get to know what is going on. If you arrive alone, you climb to the rooftop, or enter the long room if it is cold, then sit down on a low stool at the edge of the small group drinking their beer. One always sits down when eating or drinking. In the centre a woman sits on the floor, her feet stretched out in front, pouring the beer which is balanced upon a head pad (*tasir*). First she scoops off the yeasty froth on the top and sets aside the first calabash for herself. Then she pours for her clients, one of whom may have bought the whole pot, or all of whom will pay calabash by calabash. The beer is drunk slowly, with the calabash held in the right hand, the thumb being kept clear of the liquid; some people will never drink the beer from a calabash after another person has drunk out of it, and if you are asked to pass a calabash of beer to your neighbour, it is polite to take a sip beforehand, just to show you are not passing on a poisoned draught.

A woman of the house, or one who is passing by, may be called over to join the group, and formerly a man and woman who were lovers would drink together out of the same calabash, pressing their cheeks together as they did so. It is a sign of friendship that is disappearing, being regarded as unhygienic by those who have attended school. The last calabash containing the dregs ought to be shown to the man who owns the pot, that is, the person who has paid for it, or to whom it has been presented. He gestures to the pourer to drink. As in other societies, the offering of drinks works by rough reciprocity; everybody soon knows who does not pay their round and remarks are made; on subsequent occasions one may avoid that company.

The quality of the beer and the quality of the company will vary from place to place, so that men will have their favourite rendezvous. A good brewer will gain much renown and much respect; when migrants return to Birifu, they often drop down to see Brumo, who, though she has now given up brewing because of old age, likes to see her former customers from time to time.

Such a woman can become quite well off by local standards but the work is hard – collecting firewood, fetching water, going to market for grain, then the long process of turning the grain into malt, grinding the malted grain when one is ready to brew, then cooking it for two days before it is drunk on the third. At the present time specialist beer shops, extensions of the house pattern, are growing up around the bigger markets. I have known a man who, when going overseas for a course, gave his wife the money required to buy a load of firewood, the grain and the pots so that she could set up as a brewer and feed the children while he was away (though in this case he never returned to her after completing his education). In Babile, a small market and junction town, several women will share a house, each woman brewing every three days in order to provide a constant supply. These are often *feme sole* with no men around; either they have left their husbands or they have been left. These beer shops they run represent a much more commercialised operation than the village brewing, which still continues as vigorously as before. Local beer remains very much part of the LoDagaa diet, even if those who can afford to do so have turned their attention to bottled beer, brewed in the south, which is at once stronger, less nutritious and more prestigious. But these are the salaried workers, the inhabitants of market or administrative centres, who sometimes bring back a supply when they return to the village.

'Manners of the Table' are less in evidence for eating than for drinking. The table of course does not exist. Bowls containing soup and porridge are laid in front of the senior man, while others bring their stools (or squat if they are boys) and join in eating out of the same pot. In Gonja, influenced by Islam, water will first be brought to wash one's hands, a practice that is becoming more common among the LoDagaa. Eating is carried out using the forefingers and thumb of the right hand; first collecting a piece of porridge, the hand is dipped in the relish and then quickly conveyed to the mouth. Meat is picked out and chewed separately.

In centralised societies the holders of high office were sometimes given special 'protection' in their eating, being hidden from the public gaze, possibly for fear of witchcraft, sorcery or other form of evil. In December 1978, I met a highly educated chief sitting in the manager's office of a hotel. At my suggestion that it was time we ate, he was reluctant to go into the restaurant where many of our friends and acquaintances were sitting, remarking that chiefs do not eat in public; in the end we chose a side table and ate there. The reluctance was even more notable in this case, since the chief was not a representative of an ancient state but of a hierarchy that had its roots in the colonial regime; nevertheless even the newly created chiefs of formerly 'acephalous' (or 'tribal' or non-state) societies take as their model the formal patterns of behaviour characteristic of the old kingdoms. That is what chiefship is about.

A chief might have to eat special foods, as in the extreme case of the Yoruba king who had to consume the heart of his predecessor. In Gonja, the senior chiefs, and indeed the heads of dynastic segments (or 'gates'), were required to eat the food prepared for the war medicine of the kingdom (*gbandau*) and said to contain the liver of a human being. Such 'limited cannibalism', in fact an inversion of the practice of eating human flesh, was quite widespread in West Africa, for the purification of a homicide (Goody 1962: 115). It constituted a rejection rather than an acceptance of cannibalism.

The ordinary meal consists of the one dish; there are no starters, no afters; no hors d'oeuvre, no dessert. It consists of a single but filling dish, *un plat unique*. Moreover, among the LoDagaa, that dish is basically the same from day to day – porridge made from guinea-corn or millet, and accompanied by a soup, usually made from ground-nuts (*bule zier*) or leaves (e.g. *bire zier*) of one type or another. In Gonja, by contrast, yams form the basis for part of the year and grains and cassava for the rest, while more fish and wild meat are evident in the relish.

If there is little variation day by day, there is necessarily little variation in weekly diet, with no special days for special foods, except for meat on festivals. The alternation is a seasonal one. But ever here the most important variation was one of quantity, less being available at the end of the year.

Given the limitations of the diet, one would not expect great emphasis to be placed on fasting. In Gonja, the restrictions of the month of Ramadan are only observed by the most zealous Muslims. Feasting too is a matter of more of the same (but especially more meat) rather than an occasion for meals making use of different constituents, as is the case with, for example, Simnel cakes, Christmas puddings and with Hot Cross buns. A feast is a time of plenty rather than a time of difference. The Gonja speak of festivals as a time when 'even the children are satisfied'.

There is one important context of LoDagaa life, when abstinence is encouraged and certain foods are forbidden (*chiru*, tabooed), then later allowed, that is, during the Bagre performances. In one sense this happens every year at first fruit ceremonies, in Gonja and among the LoDagaa, when abstinence is followed by indulgence.

In Gonja new yams (which are linked to *gbandau*) are not eaten until the proper ceremony has been performed. The New Yam Ceremony does not have the same religious and political significance as among the Ashanti, where it was for the Odwera festival that subordinate chiefs and tributary princes came to the capital Kumasi, to do obeisance to the king, to settle disputes and to perform the festival in all its glory.[20] Among the Gonja, the Muslim calendar that encapsulates in the lunar year the whole life span of the Prophet, has been imposed on top of the round of seasonal activity. The major festival of the Gonja liturgical year, which was no longer seasonal, since the Islamic calendar is based upon a count of twelve lunar months rather than upon the solar cycle, was the Damba ceremony to which we have already referred. At this time, chiefs came to greet their superior, disputes were heard, seniority confirmed, and the populace enjoyed themselves watching the display and taking part in the dancing. But the ceremonies were necessarily divorced from the appearance of the new crop, from any kind of Thanksgiving Ceremony for the first fruits. This role was left to the New Yam Ceremony where minor offerings were made to the dead and where the important rituals of chiefship connected with the renewal of the power of war medicines were performed; in earlier days it was not a time for strangers to be abroad.

A more elaborate version of the New Yam Ceremony, however, was performed at one village in Gonja, that of Kalande near Salaga. This was a village of gunmen of Akan origin; indeed they claim to have fled from Techiman before the Ashanti advance and to have offered themselves as warriors to the Gonja state. However this may be, they still speak an Akan language and perform Akan ceremonies. At the festival the huge umbrellas beloved by the Akan are much in evidence; yams are mixed with palm-oil and given to the ancestral stools, which are entirely of the Akan pattern, for this mixture (*etɔ*) is the food of the gods as well as of humans.

Among the LoDagaa, the first fruits ceremony is the occasion for brewing beer (*Bagmaaldãã*) to the shrines in a man's house, at which time they are adorned with samples of the new crop, principally guinea-corn. The ceremony is performed during the dry season after the Bagre ceremonies have finished, but on a house-to-house basis, and on different days. In 1979, it was around mid-January that many households in Birifu brewed beer, made the offerings, sacrificed a fowl or two, and invited others to come and drink.

Both these ceremonies involve thanks to the deities for a successful harvest, but there is also some idea of abstinence from eating the new crop until these thanks have been given, though I cannot say the prohibitions are observed very strictly. Among the LoDagaa the serious prohibitions are found elsewhere, in the Bagre ceremony. Some of the main phases of the Bagre are named after foods, the Bagre of Beans, the Yam Ceremony, and so forth. All involve the lifting of prohibitions on eating certain foods that are laid down either at the start or in the course of the ceremonies. The series begins with the Announcement of Bagre, and, as the story of the guinea fowl and his mate tells us, it is the ripening of the shea fruit that sets the date. This is because the new entrants have to be released from the prohibitions on this fruit by eating it in a formal way, otherwise they will be in danger. The words of the old man, when he finds the ripe shea nut, are repeated as a refrain throughout the recitation:

> The fire blazes up.
> If we don't act,
> the children will sin.[21]

In the weeks that follow, the various ceremonies lift the prohibitions that have been placed upon the eating of bean-leaf soup, of black beans (bean cakes), of yams, of ground-nut soup. There are other prohibitions on behaviour, on sexual intercourse for example, but that on food is the most salient because the cancellation of the prohibitions takes the form of a public demonstration. That is to say, it takes the form of eating a meal in which what was forbidden now becomes permitted, an affirmation of the 'symbolic' value, the 'social' value, the value of the particular constituents as well as of food in general. For Bagre is very much about feasting and drinking. The sponsors of neophytes have to contribute grain which, before every ceremony, is measured out by the joking partners to see if there is enough to carry out the performance and effect its transformation into the proper quantities of porridge and beer.

> See the malted grain
> that has turned to beer,
> see the guinea-corn
> that has turned to porridge,
> see the leaves
> that have turned to soup.[22]

During the ceremonies the neophytes walk round the settlement begging grain and later chickens. The owner of the house where the Bagre is being performed has to send to the market to get some of the ingredients needed for the meals.

> They got up
> and told
> the neophytes
> they should go down
> and buy
> the salt
> for three times
> twenty (cowries),
> and buy
> all that
> (fresh) meat
> for three times
> twenty cowries,
> those pumpkin seeds
> for three times
> twenty cowries.
> And they should hurry round
> and speak to
> the second-graders
> and leave out
> the first-graders.
> If they hear
> a noise,

these are the hawks,
they will come.[23]

And the owner's reputation depends upon seeing that enough beer is available for those who attend, most of whom will contribute in some way to the expenses. As with many such societies, it is the contributions of the families of new entrants that helps to promote the enjoyment of the existing members.

The meal is ordinary in respect of its contents but not in respect of its procedures. In the first place the neophytes are fed (rather than feeding themselves) like little children; in the second place the meal, like other ritual meals, is in itself a test of whether the earlier prohibitions have been observed. If they have not been, then the food in one's belly could have harmful effects. One has eaten without confessing, for the very fact of accepting the food is a denial of having done wrong.

This method of feeding the neophytes, described by the verb *to*, is not unique to the Bagre, for it occurs in other *rites de passage* when somebody is being tested; for example, at a man's funeral ceremonies, the possible complicity of the widow in his death is tested by lustration and by feeding (Goody 1962: 242ff.). The procedure consists of offering the neophyte the food to reject, three times for a boy, four for a girl, the food being thrown upon the ground by the one who offers it. On the next occasion, the food is accepted, but before it is eaten it is passed under the arms and legs before being placed in the mouth.

After the neophytes have been ritually fed, the various grades of initiates get together to eat their portion of food. In the recitation of the Bagre the junior members (the White initiates, *Bag pla*) are known as 'vultures' (*dabɔɔ nibe*) because of the way they attack their food, rushing to the Bagre house whenever they are called, 'thinking it was about food' but finding when they arrived that there was work to be done as well. In any case the communal feeding and drinking is done in a formal manner, the first portions being offered to the senior members (the Black initiates, *Bag sɔɔla*) before the juniors can eat.

For these large meals, cooking is done at outside kitchens especially prepared for the occasion where women members (though they can never join the senior rank) cook for the men to eat, since here, as in the domestic setting, men and women eat (though not drink) separately. Before considering the constitution of units of consumption in the domestic setting, let me return to the matter of fasting and feasting, taboo and injunction (that is, prohibition and promotion).

In addition to the periodic prohibitions that surround ritual activity, there is an important set of taboos attached to particular groups, clans, statuses, individuals and shrines. In Gonja the most marked of these is the universal Muslim prohibition against the eating of pork and the drinking of alcohol. Abstinence from alcohol is justified by Gonja Muslims on the grounds that drink may make one forget the hours of prayer, although only the very strictest observe the rigid requirements of formal Islam. The rationale for the prohibition on pork, however, has been assimilated to other local justifications for observing similar prohibitions, that the animal in question helped an ancestor (in this case Mohammed) in a difficult situation, the same reason that is given for the curious ceremony called the Beating of the Guinea Fowl. In other cases no such rationale is provided, as with the ruling estate's refusal to eat monkey (*lakasa*).

Just as it is the 'mark' of a Muslim not to eat pork, so too it is the mark of each patrilineal clan among the LoDagaa that they observe a particular prohibition. Among the Naayile, the squirrel is the *dume* or protector of the clan because of the role that it played in saving the clan's founding ancestor from certain death. But not all clans have prohibitions relating to wild animals; some have food prohibitions of a different kind. Among the Kpiele, the inhabitants of Chaa, a ban is placed on *pie puo saab*, on eating porridge from a bowl placed in a basket. It should be insisted that these food avoidances, though very widespread, are only part of a wider set of prohibitions on human behaviour; for the Haiyuri clan, who have a tradition of migration from the Mossi Kingdom where much cloth was woven, have a prohibition against throwing a roll of cloth from one to the other.

In many cases people do not even bother to give any rationale for these prohibitions, although if pressed they may sometimes refer vaguely to their forefathers. Essentially they serve as markers of membership, and it would be a mistake to search for some semantic universe of prohibitions of which they form a highly structured part. This is not to deny they are strongly internalised, having been taught at the earliest age. But their significance lies in placing a boundary on social action beyond which members of this particular group cannot go, knowing quite well that others can.

The same range of prohibitions that apply to groups also apply to shrines which individuals have inherited or acquired, and to associations (such as the Bagre) which they have joined voluntarily or involuntarily. Each individual has a particular constellation of prohibitions (*chiru*), some of which are lifelong, whereas others, no less significant, have been acquired as the result of consulting a particular shrine. Still others may be completely individual, as when Zuko was forbidden in a dream by his beings of the wild to drink beer, a prohibition which only confirmed this eminent diviner in his solitary habits.

There is of course no absolute distinction between individual and group prohibitions on food. If the head of a household has to observe a. prohibition, for whatever reason, then his wife has to adapt her cooking accordingly if he is going to comply. So too the children will probably be confined to the same foods, implicitly observing the same taboo. In other cases where the whole family is seen to have benefited from the help of a particular shrine, an individual prohibition will be converted into a continuing family one.

Every new shrine that one consults, or wishes to establish in or near one's compound, involves some change of behaviour. Certain actions are prohibited, others are enjoined. Most of these acts have to do with food, if only because the intake of food is so often related to the problems of health; and it is for such reasons that one usually sets out to establish a new shrine. That shrine will have it own 'medicines' (*tīī*), its own tree-roots (*daanyigr*) to make the powders to eat, the tisanes to drink or an infusion to wash in. In addition, the shrine has its own negative regime, its own avoidances which are often dietary. These practices are seen as having a specific beneficial effect; at the same time they mark off attendance at a shrine or membership of a congregation in an unambiguous way, a way that is concerned with that core activity of mankind, the consumption of food, the internalisation of material objects necessary for the health of body and mind. In these circumstances, it is not surprising that so many 'taboos' centre around food. Few of the persisting prohibitions, however, touch upon central foods or central practices. Eating food in a 'basket' is fairly easy to avoid; so is the throwing of reels of cloth, for the LoDagaa do not weave. Likewise the animals are those that one is likely to need only in times of hunger, or possibly of starvation; in times of sufficiency the prohibition would present no problem.

There is of course a great difference between hunger and starvation. As a prisoner of war, one experienced hunger for weeks at a time. Rarely, except at the Christmas meal, accumulated with savings over several months, did one feel anything else, given the limited rations available. For most of the time, food was never far from one's thoughts, either awake or asleep. Individuals tried to recollect meals that they had enjoyed, making half-imagined, half-recollected Michelin guides to the best restaurants they had visited. Joking references to Freud confirmed the dominance of culinary over sexual deprivation, in dreams as well as in day-dreams. But this deprivation was very different from starvation, although at one stage some Indian colleagues did approach this point since they were not prepared to eat the tins of pressed beef provided by our captors, who were possibly ignorant of their prohibitions. The attitude of the Hindu towards the flesh of the cow differs significantly from that of the Muslim towards pork. For the Koran declares: 'But unto him who shall be compelled by necessity to eat of these things, not lusting, nor wilfully transgressing, God will surely be graceful and merciful' (The Bee, 115).

It was this situation, among others, that brought home the strength of food taboos embodied in the Hindu religion. But there was another incident, just as marked, in which the strength of the avoidance owed nothing to a specific religion. We were some dozen occupants in the room allocated to us in the camp, some old friends, others of recent acquaintance. Cooking was done in common; receipts from our captors, Red Cross parcels, food acquired in other ways, all was pooled, with the one exception of chocolate which sometimes arrived in private packages. Two people cooked for one month at a time and were responsible for the rations, for collecting fuel, for all the duties of preparation, serving and clearing up. People ate exclusively in the units to which they had attached themselves; not all groups were as large as this and some individuals organised their own food. The spread of household size lay between one and twelve, with the average toward the lower end.

Rarely did one ever consume food outside one's chosen unit. But around Christmas life became easier because of the supplies that had been saved up, and occasionally one was invited elsewhere. With a friend I was asked to take a meal with someone we had known in a different camp. A stew was offered us, which was plentiful and excellent. We understood the contents had been obtained from the guards in exchange for cigarettes; presumably one of our captors had done a little trading for a rabbit he had shot. On finishing the meal, however, our host told us that we had just eaten not rabbit but cat. The realisation that we had committed an act of quasi-cannibalism was followed not by contriteness but by congratulations; we had broken an unstated taboo and discovered a new source of food. On returning to our own room, we proposed to our companions that we find a cat for Christmas. The suggestion was met with implacable opposition. No one would share in our guilt, however tasty. Anxious to exploit our new-found freedom, we proposed to cook such a meal just for ourselves, so that anyone else who wished might join in. No, said the cooks of the month, that would not do; there was no question of using the communal vessels for such a purpose.

I recount this story partly to make the point that prohibitions of this kind can be as strong when God is not involved as when he is. Those who hold with the kingship of custom, the domination of culture, will have no difficulty in accounting for the persistence of such 'taboos' under conditions of hardship. I would add that their strength seems to rest on the fact that they are concerned with a process that, unlike many others, has dominated our lives from the beginning; the prohibitions, avoidances, taboos, have been acquired (rather than inculcated) in our infancy, and have become part of our continued interaction with and perception of the animals concerned. But for most of us, such prohibitions have their limits and given tough enough conditions, as we know from the experiences of those confined under the much worse conditions of civilian concentration camps, even cannibalism becomes a mode of survival. Conrad's Marlow in *Heart of Darkness* was not alone in his crime, and in those extreme circumstances the world is perhaps more forgiving than the individual himself.

UNITS OF CONSUMPTION

There are two basic patterns of eating, deriving from the division of the consumption unit by sex and by age. Of these two axes the sexual is the most significant. It is necessarily the case that the mother, or rather, a mother, feeds her children of both sexes at the earliest age when they are dependent upon the breast. It is not necessarily *the* mother since the institution of wet-nurses was widespread in Western European cultures until recently. St Augustine complained to Pope Gregory of the Anglo-Saxons' behaviour in this regard, attributing the practice to sexual incontinence (Bede, I, 27). In the seventeenth century it was found among well-to-do families such as the Verneys; Mary Verney put her son out to a village foster-mother a few weeks after he was born (Verney 1925: i, 380); and at the end of the nineteenth century George Moore made the abuse of the wet-nurse the central theme of his novel, *Esther Waters*. The poor had to share their milk with the children of the rich so as to preserve the features, figures and freedom of their mothers; indeed the whole system of the nursery placed upbringing in the hands of the wet-nurse, the nanny and the governess, those mother-surrogates for the upper classes. It was a system that virtually vanished with the disappearance of servants, the coming of the industrial cuisine to the nursery in the shape of feeding bottle, packaged milk and tinned baby-foods, not to speak of the influence of democratic sentiments, increasingly insistent since the introduction of universal suffrage and universal education.

But England was not the only locus of this practice, which was widespread in Mediterranean lands. Everywhere it implied a hierarchically stratified society, where differential access to resources and styles of life could be exploited to provide different feeding facilities for the children of rich and poor. There is evidence for the practice in Turkey and in Arabia, though in some parts it may reflect the relation between town and country as much as that between burgher and peasant.[24]

In Africa, co-wives may at times feed each other's children during the long period they are normally at the breast (Fortes 1949a: 130). And later on many societies in West Africa send children to be fostered by kin (E. Goody 1981). But in the early phases children are normally fed by their mothers, forming matrifocal segments of a larger unit of consumption to which they will later contribute as producers.

It is the question of what happens after weaning that is of interest. In both the African societies with which I am primarily concerned, boys and girls grow up eating with the mother until the boys eventually join an eating group consisting either of other young men in the house or else of their father and the other senior males. But adult men and women virtually never eat together. The woman brings the bowl of porridge and another of relish to the men and leaves them there to eat. The pattern is widespread in Africa and has nothing to do with the entertainment of strangers, as in some other parts of the world where women are in seclusion. And it is a pattern that is very persistent. Even in the rapidly changing sectors of society it is rare to see husband and wife eat together in a local eating house. Even in professional families the husband or other men are sometimes served alone, while the wife and other women retire to the kitchen.

In the traditional LoDagaa society the women will take their share with the children in the cooking area, while the men will be served on the rooftop, sometimes in a shade hut, sometimes in the open. They eat separately and they eat differently. For while the men squat or sit on three-legged stools, the women sit with legs outstretched or on four-legged stools.

Visiting a friend working in Morocco who was much concerned with the low status of women, I was impressed with the way that the women in Berber families sat down with the men to eat from the same dishes, and to join in the conversation. In Africa the separation that has been noted as far as property is concerned, men inheriting from men, women from women (Bosman 1705; Goody 1976), has its parallel on the more general level of male–female relations. For example, there is less social intercourse between the sexes, more separation into single-sex groups, at work, in eating, at play, than I have observed in India, Europe or the Middle East.[25] This matter is not easy to assess, given that it is based on impressions rather than quantifiable observations, and given that there is no consistent tie-up, even within classes, and certainly not within 'cultures'. In Gujerat, I have dined with the men among the poor and with men and women among the rich. Nevertheless the closer social relations of men with women, and specifically with their wives (though sometimes with their sisters) appears as a constant theme in the earliest Middle Eastern and Indian art, an art that is the expression of the values of the higher rather than the lower strata.

Units of consumption do at times exceed the size of units of production in a number of communal types of housekeeping. We need to distinguish here between the large-scale preparation of food and communal eating. For example, in a monastic community, food is prepared in a common kitchen and eaten in a communal dining hall, the long tables of which indicate the communal nature of the meal. Alternatively a common kitchen may prepare separate meals, as in a restaurant, meals that may be the same for each constituent unit (as when *en pension* or *en famille*) or which may be chosen *à la carte* in more expensive establishments.

But in simpler societies, food may be prepared separately by individual households and then brought together for common consumption. Among the LoDagaa this is often the case with the beer brewed for festivals, since no individual household would have the capacity to cater for everybody. On the other hand, the cooking of the basic porridge and soup for festivals is often done communally, either in a series of ordinary containers as at the Bagre festival of the LoDagaa or in a special pot of immense size as for the Great Porridge (*kude gbung*) of the Damba ceremony in Gonja.

However even at ordinary times there may be an element of communal consumption when the food one eats comes from different kitchens. The most notable instance occurs in Gonja, where, as Esther Goody described in her study (1973), little girls may be seen during the evening hours balancing dishes of food on their heads and walking from one side of the village to the other. This situation is typical of Gbuipe, the division closest both geographically and socially to Ashanti, where one also finds reports of the same practice (Fortes 1949b: 63–4). In Ashanti a newly married woman may remain in her natal home after marriage, cooking for her husband in the evenings, sending along his food by a small girl and visiting his room later that night. In Gonja the situation is somewhat different, for a woman joins her husband at marriage; but both spouses retain strong ties with their natal kin which take the form of sharing part of the meal with absent kinsfolk. In other words, the regular unit of consumption is not bounded here, as in many other societies, by the walls of the dwelling itself, the house or apartment; the houseful is not necessarily the household, nor is the latter always contained within the former; the unit of consumption is different from the one that eats together (the eating group).

The instance recounted above is not an example of communal eating, but rather of one man or woman consuming cooked food from different sources in the course of one meal. When men live in polygynous households, they often consume food from different kitchens, albeit all within the same household, in the course of successive meals. An essential feature of African polygyny is that each wife has her separate room which must be built for her soon after she joins her husband. The only instance of multiple occupation that I recall was in some of the villages in southern Gonja that were constructed at the time of the flooding of the Volta valley to create the Akosombo dam. This immense project involved the building of new housing consisting of small 'core' houses made out of concrete to which the occupants were invited to add extra rooms but only in the original materials. This attempt to prevent 'degradation' was fortunately abandoned after some years. For while a man had no difficulty in adding to a house built in the traditional fashion since the materials came from the immediate neighbourhood, the labour from kith and kin and the skill from his ancestors, the introduction of new imported materials required not only a cash outlay but also quite different techniques. No longer could one's mates provide the help; it was a question of employing a mason to make the concrete blocks and to construct the building. So additional rooms did not always get built for new wives who sometimes had to share a single room in conditions of rural squalor out of keeping with the obvious newness of their dwelling and the impractical dreams of distant planners.

Except in special situations of this kind, which may include temporary accommodation in town, polygynously married wives sleep and usually cook separately, certainly when they have children of their own. But wives do not usually undertake cooking for their husband at the same time, for the process is long and arduous, involves fetching firewood and water, grinding grain that is often very hard, and stirring the porridge over a hot and smoky fire. They take it in turns, just as their husband takes turns at sleeping on their mats; the cook is also the sexual partner. Among the LoDagaa, with their six-day market 'week', it is generally a question of three days on and three days off, a longer cycle if there are more than two wives.

The wife who cooks will also provide food for her co-wife. But it is sometimes the case that even if the wives of two brothers, or of a man and his son, do not form one cooking unit (unit of preparation), the men may eat together on the rooftop, sharing the bowls produced by their respective wives. In my experience this is more often the case with young men in a dwelling unit, which can get very large among the LoDagaa, than it is among their seniors whose relations are often coloured by years of quarrels over property, women, seniority and so forth – one aspect of the 'solidarity of siblings' who have lived together over a whole lifetime. Such limited commensalism does occur outside the 'household' but in most cases eating together is limited to those males who continue to farm as one unit and to store their food in one granary.

LoDagaa 'ideology' is often phrased in more cooperative terms. Members of a local lineage, consisting perhaps of one hundred persons, that is, of some twenty-five adult males, can be heard to speak of themselves as 'having one hoe', i.e. as farming together. It is true that kinsmen sometimes cooperate in certain farming tasks, such as the clearing of new land, just as women may cooperate in planting or in harvesting ground-nuts. On these occasions a man will arrange for his wife to brew beer and make food, and then call upon his friends and kinsfolk to come and aid him. But such an appeal is certainly not confined to his agnatic kin, members of the same lineage. Particularly among the LoDagaba (one of the two 'groups' I speak of as the LoDagaa), it is a man's sister's sons who are the first to be called, and almost certainly the first to signal their intention of coming. And one of the main sources of labour is one's sons-in-law, prospective and actual, who will call their kin and their kith to come along and farm (*diem kob*). Nowadays, with some prospective sons-in-law acquiring an education, and hence a salary rather than the ability to farm, such parties may be commuted to cash, unless one can prevail upon one's brothers to undertake the work alone, but as we have seen, such unreciprocated work is not a long-term proposition.

However, the idea of 'having one hoe' is something more than a description of the obligations of affinal farming; it is an expression of the closeness of lineage members to one another. Indeed the phrase is taken by some to recall an earlier state of affairs, before the external world bore so heavily upon them, before men engaged in so many petty quarrels and split up into smaller farming groups. But there is no evidence that at an earlier period units of production were larger than they are today. 'To have one hoe' is a metaphor for lineage solidarity, in the productive field, expressing the joint obligation of a lineage, for example, to contribute to a sacrifice to the local Earth shrine, though it should be said that in practice such obligations rarely emerge undamaged by incipient fission and actual tension.

The equivalent expression heard among the Vagella inhabitants of the Gonja town of Bole is 'having one bowl'. The Vagella are one of the groups of commoners who inhabited the area before the Gonja arrived. They claim to be immigrants from the Sisaala area to the north, and certainly give more of a role to unilineal descent groups (as do the other acephalous peoples of the region, including those from whom they claim to have branched off) than the ruling estate among the Gonja who are more typical of the inhabitants of the savannah states in this respect. The phrase 'having one bowl' relates to consumption rather than to production, but it has a similar significance to the LoDagaa phrase. The Vagella occupy certain wards of the town of Bole, where a large number of compounds are grouped together under one very large flat roof; it is as if the already large compounds of the LoDagaa (with an average of 16.3

in the 1960 Census) had never split apart physically, even though the same kind of internal fission of households had taken place. So the residential arrangements did lend some credence to the interpretation of the statement as referring to a past practice of eating together. Indeed people asserted that even today the senior men of the ward would get together in the evenings and eat their meal together, a meal that had been cooked by their several wives and produced in their separate fields. So convincing were these statements that I spent several nights in a room in the Vagella section (our normal abode was on the other side of the town) trying to observe this particular get-together. I never caught any glimpse of a commensal meal.[26]

In other parts of Gonja, however, the unit of consumption (the group that eats together) does turn out to be systematically larger than the unit of production and the unit of preparation. Esther Goody describes the situation in the town of Gbuipe in central Gonja where the compounds have a mean of some twenty residents, that is, from two to three households. Food preparation is based on the conjugal family, but each cook will send a bowl of food to the head of the compound, which corresponds to a farm-clearing group. While senior men eat alone, others will consume together the food sent by the wives of each (E. Goody 1973: 54). It should be stressed that while the compound generally comprises kin, we are not dealing with lineages or with a lineage-based society; the groups of men involved are relatively small and the cooking is done within the conjugal family.

The point concerning the size of extended commensal groups is of some theoretical interest in view of attempts to incorporate such an idea in the formulation of a paradigmatic 'lineage mode of production'. In the pioneering work of Claude Meillassoux on the Gouro of the Ivory Coast, the author offers a reconstruction of their social system at the beginning of the century, before the impact of cash crop production on the economy. This reconstruction involves taking at face value the retrospective claim of the Gouro to have farmed (eaten) together as a lineage at an earlier period. Discussions of this kind are always difficult to assess when we do not know either the size or order of segmentation of the lineage.[27] But we also have to consider the way that such phrases are used at present, partly metaphorically, partly with a glance backwards towards a more solidary but non-existent past. As far as units of production are concerned, an examination of a number of instances from various parts of the world (Goody 1972b) showed that the average size of such groups was relatively small, though the sample obviously did not include latifundia, monastic estates, feudal domains, slave holdings, haciendas or collective farms. The largest figures I obtained were in fact from the LoDagaa themselves, where the average size was 11.1 (for the

LoWiili). While the cross-cultural evidence on commensal groups does indicate that we may expect larger units where we find men's houses (for example, in certain societies in New Guinea and South America as well as among the Swat Pathans), the evidence for simple agricultural societies in Africa is that such groups were generally little larger, on the average, than the productive units.

But just as there were times when people farmed in larger groups, so there were occasions in which larger numbers cooked or ate together. In Gonja the main such occasion was the annual Damba festival to which we have referred. One other major ceremony of the Islamic year is celebrated by the killing of sheep (Dongi, *al-'Id al-kabīr*), though this festival is carried out on a family rather than a community level. But at most rites of passage in the human cycle and especially at funerals, large quantities of food were prepared for those attending.

The main community festival is a combination of political and religious aspects. Damba, like the *Gānē* festival of northern Nigeria, is held upon the Prophet's birthday (or day of circumcision), but it is also a political festival, celebrating the dominance of the ruling estate. The ceremony takes three days, the names for which centre around the preparation of food: the Sorting of the Rice, the Killing of the Cow, and the Great Porridge. On the first day the members of the different estates gather in front of the house of the divisional chief while the Muslims pick the stones from the rice that is supposedly going to be used for the common meal. They sit around in a circle, go through the motions of cleaning the rice and recite prayers. After this the members of the ruling estate perform a series of dances in front of their chief. On the second day a cow donated by the divisional chief is killed in the middle of his courtyard, following a series of prayers and processions round the beast. It is this meat that is eaten on the last day, the Day of the Great Porridge. Early that morning the rice is cooked and distributed. Later on, the women in the chief's house cook porridge made from guinea-corn and cassava in huge pots and portion it out in a series of small bowls which are prepared for every group that is present. At the same time the Spokesman or Linguist (*dogte* or *nsauwura*) for the division holds up portions of the meat and calls for representatives of the various sub-divisions to step forward and take their share. Not only does he call out the names of the various social divisions but also those of certain specialist occupations and other roles, including 'witches', 'thieves' and 'rapists'.[28] Everyone in the division shares in the meal, even the anti-social elements. The whole community partakes willy nilly in the commensality. It is a joint meal with clear political overtones, or rather a mixture of political and communal components, since participation reinforces the position of the ruling estate, in the general manner of the street parties that enliven the streets of Britain at the installation or jubilee of a monarch.

There is one other aspect of this meal that requires some comment. Although it is a festival, it is not a feast; there is no *Grande Bouffe*, no extravagant blow-out, no meal of many courses. The actual content of the meal is that of everyday life. For some there may be more meat, but it is at most a question of more rather than different. In these communities there is no special menu for festive occasions, though clearly some dishes are preferred to others; indeed there is a minimal differentiation, not only between festival and weekday, but between the various estates of this stratified community.

One indication of this state of affairs is the position of rice. For although the preliminary preparation of the meal centres on the sorting of rice, this cereal plays little part in the meal itself. It is an indication of the northern origin and Muslim affiliations of the ruling estate; in the pagan context of *gbandau* they eat yams, a local food with southern links; while for ordinary ceremonies it is porridge that forms the basic diet. In fact the Gonja, like other peoples in northern Ghana, neither grow nor eat much rice. Both these conditions are changing quite rapidly. Rice is becoming a common element in the diet of the middle class, and indeed Uncle Ben's American rice forms one of the country's food imports, though it is still not a favourite food in the north. However a great deal of rice is beginning to be grown there, starting in 1969 when the mechanised cultivation of high-yielding varieties began in earnest, leading to some revolutionary changes in the holding and distribution of land. However, west of the Comoe river in what is now the Ivory Coast, rice has long been produced and consumed as the most important cereal. Whereas many of the present staple crops such as maize and cassava were brought in from other continents, one variety of rice (*oryza glaberrima*) was a domesticate of West Africa with a long history of cultivation. It was from the north-west, the ancient rice growing area, that the ruling estate of Gonja claim to have come, and it is a claim one has no reason to doubt despite the fact that they have changed both their language and their diet in tune with local demands. However, for the purposes of the ceremony rice has to be acquired and cleansed. While it does not have the same symbolic significance, similar factors lie behind the continued use of wine in the rituals of Christians and Jews even in those areas of northern Europe where the grape cannot be grown and had little local significance. In northern Ghana, too, I have attended a Catholic Mass where both the bread and the wine have had to be imported, as well as a Jewish Seder, made possible by the advent of Israeli wine and unleavened bread (*mazzot*) in the diplomatic bag.

The explicit connection of the bread and the wine with the body and blood of Christ clearly encouraged the continued use of these agricultural products when Christianity moved outside its place of origin and their centre of cultivation. As Duby (1974) has pointed out, religion, and the desire to imitate Roman models, encouraged these cultigens to spread outside their home areas into regions for which they were little suited at the time. There is little explicit symbolism in the use of rice, except in a general sense to reinforce the ideology of the ruling estate as a group of conquering warriors coming from afar, and linked to the great states of the Niger Bend. The conservation of this feature of the Damba ceremony is part of the intrinsic conservatism of 'ritual', whose formality ensures the continuation of what might otherwise have fallen into desuetude. Ritual can be said to preserve for the sake of preserving, that is, for its own sake.

For the Gonja, large communal meals play a more important part in social life than for the LoDagaa, with the exception of the Bagre ceremony itself. At funerals, too, porridge will be cooked and served to the multitude attending; indeed the actual preparation of the food is once again an important part of the ceremony where women's roles come very much to the fore, leading to a similar distribution of food and meat. Since the state of Gonja includes an important Muslim component, and since the ruling estate themselves acknowledge their links with Islam as well as with the local religious practices, the brewing and drinking of beer, so significant among the LoDagaa, plays little importance in such ceremonies. The sharing of food has a somewhat equivalent role to the sharing of drink at the funerals and other ceremonies of the LoDagaa. But this phenomenon is not only linked with the substitution of porridge for beer (they are after all only alternative ways of treating the same grain), or with the fact that the Gonja live in tight nucleated villages where food sharing is common, rather than the dispersed settlements of the LoDagaa. The increased stress on the communal collecting, cooking and consumption of cooked food among the Gonja is also linked with the existence of a centralised regime. It is an aspect of what Polanyi called 'redistribution', and of what Pryor (1977) calls 'centric transfer'; and it is characteristic of a regime where, despite political and religious divisions, and the existence of a form of stratification, there is no great difference in what Max Weber termed 'styles of life'. All members of the state eat together, just as they sleep together; they interdine, just as they intermarry; kinship ties and the distribution of food cut across estate membership. Indeed the interchange of food and sex are aspects of the fact that domestic life is not separated into groups exclusively or even largely composed of members of the same caste or class. This fact is critical to the relation between cuisine and hierarchy that we develop in the next chapter.

While we have discussed market activity in relation to the supply of the raw materials for the kitchen, today there is also a vigorous sale of cooked food. In principle there is nothing new about this trade. Women have traditionally prepared not only beer, an important form of cooked food, but also special dishes such as fried bean cakes, which would normally be available only at markets. This was the case in pre-colonial days, and today the smoky section selling cooked food is a prominent feature of every market, though it is men who sell cooked meat.

In the larger towns, such as Salaga, the weekly markets were supplemented by daily ones at which cooked food as well as raw produce was continually available. In Salaga, according to Binger (1892), the market began at seven o'clock when women brought their *akoko* (gruel) or *to* (porridge). While young girls sold kola and cooked meat, others brought pots with boiled yams, to which salt and pepper had been added. Every day in the big market, even in the wet season when the town had few merchants, two or three cattle were killed and the meat chopped up for sale in hundred cowrie lots.

Moreover, surrounding the market-place were houses dedicated to trade, where landlords provided the housing and similar services needed by traders and other travellers. While not yet shops, they were already stores. The coming of colonial rule brought with it the shop. The establishment of Government shops at Gambaga and Wa was followed by private enterprise in the shape of larger expatriate firms such as United Africa Company as well as smaller traders, mainly of Yoruba or southern Ghanaian origin. It was these latter traders who visited the smaller villages around on their market days and who also undertook some peddling at other times, especially in imported manufactured goods. Nowadays such activity is more common in Gonja than it is among the LoDagaa, whose system of local markets is more developed. Possibly because of the greater distances between villages, weekly markets were rare in Gonja (E. Goody 1973: 18–19). Instead, peddling was more common, and even members of the ruling estate, men as well as women, may be found carrying their wares around the outlying villages. But while cloth and imported goods are often sold in this way, with the exception of salt, food products play little or no part in this trade.

However, a mini-market in cooked food develops at many ceremonies and rites of passages, especially at LoDagaa funerals where men and women come from afar and spend the best part of the day sitting, participating and paying their respects. Women will bring their cooking pots, set up three stones as a hearth, light a fire and make food for sale. Nowadays this is done in all permanent markets and in most villages and towns where passing truck drivers, full-time employees or local schoolboys create a demand for ready-made food. It is the counterpart of the permanent beer-bar, both being developments of traditional institutions where food and drink were prepared for sale. It is as well to remind ourselves of the fact that consumption was never limited to household or ceremony but always had a 'market' element which expanded under impact with wider systems of market exchange and division of labour.

To summarise the problems of difference in food and the cuisine among the LoDagaa and Gonja, I referred first to the direct influence of environmental factors, the LoDagaa being situated to the north, leading to a greater concentration on cereals as against root crops. Though rainfall was slightly less, they had better sources for drinking water; since they had fewer tsetse, they could support more livestock. The Gonja did import horses for military purposes and for prestige but they could not breed them, whereas the LoDagaa bred cattle and smaller livestock, but had no use for the horse.

From one point of view it appears paradoxical that the Gonja, organised in a state system with market towns and greater craft specialisation, depended to a greater extent on wild animals and other natural resources. Ecologically their land was poorer, not only in soil but in dry season water. It was also much less densely populated than the tribal regions to their north. This fact has perplexed some scholars who, taking their model of the state from the Middle East, have seen political centralisation as linked to the increased surplus gained in agricultural production and hence in higher densities (Goody 1978). It is critical to my argument about cooking to point out that African states were not like this. Their agriculture was probably less productive than that of most tribal peoples and certainly of some hill areas where a form of intensive cultivation was practised. Simple forms of irrigation were more common among the LoDagaa than the Gonja. The latter lived partly by booty, raiding the resources of their stateless neighbours for slaves, for cattle and anything else they could take away. The gains from their raids meant that the warrior rulers themselves could undertake less agriculture, a task on which they tended to look down. Their activity created devastated areas, driving the tribal peoples into denser settlements and finding the emptier areas easier to conquer. As a result they had more open land for 'communal' exploitation, especially for hunting and fishing.

Meanwhile the 'tribal' peoples in northern Ghana occupied what were in some ways better lands on which they clustered together at higher densities, partly in refuge, partly as a means of defence, partly because the lands were often more fertile. The heavier densities and better land of the LoDagaa meant farms around the compounds and cattle in the bush.

95

In Gonja it was just the opposite, with most food being stored away from the village.

Thus the state's dependence on gathering (including the gathering of humans) was greater than that of the tribe. In Gonja, there was more wild meat and less slaughtered livestock. Not only was there more empty space but the Gonja were better able to exploit it with horses, some guns and a tradition of war and the chase. Wild vegetable produce, including shea nuts, was more readily available. So too was honey, essentially a product of the wild. In the sphere of drink, the Gonja tapped palm wine in the woods, while the LaDagaa brewed and drank that basic product of domesticated crops, beer.

Beer was always offered at LoDagaa festivals, to visitors as well as to the gods. Otherwise the food exchanged was raw rather than cooked, except at the series of Bagre festivals. Whereas among the Gonja, both national festivals (the equivalent of the LoDagaa religious rites) and family ceremonies were marked by the preparing and distribution of cooked food. Porridge was partly a non-alcoholic equivalent of beer in a Muslim society. But communal cooking was also related to the existence of nucleated villages rather than the dispersed settlements of the LoDagaa, to aspects of centralised organisation which contrasted with the 'ordered anarchy' of their neighbours.

The differences in social organisation affected the course of events in the colonial and post-colonial worlds, and these in turn the nature of production and consumption. Their dependence on slaves, on booty production and on a warrior (or chiefly) tradition meant that the coming of colonial rule hit the Gonja much harder than the LoDagaa. The state had everything to lose, until the ruling class learnt to adapt to the new political openings offered by Independence. For the LoDagaa opportunities opened up all around. Not only were they more ready to accept education as a way of advancement, but their agricultural produce was in increasing demand. High population densities left little room for increases in production. But like the Konkomba in the east, some of them moved into the underpopulated lands of Gonja to grow the yams and other crops required by the south, entering early on into commercial farming. At the same time some of the inhabitants of the Gonja towns, who had always been busy in the market, entered into the commercial exchange of livestock on a much greater scale than before in order to supply their own needs and those of urban markets of the south.

But despite these various differences that affected food in general, the actual shape of the cuisine in both societies was surprisingly similar. We did not discover any major differentiation of cooking either on a periodic basis, for festivals, or in relation to the different strata of Gonja society. Let us turn now to examine briefly the nature of the cuisine in the major Eurasian societies, where the differences are of another order.

4

The high and the low: culinary culture in Asia and Europe

In the traditional societies of northern Ghana there was little internal difference in the food, whether raw or cooked, of the various members. Even a state like Gonja that consisted of distinct strata organised in a hierarchy and differentiated in terms of access to political office, socio-economic role and religious affiliation, had a simple cuisine. There is little evidence of differentiation in the accounts of pre-colonial travellers or early administrators, and it is significant that visitors of high status, not only Europeans, were often offered food in its raw rather than its cooked state.

The provision of food for strangers was usually the responsibility of the local chief or headman. However in urban centres where merchants gathered, the landlord would provide cooked food for his 'strangers'. When Binger visited the Gonja town of Salaga in 1888, he found the compound of his host had a cooking pot and a stirring stick fixed on the roof as a sign of the hospitality that this well-to-do merchant was prepared to offer (Binger 1892: ii, 85).

The situation is not very different today, although the impact of a new type of stratification that results most immediately from literacy and education and is associated with teaching, administration, military rank and political office, is having its effect, more especially now that new forms of primary production, the tractor cultivation of high-yielding varieties of rice for the market, have made their mark on the savannah area (Goody 1981). These factors – the impact of colonial rule, the creation of an 'independent' nation, the links with the world economy – have brought the inhabitants in touch with different types of cuisine, and in particular with the products of the industrialisation of cooking. Into the nature of industrial food and its impact on northern Ghana we will enquire in later chapters, before we try to explain the general state of the African cuisine in contrast to the major societies of Eurasia. But first we must try to specify some of the common features of that Eurasian cuisine. In doing so, I will deal only with a small segment of the processes I have described in the last chapter, that is, with the cuisine itself. Even here I am concerned with one basic point, the characteristics of a truly differentiated cuisine marking a society that is stratified culturally as well as politically.

The nature of a cuisine is clearly related to the particular system of producing and distributing food. In discussing the emergence of the Chinese cuisine, which he sees as occuring in the Sung period (960 – 1279), Freeman distinguishes three prerequisites. First, there is the availability of a number of ingredients, some imported, together with a wide variety of recipes; 'cuisine does not develop out of the cooking traditions of a single region' (1977: 144). In China it was an imperial venture, a product of the great capital cities, first of Keifeng in the north, then of Hangchow. Secondly, 'a cuisine requires a sizeable corps of critical, adventuresome eaters', not simply a palace clientele such as already existed in China, but a broader elite which in this case consisted of the growing body of officials as well as the merchants who supplied not only the products of distant lands and diverse regions ('the golden peaches of Samarkand', the grapes from the Middle East) but also the huge quantities of grain and other foods needed to maintain 'the greatest city in the world', the extent of whose markets are described by Marco Polo and pictured in that fascinating scroll, Spring Festival on the River (Freeman 1977: 143). Thirdly, there were the attitudes which gave first place to the pleasure of consuming food. A fourth prerequisite was also 'decisive', namely the important developments in agriculture and commerce that occurred during this period. The introduction of new species of Vietnamese rice allowed for some double-cropping and opened up new areas for farming; the development of a commercial agriculture helped to increase production in the country and consumption in the towns; there was a change in patterns of mass as well as of elite consumption, leading to the inclusion of rice, tea and sugar in the diets of the many as well as the few.[1]

In this chapter, I am concerned with a wider development and one which certainly took place earlier in Chinese history as well as in other cultures. While I speak of the development of a differentiated cuisine, an *haute cuisine* as compared with a low cuisine, it might be better to refer to a higher and lower cooking in order to avoid some of the more specific implications of the French usage to which Freeman calls attention. In any case I see this differentiation as occurring earlier, and as based upon a system of production and stratification that was not to be found in the Black Africa of pre-colonial times, with certain limited exceptions. It is the absence of this productive system that makes the application of terms like feudalism or Asiatic mode of production quite inappropriate to the social systems of that continent, a fact that profoundly affects their cultures as well. In order to clarify this contrast with the major societies of Europe and Asia, I want to look at the way that cooking is

differentiated in the latter group of societies. In doing so, I draw attention
to the fact that those societies have two characteristics that are
particularly relevant for my purpose. First, they practise forms of
intensive agriculture, harnessing animal energy through the plough or
controlling water through irrigation and other means. Secondly, they
employ writing for a whole variety of purposes, economic, administrative, literary and 'practical'. It is in this last field, the 'practical' one,
where we find the uses of literacy developed in connection with cooking,
and more specifically with diet, where early on we find the elaboration of
ideas about food and eating in the context of cosmological and
physiological systems. The discussion about man in relation to heaven
and earth is part of the background to the specialist production of dietary
manuals and cookbooks in the contemporary world.

A salient feature of the culinary cultures of the major societies of Europe
and Asia is their association with hierarchical man. The extreme form of
this differentiation is found in the allocation of specific foods to specific
roles, offices or classes, swans to royalty in England, honey wine to the
nobility of Ethiopia. But there were more complex, more subtle forms
of differentiation than these, and to try and distinguish some of the main
features of the hierarchical cuisine we should first turn to the Ancient
Middle East, the cradle of Bronze Age 'civilisation', where the advent of
writing and the elaborateness of graphic and sculptural forms enable us
to distinguish the outline of a cooking very different in its social
implications from that which existed in Africa. Egypt was not the first
culture to acquire writing; that honour appears to belong to another
society based on irrigation and the plough, the Sumerians of Mesopotamia. But the evidence for early social life in Egypt is richer because of
elaborate graphic testimony associated with the cult of the dead.

Right at the beginning of the fourth millenium B.C. the tomb paintings
of the priest Thy, near Saqqara, display a considerable variety of foods,
the result of a wide range of agricultural pursuits, a host of servants and a
developed system of trade and tribute. In her monograph on the
Mastabas at Saqqara, Margaret Murray distinguishes fifteen kinds of
bread and cakes.[2] There was a great gulf between the frugal diet of the
peasantry, consisting of dates, vegetables and occasionally fish, and the
elaborate tables of the ruling classes[3] – a gulf that was not simply a
matter of quantity but of quality, of complexity and of ingredients.

Some indication of the complexity of the kitchens of the upper classes
at a later period is given in the list of different kinds of bread that appears
in the Onomasticon of Amenope (Twentieth Dynasty, c. 1000 B.C.).
This document purported to include the name of everything that existed
in the world, although we do not possess the complete inventory, if

indeed it ever was completed. A list of types of agricultural land and their produce is followed by over forty items starting with flour (no.506). With only the rare exception, these entries have a determinative that shows them to be kinds of pastry, bread or cake made from the cereals mentioned earlier in the catalogue (Gardiner 1947: ii, 228). Cereals also form the basis of 'beer', which is the first entry of 23 varieties of beverage. Then it goes on to enumerate 29 parts of an ox, beginning with the generic term 'meat', then descending to 'head', 'neck', etc. The incomplete Onomasticon ends with three kinds of meat, 'raw meat', 'cooked meat', and 'spiced meat' (literally, 'sweetened'), a triad of processes that may have originally been followed by a listing of the cooked dishes that contained these various types of meat. The progression would then have been from field to kitchen to table.

In Egypt cereals formed a substantial proportion of the diet and were prepared in many different ways. The Papyrus Harris (c. 1200 B.C.) again mentions over thirty forms of bread and cakes. By this time modes of preparation and combinations of ingredients seem to have become yet more complex. Mixtures of flour, honey and oil were common; sweets played an increased role; pickling and salting supplemented the culinary processes. As the cuisine became more elaborate, it also became differentiated in line with the social hierarchy. In Egypt pickled and salted fish appears to have been the food of the poor as far as animal protein was concerned (Forbes 1954: 272). In Mesopotamia, a similar differentiation took place; beef, for example, was typically the food of the rich. A Sumerian proverb expresses this contrast in culinary terms:

> The poor man is better dead than alive;
> If he has bread, he has no salt,
> If he has salt, he has no bread,
> If he has meat, he has no lamb,
> If he has lamb, he has no meat.

> (Kramer 1956: 154)

Techniques also became increasingly complex over this period. Ovens were developed for pottery and bricks as well as for cooking. These first ovens were of course back ovens. That is, the fire was built inside the ovens and the embers were then withdrawn to make way for the item to be baked, which cooked while the oven cooled, as is still the case with bread and pizzas in the Mediterranean area. Baked meats were cut up before placed in the heated oven, even when this was heated externally. Meat had to be roasted on a spit and oven-roasting had to await the advent of continuously heated ovens made of metal (associated with the stove) which was a product of the Industrial Revolution. Until that time baking and roasting were very different processes.

In Egypt, the technique of baking became common, especially as a way of preparing bread. But there also developed this new form of treating meat by cutting it up and baking it in an oven. During the time of the building of the Pyramids, the larger estates were equipped with brick furnaces, braziers with special pans for frying and various other kinds of culinary equipment. In Mesopotamia, too, bakeries were found in the temple estates; the growth of temple and royal households led to larger units of food preparation and to the development of a technology able to cope with the change in scale. Such 'common kitchens' were the precursors of the army catering, the monastic refectories, the College Halls and the industrial canteens of later times. The organisation of such consumption units was accompanied by the specialisation of culinary roles and by the sexual transposition of domestic tasks in the kitchens of the rich. The walls of the tomb of Ramses III are covered with representations of men working in the kitchens, baking, cooking, preparing joints and kneading dough, carrying out the work assigned to women in the ordinary domestic context. The new technology of cooking and its associated specialisation spread outside the kitchen itself into craft activities such as the male preserve of metal working. 'The pharmacists and perfumers drew heavily on kitchen utensils and operations, and developed them to react on cooking, to influence the worker in metals, and ultimately to determine the laboratory equipment and terms of the first alchemists' (Forbes 1954: 290). As among the LoDagaa, the kitchen was the first 'laboratory', although the latter was taken over by men.

The aspect of the sociology of cooking that bears on the sexual division of labour was a highly generalised one. From Egyptian times, the great courts of Europe and the Mediterranean employed men as cooks. It was they who took over the women's recipes for daily cooking and transformed them into a court cuisine. Stratification took a very different form in Africa. There it was women who cooked at the courts of kings, and there were few if any culinary changes from the recipes and processes of ordinary life. For such women were not cooking as household servants but as wives. Chiefs were responsible for providing food and shelter for traders and other travellers, so that the more guests the more wives were required to carry out the often very onerous task of preparing food for visitors. Even captive women were transformed into wives, although captive men also performed female tasks such as gathering firewood; they were perhaps the true slaves. In any case the sexual and culinary roles of women were rarely separated in the way that occurred among the hierarchies of Europe and Asia. Space was not divided into the quarters for sexual partners, that is, the harem and the bedchamber, on the one hand, and the quarters for kitchen staff on the other, a layout that is typified in the great Topkapi Palace of Istanbul. The architectural features of the palaces of Africa, Europe and Asia obviously differed according to the numbers of clients, followers, dependents and visitors, but they were also influenced by the nature of the tasks of the royal wives and other retainers.

The gap between Africa and the Ancient Near East makes itself felt in the market-place as well as in the palace. We have seen that in most rural markets in Africa today one can buy food and beer prepared for sale by the women of the village. In the Ancient Near East, however, cooked food became the subject of specialised commercial exchange. Preparing food was often a full-time occupation, both for men and women. Specialists carrying out one type of trade or manufacture were often grouped together in a distinct part of the town or village. When he committed the prophet Jeremiah to prison, King Zedekiah commanded 'that they should give him daily a piece of bread out of the bakers' street' (Jer. xxxvii: 21). Street of bakers implied some type of organisation based on the craft, although guilds were not only found when its members lived together. However, here, as in parts of medieval Europe, specialised tasks had taken on a spatial dimension and become the basis of residential clustering.

The Egyptian tombs demonstrate the arrival of the prerequisites of the *haute cuisine*. But it was in Greece and Rome, when logographic and syllabic forms of writing had given way to the easy art of the alphabet that here, as in so many spheres of human action, cooking was embodied in the written form so as to create a core of practices and recipes that could be subjected to further elaboration in the kitchens and libraries of the rich.[4] The claim to be the first work on cooking is disputed. There is a description of an Athenian banquet by the Scythian visitor Anacharsis in the fourth century B.C. (Barthélémy 1824). Later on, Petronius provides us with the well-known fictional, indeed satirical, account of Trimalchio's dinner. Here the elaboration of food took a whimsical form characteristic of much conspicuous consumption and included dressing up one meat to look like another, a culinary trick typical of banquet food.

There would have been no end to our troubles if a last course had not been brought in, fieldfares made of fine meal and stuffed with raisins and nuts. There followed also quinces, stuck all over with thorns to look like sea-urchins. We could have borne this, if a far more fantastic dish had not driven us even to prefer death by starvation. What we took to be a fat goose, with fish and all kinds of birds round it, was put on, and then Trimalchio said, 'My friends, whatever you see here on the table is made out of one body. . . . As I hope to grow in gains and not in girth, my cook made the whole thing out of a pig' (1913: 157).

However, the main sources on early cooking are Athenaeus and the much discussed cookbook by Apicius, which some have taken as a medieval forgery (Vehling 1936). The book by Apicius, unmentioned by the former writer, was possibly a trade manual that at first was only for the use of cooks. Or possibly a number of manuals, largely of Greek origin, may have been collected together under the name of a well-known gourmet in the third century A.D. Whatever its origin, the book continued to be of great interest right down to Renaissance times. In Italy, the fourteenth and fifteenth centuries produced a dozen manuscripts. The book was no guide to ordinary eating but essentially a book of gastronomy, directed at the 'favoured few'. 'Apicius', Vehling remarks, 'cared nought for time or labor' (p. 24).

The gastronomic pretensions of Rome led to a series of sumptuary laws through which an attempt was made to control the expenditure on food and to limit the extent of conspicuous consumption. While such legislation appears to have had little effects, it shows the constant strand of opposition to the *haute cuisine*, whether in moral or political terms, under the guise of puritanism or egalitarianism. For even if such laws are construed as attempts to preserve the structure of existing inequality, their very introduction implies a threat to the hierarchy. Indeed it is a resentment virtually inherent in the existence of a publicly differentiated cuisine.

Earlier than Apicius and probably the first culinary treatise that has come down to us is the work by Athanaeus, a native of the Egyptian town of Naucratis; composed about A.D. 200, this was called *The Deipnosophists*, 'Connoisseurs in the Art of Dining' or 'The Banquet of the Learned'. Using the customary academic technique of plagiarising earlier writings, he gathers his remarks on the manners and the customs of the ancients from 800 different authors. Much of the treatise has to do with food and its elaboration. At one point the author enumerates 72 kinds of bread made in Greece. The distribution of these varieties is largely geographical; different local names may have been used for the same kind of bread. But other variations in the nature of the available foods marked out the social hierarchy, the emphasis being placed on riches, luxury and on difference itself. Significantly the book itself is presented as a conversation at a dinner party given by a rich Roman, reflecting the great interest in gastronomy among the upper classes; the word *symposium* originally meant a wine party. The essential elements of conspicuous consumption, of servile labour and of culinary elaboration that characterised high society are brought out in the following passage from the versified translation (Bohn i, 238).

And then two slaves brought in a well-rubb'd table,

103

And then another, and another, till
The room was fill'd, and then the hanging lamps
Beamed bright and shone upon the festive crowns,
And herbs, and dishes of rich delicacies.
And then all arts were put in requisition
To furnish forth a most luxurious meal.
Barley-cakes white as snow did fill the baskets,
And then were served up not coarse vulgar pots,
But well-shaped dishes, whose well-ordered breadth
Fill'd the rich board, eels, and the well-stuff'd conger,
A dish fit for the gods. Then came a platter
Of equal size, with dainty sword-fish fraught,
And then fat cuttle-fish, and the savoury tribes
Of the long hairy polypus. After this
Another orb appeared upon the table,
Rival of that just brought from off the fire,
Fragrant with spicy odor. And on that
Again were famous cuttle-fish, and those
Fair maids the honey'd squills, and dainty cakes,
Sweet to the palate, and large buns of wheat,
Large as a partridge, sweet, and round, which you
Do know the taste of well. And if you ask
What more was there, I'd speak of luscious chine,
And loin of pork, and head of boar, all hot;
Cutlets of kid, and well-boil'd pettitoes,
And ribs of beef, and heads, and snouts, and tails.
Then kid again, and lamb, and hares, and poultry,
Partridges and the bird from Phasis' stream.
And golden honey, and clotted cream was there,
And cheese, which I did join with all in calling
Most tender fare. And when we all had reach'd
Satiety of food and wine, the slaves
Bore off the still full tables; and some others
Brought us warm water for to wash our hands.

The author quotes frequently from the Sicilian, Archestratus, who wrote a yet earlier treatise on *Gastrology*:

But this Archestratus was so devoted to luxury, that he travelled over every country and every sea with great diligence, wishing, as it seems to me, to seek out very carefully whatever related to his stomach; and, as men do who write Itineraries and Books of Voyages, so he wishes to relate everything with the greatest accuracy, and to tell where every kind of eatable is to be got in the greatest perfection.[5]

The quotation draws attention to a further point about the development of the *haute cuisine*, namely, its dependence upon a variety of dishes which are largely the inventions of specialists. But by no means entirely.

The high and the low

For the higher cuisine also incorporates and transforms what, from the national standpoint, is the regional food of peasants and the cooking of exotic foreigners. In terms of class and cuisine, the higher in the hierarchy, the wider the contacts, the broader the view.

Thus the higher cuisine inevitably had to acquire ingredients from 'outside'. Of nothing was this truer than for that most valuable element in cooking, those exotic spices in which the trade expanded so rapidly following the eastern conquest of Alexander. The word itself derives from the Latin *species*, meaning a commodity of special distinction or value in contrast to the articles of ordinary commerce.[6] Spices from China, South-East Asia, India, Persia, Arabia and East Africa formed a substantial part of Roman trade, and the Spice Quarter became a well-known part of the capital city. The extent of the trade in exotic luxuries was an indication of the great wealth of the Empire, for these commodities were normally exchanged for precious metals. Internally, the distribution of these valuables had a strong link with hierarchy, like other foods. The recipes of Apicius, presuming that these date from the Augustan period, were the first to discuss spices as condiments in the modern sense; they 'were primarily for the rich man's table' and 'introduced to the West a new mode of life' (Miller 1969: 10). These imports accompanied 'such exotic dishes as boiled spiced ostrich, crane, parrot and flamingo, and a rich ragout à la Baiae, consisting of minced oysters, mussels, sea-urchins, chopped toasted pine-kernels, rue, celery, pepper, coriander, cumin, sweet cooking-wine (*passum*), fish vinegar (*liquamen*), Jericho dates, and olive oil' (p. 11). The hierarchy of food had become well established in Roman Italy, in literature as in life.

This culinary differentiation of culture was not only a phenomenon of the classical world but of all the major societies of the Eurasian continent. For it is linked to a particular kind of hierarchy, with distinct 'styles of life', a hierarchy that is in turn based upon a certain type of agricultural system. The kind of differentiation we have seen in the Mediterranean world, together with the kind of opposition it engendered both at the conceptual and at the political level, are apparent in perhaps the most complex cuisine of all, the cuisine of China.

Here the differentiation in cooking took both private and public as well as regional and hierarchical forms. Many of the differences in this vast country were geographical. In the thirteenth century, at the Southern Sung capital of Hangchow, known to Marco Polo as Quinsai or Kinsai, the 'City of Heaven', without doubt 'the first and most splendid city in the world' (1958: 213), or in the twelfth century, at the Northern Sung capital of Kaifeng, restaurants served a variety of regional cooking, catering for refugees as well as for the grand families who had come there from distant parts of the kingdom. It was these regional restaurants at the capital that seem to have formed the basis of the various 'schools' into which the higher cuisine was divided. For this cuisine was not only a distinctive feature of the rich as against the poor. It reached a wider public through the restaurants in which even those of more modest means celebrated family festivals by means of an elaborate banquet.

Chinese cooking is often divided into four main regions, although in Sung times these seem to have been only three (Freeman 1977: 168). In northern cuisine, the dishes tended to be bland and to include much lamb and many preserved foods; some claim them to be 'sour'. Their basis was wheat and millet which were converted into noodles, buns, dumplings and cakes, often with a filling. Southern cooking, as found for example in the Yangtze delta, used pork and fish, and was based on rice; it was more highly seasoned and sometimes included frogs, a dish that the northerners found as incompatible as the English do in France. Szechwanese cooking was also based on rice but was hotter because of the use of chillis; it is often associated with tea and medicinal herbs since Szechwan was the great centre for their production. To these three has now been added Cantonese food, characterised by sweet and sour dishes.

Other authors claim that the traditional division is into five regional cuisines, which they see as an example of the general concern with fives. The northern cuisines are Honan and Shantung, the southern ones, Szechwan, Fukien and Canton. But some see even this categorisation as much too limited, even if one uses Wei's criterion for a school, that its restaurants can 'offer... patrons on demand on any night more than one hundred different courses prepared from local products' (Anderson 1977: 354).[7] For Chang also points out (1977: 14), while we hear of Ching *ts'ai* (Peking dishes) or Ch'uan (Szechwan) *ts'ai* as major sub-divisions of the Chinese cuisine, these styles are more a classification of restaurants than of local cooking; Peking *ts'ai* for example is the food served in restaurants *outside* Peking and combining many local specialities throughout North China.

However, regional differentiation was clearly not only a matter of restaurant styles. Among other things, it depended upon the staple foods, rice in the south, wheat and millet in the north. As in most cuisines outside Europe, meat played a relatively small part in the diet. But although influenced by Buddhism, the Chinese did not reject meat, as many Indian groups do, for spiritual reasons; there was just not much available. What there was, including dog, was eaten and even human flesh was not altogether taboo. Anthropophagy was practised in China during the T'ang period in quite deliberate ways:

The high and the low

It was by no means an uncommon occurrence for outraged T'ang citizenry to chop up the body of a corrupt or tyrannical official and eat him.... In 739 an officer of the court, who enjoyed the monarch's favor, accepted a bribe to cover up the crime of a colleague; the affair came to light, and the ruler had the offender beaten severely, after which the official supervising the punishment cut out the culprit's heart and ate a piece of his flesh.

Schafer speaks of this incident as an example of 'ceremonial cannibalism' (1977: 135), but other factors too were present. 'In 803 a military officer led a mutiny against his commander, killed him, and devoured him.' This final solution appears to have been a way of securing revenge, not unlike the displaying of a victim's head on a post or spike or the cutting up of his body, both of which were practised in Europe and in sub-Saharan Africa. One recent example of the latter is given in J.-F. Rolland's account (1976) of the astounding expedition of Voulet and Chanoine to Chad in the late nineteenth century, while the former was also practised by the punitive expeditions of colonial regimes (Weiskel 1980, frontispiece). In the Yuan and Ming periods human flesh again appeared as an item of diet, and we hear of steamed dumplings filled with minced humans. But 'revenge cannibalism' and 'gourmet cannibalism' seem less frequent than the 'cannibalism of desperation' that is regularly recorded in times of famine and disaster (Mote 1977: 243). In the Ch'ing period (1644 – 1911), local gazetteers often repeat the sentence, 'In this year people ate each other', when referring to famines, although it has been suggested that this expression should be taken as a metaphor rather than as actuality (Spence 1977: 261).

Leaving aside animal protein, there is a line dividing eastern Asia into two groups, those who depend upon milk products (India, Tibet and the Central Asian nomads) and those who reject these foods, a category that included the Chinese, at least at certain periods. In India the main source of protein comes from pulses and from milk products. In China the absence of milk products was linked to the prevalence of the soya bean which provided the same kind of nutrition but more economically (Anderson 1977: 341).[8] The cultivation of wet rice achieved high yields in the south; but the Chinese also found in the soya bean a much more efficient way of producing protein than by herding livestock. The absence of livestock and the presence of the soya bean permitted high population densities in town and country. The Chinese themselves have sometimes claimed that the rejection of milk products was a way of differentiating their ways from the border nomads, by which means they could remain independent in terms of food. The two notions are not incompatible. However, today, faced with that key product of early industrial cooking, namely sweetened condensed milk, the attitude is changing rapidly.

As well as regional variation, cooking differed according to the stratum to which a domestic group belonged. An extreme case was that of the exotic luxury of wine which from the seventh to the tenth centuries was reserved for emperors. But the diversity extended much further. Marco Polo noted that the flesh of the bigger animals 'is eaten by the rich and the upper classes. The others, the lower orders, do not scruple to eat all sorts of unclean flesh.'[9] As Gernet comments: 'There were such extremes of wealth and poverty in the classes forming the population of Hangchow that a distinction must be made between the food eaten by the rich and the food eaten by the poor.'[10] Indeed, according to Chang (1977: 15), there was a wider disparity in China between rich and poor than in any other country of the world. Frugality among the peasants is a function of their socio-economic position. Among the rich, frugality is considered to be a virtue, but one that is observed intermittently, as periods of fast alternate with those of feast; at this level a frugal diet is associated more with fasting and voluntary denial than with famine and the ineluctable elements; abstinence was internalised as a way to grace rather than the result of external pressures that heralded starvation.

The importation of Indonesian and other spices during the T'ang period emphasised the differences in the cuisine of the rich and the poor (Schafer, 1977: 110). Rich households were generally addicted to foods from abroad; 'foreign food (to say nothing of foreign clothes, foreign music, and foreign dances) was rigorously required at tastefully prepared banquets and this necessarily included dishes cooked in the Indian style' (p. 127). And it was aristocratic households of the same period that attempted to overcome seasonal deficiencies by the use of ice on a large scale. Nor was this differentiation limited to the secular sphere. Of the Sung period Freeman writes: 'Abbots lived in great luxury; temples gave rich and elaborate maigre feasts on Buddhist holidays' (1977: 164).

The hierarchy of the cuisine was a matter of public as well as private consumption. Publicly, food was provided by a great range of restaurants; these were officially classified into two groups, but in fact eating places and inns offered a variety of facilities appealing to all pockets. An idea of the extent can be gained by examining that magnificent twelfth-century scroll, 'The Spring Festival on the River', depicting life in the Northern Sung capital.[11]

In Hangchow the tea-houses frequented by the rich had a sumptuous decor, with displays of flowers, dwarf evergreens and works by celebrated painters and calligraphers. Others had singing-girls on the top floor and were avoided by the best people. Taverns varied in the drinks and menu they offered. Some served nothing but pies with the drinks, and the more plebeian of them were nothing but rough and ready shelters. 'Others again, where only the lowest class of people were to be met (porters, shop-hands, artisans, servants), did not serve anything along with the drinks except beancurd soup, oysters and mussels'.[12] Restaurants catered for the same range of society as the tea-shops and taverns, all being part of the urban scene that was 'entwined with the world of prostitutes' (Freeman 1977: 159). Every restaurant in the capital had a menu offering a considerable choice of dish. Other shops, such as those selling noodles, catered for a humbler clientele.[13] The range of cooked food was very broad, some even being manufactured in workshops which supplied the vendors and hawkers who flooded the streets of the larger cities.

The other institution providing food to the public was the inn, so widely used by travellers. These inns acted as a social centre for the local population, as in other regions of the world, playing an important part in the exchange of news and gossip, and providing a meeting-place where discussion could take place and even uprisings planned (Spence 1977: 290).

Clearly, the organisation of distribution that accompanied this elaborate differentiation of ranks and restaurants was highly complex. According to Marco Polo who visited the Southern Sung capital in the thirteenth century, the town was some hundred miles in circumference and had ten principal market-places, not to speak of innumerable local ones, in which for three days in the week there were gatherings of forty to fifty thousand people 'who came to market carrying everything that could be desired to sustain life' (1958: 214). Huge imports of food by river and by road were required to feed the population whose size was such that 'anyone seeing such a multitude would believe it to be a stark impossibility that food could be found to fill so many mouths' (p. 216). The amounts were indeed staggering, and the visitor estimated that the city required 43 cart loads, nearly 1000 lbs, of pepper every day.

In the organisation of supplies, of government, of crafts, of leisure, in its clothing, in the sumptuousness of the houses and in the extent of its trade with merchants from India and elsewhere, in its use of paper money, in all these features the world of China far surpassed that of Europe of the thirteenth century. It is against this 'backwardness' of the West that, at a time when some have seen it as already 'unique', its later achievement has to be judged. The 'uniqueness of the West' was perceptible only three hundred years later; its supremacy lasted for about the same span of time, until the rise of industrial Japan.

While Chinese cooking was differentiated by regions, there was also a kind of national tradition, based upon the cuisine of the court but partly originating in peasant life.[14] The court itself was an extraordinarily complex organisation which had to devote much activity to obtaining and preparing supplies for the residents as well as offerings to the ancestors. Especially was this true of the Ming period. Founded by 'a ruffian from the lowest stratum of Chinese peasant society' (Mote 1977: 210), the dynasty made great efforts to restore the traditional norms. The palace kitchens were run by three groups of people, the kitchen servants,[15] the eunuchs and the palace women.[16] The kitchen servants numbered between three and six thousand at different times. The eunuchs became increasingly important not only in connection with food but throughout the entire administration; one estimate gives a figure of 70,000. From the beginning of the period the eunuch staff were allotted to separate bureaus for dealing with food and drink, that is, the palace pharmacy, the imperial wine bureau, the flour mill, the vinegar works, the bureau of herds and flocks, and finally, of vegetable gardening. The eunuchs supervised the procurement of everything needed in the palace, as well as controlling foreign trade, managing the imperial estates, factories, warehouses, gardens and herd grounds, and making purchases in the markets (Mote 1977: 212–13).

In Ming China, the Ministry of Rites was responsible for both the feasts for the dead and the great banquets for the living; two characters with the same transliteration were used, even though one referred to 'the ways of the spirits' and the other to 'the ways of men', drawing a parallel between sacrifice and hospitality (Mote 1977: 218); the difference lay in the fact that food for the dead had to be unblemished. Offerings to the gods seem to have consisted of stewed meat, but they also included the flesh of wild animals (p. 134). The animals for both were provided either by levies or from the imperial estates; they were transported to the capital by the fleet of canal barges organised by the eunuch bureaucrats. In such ceremonies, whether religious or secular, the emphasis was placed on traditional foods (Schafer 1977: 133), a mark of ceremonial conservatism.

One of the main reasons for the great banquets, then as now, was the entertainment of foreign visitors (p. 133). As with other major feasts, it was customary for women to be excluded from these banquets. However the Empress ran a parallel dinner at the imperial court for the wives of ambassadors and other guests in the Palace of Female Tranquillity.

In contrast, ordinary meals were eaten in the company of one's wife and other family members, in the homes of commoners as well as of the elite.[17] It is recorded that one particular clan did separate husbands and wives at meal times and on other family occasions; but while they were honoured for supposedly following the ways of antiquity, they were not emulated by others (Mote 1977: 254). Essentially similar patterns of familial eating seem to have been practised in medieval Europe, and while the same conjugality did not always exist in Indian homes, these societies still provide a general and valid contrast with Africa where men and women regularly eat in separate places, where there are sexual but few horizontal inhibitions on eating together. The structure of the table is linked to the structure of the marriage, which in turn correlates with the presence of dowry and the system of inheritance. Where women are endowed and ranked, they tend to eat with men of equal status, enjoying the same cuisine.

The differentiation of the cuisine is clearly expressed in the written works on Chinese cooking. During the T'ang period (618 – 907), and even before, a considerable number of books appeared known as Food Canons which constituted definitive texts on food. These were not cookbooks but rather guides to diet whose main intention was to instruct members of the elite about the correct preparation of balanced dishes. Influenced by the recommendations of learned pharmacologists, such as Meng Shen in the seventh century, the dishes were initially prepared for medical purposes, but many of them later came to be regarded as gourmet foods (Schafer 1977: 87).

Much of the earlier Chinese writing in this area was concerned with medical matters. *The Principles of Correct Diet* by Hu Ssu-hui (1330) proclaimed that 'many diseases can be cured by diet alone' and marked an important advance in dietary medicine. More typical perhaps is Chia Ming's *Essential Knowledge for Eating and Drinking* (1368); it stresses prevention of disease and includes much knowledge that comes from earlier herbals. Most Chinese, learned or not, were partly aware of the concepts on which the book was based, but to observe all the taboos and warnings in the book would, Mote remarks, 'make eating virtually impossible' (1977: 233). As with many other products of early literacy, the 'urge to classify' overwhelms reasonable human purposes and produces the over-systematisation that influences the cosmologies and religions of the book so profoundly that their prescriptions can sometimes be fulfilled only by a small elite of religious men and women, most often themselves literates. From one standpoint (which is certainly theirs) this elite can be regarded as 'orthodox', from another they are 'extremist'. Anthropologists and sociologists are often tempted to view the formulations of the customs and belief of such groups as presenting the essential features of a particular culture. Mote himself speaks of Chia Ming's assumptions on the 'philosophical underpinnings of the concepts surrounding foods as active agents in the cosmic process' as bringing us 'face to face with the sources of authority on which all the Chinese drew in ordering and maintaining all the constituents of their civilization' (p. 234). But there is an alternative view that sees such written products, like some oral ones, as efflorescence rather than revelation, as erecting one possible philosophy out of a set of generalised constituents rather than revealing the underpinnings of a conceptual system.

Whatever view one takes, it is clear that, by and large, the written expressions of Chinese cuisine represented the culinary culture of the upper classes, whether those expressions were literary or technical. One striking example of the former is the poem written by a poet of the third or second century B.C., many centuries before Athenaeus, on the subject of his favourite dishes.

> Where thirty cubits high at harvest-time
> The corn is stacked;
> Where pies are cooked of millet and bearded-maize
> Guests watch the steaming bowls
> And sniff the pungency of peppered herbs.
> The cunning cook adds slices of bird-flesh,
> Pigeon and yellow-heron and black-crane.
> They taste the badger-stew.
> O Soul come back to feed on foods you love!
>
> Next are brought
> Fresh turtle, and sweet chicken cooked in cheese
> Pressed by the man of Ch'u.
> And pickled sucking-pig
> And flesh of whelps floating in liver-sauce
> With salad of minced radishes in brine;
> All served with that hot spice of southernwood
> The land of Wu supplies.
> O Soul come back to choose the meats you love!
>
> Roasted daw, steamed widgeon and grilled quail –
> On every fowl they fare.
> Boiled perch and sparrow broth – in each preserved
> The separate flavour that is most its own.
> O Soul come back to where such dainties wait![18]

In contrast to such rapturous celebration of the rich and rare, here, as in the Ancient World, a parallel theme runs through the literature, one that emphasises the need to look at cooking from a 'sociological' as well as from a 'cultural' point of view. For expression is also given to the resentment against the sumptuary expenditure of the rich or the reaction to the 'relative deprivation' of the poor, the point of departure depending upon one's social position. The feeling is most clearly expressed by the intellectuals, philosophers and sages whose role was to promote spiritual as against earthly values. One common complaint is that 'while the wine and the meat have spoiled behind the red doors [of rich households], on the road there are skeletons of those who died from exposure' (Tu Fu, A.D. 715–770, quoted by Chang, 1977: 15). Similar contrasts are drawn by Mencius in the fourth century B.C. 'There's fat meat in your kitchen and there are well-fed horses in your stables, yet the people look hungry and in the outskirts of the city men drop dead from starvation' (Mencius 1970: 52). Mencius was certainly not backward in recognising the value of 'government', rank and respect between the orders. But he was also critical of what he regarded as conspicuous consumption:

When speaking to men of consequence it is necessary to look upon them with contempt and not be impressed with their lofty position. Their hall is tens of feet high: the capitals are several feet broad. Were I to meet with success, I would not indulge in such things. Their tables, laden with food, measure ten feet across, and their female attendants are counted in their hundreds. Were I to meet with success, I would not indulge in such things... Why, then, should I cower before them? (Book VII, Part A, 34)

Such sentiments obviously became more pronounced in times of shortage. But the theme of denial, of restraint, of asceticism, is a persistent undercurrent of the ideology of these civilisations with which we are dealing, standing in stark contrast to the gluttony of court feasts and the elaborate dinners of the academics that we encounter in Wu Ching-tzu's novel, *The Scholars*. Both the attitudes of criticism and denial inevitably receive their most potent expression, in action as well as in words, at times of radical social change, of revolution but even of rebellion. From their Hunan base the Communist-led Peasants' Association of the 1920s issued the following rules about banquets:

Sumptuous feasts are generally forbidden. In Shao-shan...it has been decided that guests are to be served with only three kinds of animal food, namely, chicken, fish and pork. It is also forbidden to serve bamboo shoots, kelp and lentil noodles .... In the town of Chiamo...people have refrained from eating expensive foods and use only fruit when offering ancestral sacrifices. (quoted by Chang 1977: 15)

The abnegation of rich foods takes on a moral quality. In Mencius resentment of sumptuous living takes the more positive form of valuing asceticism for the good it does to the individual: 'There is nothing better for the nurturing of the heart than to reduce the number of one's desires.' This general attitude, which contrasts with the specific prohibitions an individual acquires through attachment to shrine or clan, because of fast or illness (which constitute the taboos of anthropological discourse), is characteristic of societies where differences in styles of life infuse the social scene. The hierarchy between ranks and classes takes a culinary form; the conflict and tension that this implies and generates are embodied in resentment against luxury that comes out of the writings of scholars of philosophical bent and in one form encourages renunciation of the 'high life' in favour of the 'good life'.

Similar themes are found in the culinary culture of that other great Oriental civilisation, India. The link between food and sex is brought out in the whole ideology of caste. In a different way we find it too in Chinese culture, at least as brought out in that sixteenth-century novel, *The Golden Lotus*, which has been characterised as displaying a 'bi-sensual modality' (Mote 1977: 278). Of the Ch'ing period it has been said that 'the vocabularies of food and lust' overlapped and blended into a language of sensuality (Spence 1977: 278). But in India the association of cooking with sex and marriage is at once more intimate and more political, pervading as it does the whole sphere of hierarchy. In a general way, as we have seen in an earlier chapter, many anthropologists have drawn attention to the link. Lévi-Strauss, for example, has insisted upon the identification of copulation and eating: both involve 'une conjonction par complementarité', when two separate but complementary units unite. Looking at the question from a more concrete point of view, both activities involve a division of labour on a male – female basis, the one physiologically, the other socially, both of which are effectively universal in human societies. Since both activities centre upon the domestic domain, the same individuals are frequently involved, and the cooking of food by the woman is often seen as the reciprocal of the coital acts of the man. The word for eat (*di*, LoDagaa, *dzi*, in Gonja) is frequently used for sex, and covers much of the semantic field of the word 'enjoy' in English. As we have remarked, this reciprocity as especially marked in many African societies; since marriage is polygynous, the woman has to safeguard her share of male attention, and the wife with whom the husband is sleeping is normally the one who provides him with food. In polygynous households, cooking and sex takes place on a rotational basis,[19] with menstruating women being left out of both schedules.[20]

In India, the connection between the two is projected into the domains of politics, religion and indeed economics, being clearly brought out in the prohibitions on intermarriage and interdining, on commensality and *conubium*, that are such central features of the caste system. While we may follow Dumont and see the separation between castes as an aspect of 'interrelations and hierarchy' (1970: 130), as resulting from 'the organisation of the whole' (p. 131), the specific features of the relationship centre around prohibitions on interdining and intermarriage, that is, on separation rather than integration. Indeed it has been argued (Stevenson 1954) that the importance attached to marriage and to food and drink in the separation of castes is linked to the fact that sex and eating represent especially serious forms of contact. Any external and internal pollution that results has to be removed by acts such as bathing. Contact of this kind with members of other groups has to be thoroughly cleansed both for individual and collective reasons. The separation of hierarchy has to be maintained.

India, then, presents the clearest example of the link of hierarchy with food and sex, both topics receiving prolonged attention in life and art. As in China, the earliest records show a widespread concern with the properties of food. There was a firm belief, writes Prakash, that a man is what he eats and that purity of thought depends on purity of food.[21] Works like the *Bhagavadgītā, Kāmasūtra, Smṛtis and Purāṇas,* lay down what is to be eaten, at what time and by whom. Students, widows and ascetics are advised to avoid exciting foodstuffs just as they had to avoid sex. Moreover the caste system itself is partly defined in terms of the type of food a man is allowed to eat. To move upwards meant changing one's diet, usually by becoming more vegetarian.[22] In addition there was a straightforward distinction in economic terms: 'the mass of the people lived on simple and nourishing food. The rich however enjoyed dainty dishes'.[23]

Already in the Vedic period there was differentiation of food according to caste, each of the four main *varṇas* having its proper drink. But there is evidence too that members of different castes were already forbidden to eat food with one another, just as they were forbidden to marry. 'In the Brāhmanas we find some traces of the idea of pollution of food by contact with persons of low caste. People refuse to dine with Kavasa because he was the son of a maid servant.'[24]

For the period around the beginning of the Christian era, the *Arthaśāstra* of Kautilya formalises the distribution of food in hierarchical fashion.

The meal of a gentleman, according to Kautilya, consisted of one *prastha* of pure unbroken rice, one fourth of a *prastha* of pulses, one sixty-fourth part of a *prastha* of salt and one sixteenth part of a *prastha* of clarified butter or oil. For menial-servants the quantity of pulses prescribed is one sixth of a *prastha* and the quantity of oil or clarified butter half that prescribed for a gentleman. He lays down that women should be provided with three fourths of the above quantities and children only half of what is prescribed for a gentleman. Bran was given to blacksmiths and labourers and broken pieces of rice to slaves, servants and cooks who cooked soups, rice and cakes. The rice used by the king was so highly polished that only five parts of polished rice were considered edible by a king out of twenty parts of unhusked rice.[25]

The epics show that these differences in distribution were accompanied by the growth of an *haute cuisine*, with its expert cooks, waiter service and the preparation of special dishes.[26] At the same time there is an elaboration of the rules of etiquette and hospitality. According to Manu, a person who cooks for himself is a sinner.[27] In towns and villages a man was employed to lay out special food for the gods as well as for the poor. Meals for the rich were very different; the order of courses was formally laid down and it became the practice to listen to music while eating dinner. At this time, according to Prakash, we have a society 'divided' into three broad culinary strata: 'the rich enjoyed many meat preparations and dainties. The food of the middle classes generally consisted of milk and articles cooked in clarified butter while the poor were satisfied with food articles cooked in oil' (pp. 130–1). The art of cooking was further developed because of the keen interest taken by royal princes, especially in the great feasts produced at marriages and as offerings to the gods.

Since cooking involves contact, which creates pollution depending on the position in the hierarchy, individuals are prohibited from eating food prepared by the lower castes. Hence a banquet had to be prepared by the ritually highest caste of Brahmans whose cooking can pollute no one. But while cooked food enacted hierarchy, raw food was liberated from such constraints and represented the 'food of gifts'.

The concern with food took two other somewhat contradictory directions but similar to those we noted in China. Positively this interest led to the elaboration of cuisine and categories in a body of written works; negatively the rejection of food was seen as a way to health and holiness. The literary works are largely medical compositions which attempted to incorporate edibles into classificatory schemes for remedial purposes; as in medieval England, recipe and prescription were virtually one and the same. In the Sunga period, around the beginning of the Christian era, medical works indicate that Indians used more than forty varieties of rice, sixty varieties of fruits and more than one hundred and twenty vegetables. 'Treating the subject scientifically', writes Prakash, 'they give a list of food articles which suit people residing in different regions, as also the articles which one should consume in a particular season' (p. 244). Regional dishes were partly incorporated in a national cuisine. At the same time increased trade brought in foreign foods and new recipes, which, like the national cuisine, was food for the rich rather than the poor.

The other side of the hierarchical cuisine was the extended notion of the fast, the rejection of food for religious, medical or moral reasons. The denial of food to the body, whether some or all foods, was partly associated with the rejection of violence, with avoiding the killing of animals and the culling of plants. But vegetarianism is only one element. Abstinence and prohibition are widely recognised as ways of attaining

116

grace in hierarchical societies such as China and India. The idea is clearly expressed in a verse in the *Manusmrti*: 'there is no harm in eating meat or drinking intoxicating liquors as it is the natural craving of man but abstaining from them is meritorious'. The great Indian religions, Buddhism, Jainism and Brahmanism, all developed this ethical injunction into a way of life, and total abstention from meat was considered meritorious. Blood sacrifices were now seen as in inappropriate means for communicating with the gods. Vegetables and milk replaced meat and liquor, at least in those upper castes with a specifically religious orientation. Indians generally recognised abstemiousness as, in Gandhi's words, 'a great aid to the evolution of the spirit'. Such a philosophy of rejection could develop only within the context of hierarchical society with its stratified cuisine, since abstention only exists in the wider context of indulgence.

At the same time as being spiritually valuable, restraint was also thought to assist the body in a practical way. Marco Polo thought that Brahmans lived longer than anyone else in the world, and attributed their longevity 'to their light feeding and great abstinence' (1958: 278). Of course, in all societies the control of diet is seen as an important aspect of medical treatment, but nowhere in my experience are doctors of all persuasions so prone to act on the notion that a cure can be affected by manipulating the intake of food, though contemporary California may run India a close second. In Africa, by and large, cures are obtained by the addition of 'medicines' (*tīī* in LoDagaa, *aderu* in Gonja – a very widespread concept); these are special substances not consumed in the course of an ordinary meal. Some general adjustment is often made for the sick and for infants, but there is little development of the idea that particular foods or dishes have special curative properties. That is the domain of the wild, uncultivated plants rather than the domestic ones on which human life depends in a different way.

One interesting aspect of contemporary Indian fasts, which as elsewhere often demand an alternative diet rather than total denial, is the abstention from foods raised through ploughing (*jota anna*), arising from what has been called 'the most fundamental dichotomy for appropriate and inappropriate foods for fasting' (Khare 1976a: 130); fruits, *phalahar* (literally, 'food of fruits') are separated from grains and cereals. I have friends who restrict themselves to 'fruit' on one day of the week, not unlike the earlier Christian abstention from meat on Fridays. In his detailed study of food in the North Indian town of Lucknow, Khare notes that the main characteristics of these fasts are 'austerity, self-discipline and devotion, to seek aims ranging from "self-realization" to the possession of worldly riches and pleasures' (p. 132). Individual fulfilment through denial can lead to general or specific benefits for oneself or for others, including the gods themselves. But whereas men's fasts are mostly directed towards improving or upholding their own purity and spiritual status, the fasts of women are largely aimed at enhancing and maintaining auspiciousness for 'the social collective', that is, for the family.

Just as fasting implies withdrawal from eating certain normal foods, so it involves withdrawal from other aspects of ordinary human intercourse which are replaced by meditation and silence, sleeping on the ground and in a celibate fashion (p. 134). Khare describes a case where the mother of a man undertaking a fast refused to speak while the cooking of the 'fruit' was going on but communicated with her daughter-in-law by means of sign-language alone (p. 136). The food, of course, was an offering as well as a meal of self-denial, a sacrifice in both senses. For when the food was ready, a portion was first offered to the sacred cow, while the next was given to the crow so that he could feed her husband's ancestors, the crow being the messenger to their world (p. 137).

The offering to the sacred cow, that prominent feature of the iconography of the Hindu temple, indicates its religious significance which also has dietary implications. Embedded in the rejection of all meat by upper-caste Hindus is the much stronger rejection of the flesh of the cow. Both the general abstinence from meat and the special position of the cow can be seen as extreme cases of wider tendencies in man's relation with the animal and vegetable world around him.

Other areas of Asia displayed an ambivalence about the killing of animals, especially domestic animals and especially the cow whose powers of traction were so important to a plough agriculture. While the meat of domestic animals was included in the Chinese diet of the T'ang period, pharmacologists did not rate their flesh, and specifically that of the cow, very highly. Meng Shen advised against the consumption of the flesh of yellow or black ox, the proper use of such bovines being to assist in the cultivation of crops (Schafer 1977: 99). In Egypt too the flesh of the cow was at times avoided, and the avoidance of an animal whose role in domestic production was so central cannot be altogether accidental. Of the T'ang period Freeman notes that the Buddhist influence meant that beef was relatively unpopular; while cattle were brought to the market, beef is not explicitly mentioned in the lists of banquet dishes. 'Purely aside from religious feelings, their flesh must have been tough, stringy, and dry after a career of pulling a plow' (1977: 164). In Europe the rejection of meat was not confined to the monastic orders of Christendom. It had been vigorously advocated by some of the great 'pagan' philosophers such as Porphyry, who justifies abstinence on the grounds that justice 'is due from us to the ox that ploughs, the dog that is fed with us, and the animals that nourish us with their milk, and adorn our bodies

118

with their wool' (1965: 129). This passage seems to show that we are faced with a specific ambivalence about eating or sacrificing some animals, not so much because they are close to mankind but because they assist him in his work. It is a matter of production as well as distance. On a yet more general level the ambivalence is about killing any animal that, like man, lives, moves, generates and breathes, and that may, like him, have a soul (*anima*).

Just as abstinence from food is the path to holiness, so too is abstinence from sex. For holy men, this is as true in Hinduism as in Catholic Christianity. In his visit to the Indian kingdom of Maabar which lay along the Coromandel or Eastern Coast, in the district round Tanjore, Marco Polo observed the self-denial of those who devoted themselves to the holy life. The 'regular religious order...of Yogi...carry abstinence to the extremes.' They go without a stitch of clothing and when asked why they display their private parts, reply that we are not ashamed since we commit no sin with them. Not only will they not kill any animals, because they say that they have souls, but that they eat nothing fresh, either herb or root, for the same reason. 'They fast all the year round and never drink anything but water' (1958: 279–80). When a probationer is installed as a monk 'to serve the idols' at the death of the previous servitor, he is caressed by the temple virgins. 'They touch them on various parts of the body and embrace and fondle them and instil into them the uttermost of earthly bliss. If any man thus caressed lies completely motionless without any reaction to the maiden's touch, he passes muster and is admitted to their order' (p. 281). The story is similar to the one Marco Polo tells about Buddha. In his effort to get his only son to think of earthly things, the king his father

housed him in a very luxurious palace and provided 30,000 maidens of the utmost beauty and charm to minister to him....They sang and danced before him and did all they could to delight him as the king had bidden them. But...all these maidens could not tempt the king's son to any wantonness, but he lived more strictly and more chastely than before (p. 282).

For the European visitor what was remarkable was the supposed contrast between unrestricted sexuality ('they do not regard any form of sexual indulgence as a sin', p. 267) and its total rejection, which like abstinence from wine and flesh meant the gaining of power.

In spirit, these incidents from the thirteenth century are consistent with the contemporary Gandhian doctrine of *Brahmacharya* which is brought out in the whole history of his relations with his wife. Nor is this only an elite sentiment; like the prohibition on killing and eating animals, it is not confined to Brahmans alone. In the villages of the Degham *taluka* (district) of Gujerat, where we spent a short period in

1977, prohibitions on the consumption of meat were observed not only in farming groups, such as the Patels or Patidars, but also among the service castes, such as the Barbers, who had here adopted the name of Sharma. Widespread too was the positive view of sexual abstinence. While assisting in a survey of merchants in the town of Degham, I was struck by the occasions on which people talked, in a quite unsolicited manner and to a near stranger, about the virtues of Yoga and of abstinence from sex. 'Why waste in two minutes', a youngish but successful merchant asked me, 'what you have saved in twenty-four hours?' For him power came from saving, from abstinence.

In most cultures, there exists a set of close and extensive relations between food on the one hand and the cosmological and ideological beliefs on the other. In India, these relations are particularly elaborate and form the central focus of Khare's detailed studies of food in the northern city of Lucknow, in the course of which he tries to offer a 'cultural' account of the Hindu hearth and home. As with other proponents of the radical autonomy of social or cultural systems, his approach leads him to play down constraints of a biological kind (e.g. p. 109). Economic factors are similarly given short shrift; the money given to a Brahman for the purchase of food is regarded as 'a symbolic substitution for food' (p. 110). So at one level it is, but that level is rather meaningless. More importantly from the present point of view, in his concern with explanations phrased in terms of particular cultures he is led to reject the Western nature/culture dichotomy as applicable to Hindu conceptions of food (1976b: 119). He argues more generally against such dichotomising tendencies, inferring that they are features of particular cultures rather than attributes of the human mind. In particular, he does not see the dichotomy of cooked and raw/uncooked as being critical to Indian concepts partly because fire is not intrinsic to the 'cooking' of Indian food (1976b: 2, 10). The folk taxonomy of culinary processes, to which he refers as an 'analytical cultural construct' (p. 10), is based on axes of a different kind. And it is this folk taxonomy, the character of explicit constructs, that forms the basis of his own analysis and that leads him to be critical of other observers.

Commenting on Beck's analysis (1969), he claims that she 'stretches symbolic extensions, at times, too far to obtain a satisfactory category opposition. This feature often violates the established cultural meaning domains, and thereby defeating the very purpose for which she postulates category distinctions' (1976b: 84). Such a comment is perfectly justified when the author is trying to remain at the actors' own level of semantic operation, although even here we have to allow space for commentaries by members of that society as well as for those of outsiders. These are part of the scene. But there is no reason why a study has to remain encapsulated in a particular cultural context or has to be rooted to the actor level. In fact no study ever is, if only because we are using another 'natural' language to 'translate' action. Such studies have their own problems, for example that of 'verification', of a plurality of observers making a similar analysis. But the resort to an already compromised 'cultural' commentary does not cut out the need for more general approaches in different terms, even though the level of *verstehen*, the understanding of the actor's point of view, often provides an important point of departure.

According to Khare, 'the cultural significance of cooking... within the Hindu system remains incidental' (1976b: 63). Behind this surprising statement lies a distinction between 'sophisticated cookery and cooking techniques' (i.e. 'cooking') on the one hand and 'the ontological modes of handling food' on the other. For Khare the former is undeveloped, the latter developed. By this he means that while there is a general pan-Indian idea about the ritual purity and impurity of foods, 'there are no culinary cultures common to all parts of the country'. He recognises regional diversity in cooking. But his concern with the 'cultural' order leads to a holistic stress on unity, on 'culturally valid reasons', on 'the unitary principle that the entire culture highly emphasizes' (p. 106). Such a preoccupation with unity leads him to ask whether the giving of *prasad* violates the ideology (of caste), and if so are we dealing with a 'spurious or genuine breakdown'? The answer, predictably, lies in constructing a wider, all-embracing level of ideology that becomes so general in its formulation that it includes all sectarian and other oppositions. At one point the author remarks:

A cultural announcement of the Hindu food must, therefore, contend with a general system of the Hindu thought, where, if on the one hand all cognitive diversity must be ordered by a set of dominant cultural principles, then there is, on the other, the task to discover a more fundamental intellectual *process* of reduction of diversity (of contexts) in terms of the same, stated cultural principles (1976b: 118).

The question one must face here, as in a great deal of social and cultural analysis, is the status of these principles. Are they to be seen as active forces or descriptive devices? If they are descriptive, who is using them as tools – the actor (which actor?) or the observer (which observer?)? These categories cannot be viewed as completely separable and opposed – the actor is observer as well as participator, the observer is often a participant observer. Nor of course are the categories of 'forces' and 'devices' to be absolutely divorced one from another, if only because a description of behaviour may lead to its modification. But it seems quite another thing to assume that all behaviour (all cognitive diversity) must be *ordered* (a very strong word compared with 'modify') by dominant principles, when these notions seem to pertain to the descriptive level. It is a question that raises, in acute form, the nature of the group or culture in which these dominant principles obtain – the local caste segment, wider caste, Lucknow, North India, Hindu culture....

In his own study of the contemporary Hindu cuisine, Khare sees even internal differences as being ordered by this set of dominant cultural principles. He does acknowledge the difference in cuisine not only regionally (indeed he denies the existence of a distinct Indian cuisine) but also hierarchically. For example, among the lower castes there was not the same concern with specified hours for eating.

Compared to the twice-born pattern... the cooking, serving and eating phases of a food cycle are thoroughly simplified, making the daily twice-born version look quite formal.... Cooking, serving, and eating, the three distinct stages of the twice-born food cycle, here undergo compression, simplification and attenuation (1976a: 95–6).

Even the well-known and pervasive distinction between *kacha* and *pakka* is 'aborted here' (p. 98);[28] indeed the author speaks of 'aborted Sanskritization' and it is in these terms that his analysis is made. But the use of this phrase suggests an alternative view of the relation of caste to cooking. Wherever he can, Khare takes a 'cultural' view; and culture for him has its 'orthodox' expression in Hindu cosmology. But at least at the level of 'manners of the table', the word 'formal', or rather formalised, may be more appropriate than orthodox. For the lower-caste cuisine should not only be seen, except by the Brahman, as an aborted form of upper-class 'orthodoxy'. For the Brahman mode may also be understood as a specific formalisation of a more general and less structured pattern of action which, in their attempts to attain higher degrees of political, economic or religious grace (the latter process being referred to as Sanskritisation), the actors may adopt and adapt, taking on the manners of their caste superiors.[29]

Evidence for such a view comes from the court cuisine in earlier Lucknow, the town in which Khare carried out his study and which in the late eighteenth and early nineteenth centuries was the seat of the independent court of Oudh (Sharar 1975). The rulers of this Indo-Mughal civilisation were Muslims, and an important part of their cuisine was derived from Arab sources. Other elements came from the Hindu cuisine. 'Seeing the Hindus frying their puris, Muslims put some ghee into their griddle-baked bread and invented parathas' (Sharar 1975: 161). So it was with many other dishes; the high-status cuisine of the court included meat curries (*qaurma*) as well as pulaus, kebabs as well as biryanis.

The court cuisine, which did not fit well with Brahman models, was elaborated in ways common to the rich of various cultures. The books of the wealthy invented extravagant dishes; one produced a pulau in which half of each grain of rice was fiery red like a ruby while the other was white and sparkled like a crystal. Another cooked rice to reproduce the nine well-known gems; *moti*, the pearl pulau, was made to look as if the rice contained shining pearls. In Hyderabad visiting Englishmen were regaled with a large pie from which, when opened, small birds flew out, like the blackbirds of the English nursery rhyme (Sharar 1975: 158, 162). The varieties of cooked food were linked to the rank of the household, especially the food known as *tora* which was chosen to be sent out for various festivals as well as served for feasts at home. In the royal palace the king's *tora* consisted of one hundred and one trays, the cost of which was about five hundred rupees. Such cultural diversity and sumptuary differentiation has little place in a 'cultural' account that is searching for structural continuity.

In looking at more recent changes, however, Khare makes the interesting point that Indian food practices are changing more quickly than marriage. Endogamy continues even where people have dropped many barriers of interdining and ceased to observe the earlier orthodox rules, regarded by Khare as of central moral concern. Leaving aside his question as to whether or not this constitutes 'a *basic* change in the system and its underlying cultural constructs' (1976a: 271), if only because there is no apparent way of answering the query, the observation raises important issues.

Why should cuisine change more quickly? We might argue, contrary to Khare, that this evidence suggests that food practices are more peripheral than has been supposed. The argument could also be turned on its head, for the peripheral might persist unchanged simply because of its lesser degree of entailment. But such a line of argument does not apply in the present case. In a heavily stratified (or hierarchical) system, it is understandable that in-marriage should be more resistant to change. With pressure from a democratic political system, dependent upon mass votes, the more obvious observance of separation (differentiation, apartheid, discrimination) are clearly the ones most likely to come under attack. Since like marries like in most societies, endogamy is less easy to dispel as well as to spot and criticise.

The limited observations made by Esther Goody and myself in Gujerat confirm Khare's remarks about the changes. But at the village level at least, much of the 'traditional' system of food-ways lives on. By comparison with an African village, one of the most striking contrasts lay in constant invitations to come and eat. At the very same time some inhabitants, at least among the older Brahmans, refused to accept the food we offered them. On my first evening in Nandol, a number of people came to greet us, including the elderly scholar, Kalidas, who had been a clerk in the Education Service of the Government of the Gaekwod of Baroda. On his arrival I fetched some water to offer him, as I would have done in Africa and elsewhere. When I handed him a glass, he set it aside, firmly but politely, saying that he only ate in his own house, by which he meant in his own caste. All other food he considered polluting, not because of the nature of the constituents but because of the status of the person who had prepared or offered it.

Of course, what went into a meal was also of concern. But even the service castes were vegetarian, so that there was no great differentiation of one caste from another from the standpoint of culinary rules. It was the handling of food that differentiated. In our Brahman house the kitchen was the most sacred, the purest part, on entering which it was necessary to remove one's shoes. As elsewhere outsiders were not allowed to come in (Pocock 1972: 12). Indeed even members of the household not directly involved in cooking have to keep their distance (Khare 1976a: 136).

While most castes were vegetarian, the former 'untouchable' castes were certainly not. It was the harijan of the Dedh caste from the next village, as there were no longer any leather workers in Nandol, who came at night and disposed of the buffalo that died at the end of the street and whose death brought mourning prohibitions on us all. The ban on eating after a cow has died is one of a number of prohibitions on the way Hindus could eat.

Thus one cannot eat standing, lying naked, or in wet clothes, nor out of a broken or impure vessel, nor out of the hand; one cannot eat in the open air, in a temple, or in an empty house in mid-day or mid-night or at dawn, nor at the time of solar or lunar eclipse [or when any misfortune has occurred to the king, to a Brahman, or to a cow]; nor can one eat during a period of indigestion or to surfeit or more than twice a day or too late or too early.

The list of prohibitions comes from Jolly's account of Hindu law and customs (1928: 339ff.), and Khare comments that he himself encountered them all during the course of his research except those he placed within brackets. The widespread character of the prohibitions, their association with the astrological system, the manner of their formulation, makes the list seem like the product of that religious literacy which has so strongly marked Hindu – Brahmanical culture.

Other groups of former 'untouchables' made the wine (*dāru*) from the flower of the *maura* tree, forbidden to the upper castes, and ate that which was uneaten by those who had direct access to the land. The well-off farmers, the Patels, whose wealth had greatly increased since land reform, the Green Revolution and rural electrification, got milk and clarified butter from their own cattle, and grain and fresh vegetables from their fields. The buttermilk was put outside the house each night so that 'their' untouchables would come and take it away for their own families. Such dependence was much lessened by the fact that many of this particular group of harijan, the Bhangi of the Vankar section, formerly a caste of weavers, had jobs in the cotton mills of Ahmedabad, some thirty miles away, so that their housing had become as good as any in the village and their standard of living had greatly improved. Nevertheless, they all still lived on top of a steep hill in a segregated part of the village, using a separate supply of water. When the former *sarpañc* or mayor of the village asked some of their members to come and talk to us in his house, this progressive man served them tea in chipped cups, apparently kept for that purpose, a gesture that did not go without notice by his guests.

Given the absence of meat from upper-caste diets, the consumption of buffalo milk, collected fresh twice a day, was an important component of their diet. It was drunk as milk, or eaten in the form of yogurt (*dahi*) or clarified butter (*ghī*). In addition fresh vegetables (*shāk*) were gathered from the fields, bought from an itinerant trader or purchased in the nearby market town. The basic cereals were millet (*bājara*, pennisetum) or rice (*danger*) and lentils (*kathol*, specifically *mog*). Rice served to distinguish upper from lower diets. While millet plays a greater part in lower diets, so rice does in upper ones. A doctor, who was a member of the Patel caste, once remarked to me over dinner that a Gujerati meal consists of four elements, *dal* (pulse), *bhāt* (cooked rice), *roṭli* (pastries) and *shāk* (vegetables).[30] Special attention was paid to the rice as well as to the many small dishes of pulses and vegetables that were laid out on the *thali* (metal dish) or served separately. The 'bread' consisted of delicately – prepared *puri* and *roṭli*, thin pastries carefully fried in oil or cooked on the griddle. But in the lower cuisine, and often in the fields, the basis of the meal would be a thick millet pancake (*thepla*), filled with vegetables.

One's diet also depended on the difference between what one eats (privately) in the fields and what one eats (in a sense publicly) in the village. In another part of Gujerat, it has been observed that even vegetarian farmers may eat the meat of small animals in the fields (Pocock 1972: 44–5).

In ritual meals (*puja*), when the sugary *prasad* or offering to the gods is given to guests and passsers-by, the emphasis would often be on sweetness. Such a meal has to be sacralised by the particular Brahman attached to the house who would read or chant the appropriate scriptures. We spent a long time at the house of a senior electrical engineer, waiting for a tardy Brahman to turn up before proceedings could begin; he had to make the offering which was then handed over to the congregation to consume.

Such ritual meals are often very large affairs, sometimes being held in a private house but at other times in a temple. One Brahman migrant to Bombay, who had made a tidy fortune in the bristle business, arranged a *puja* for all the Brahmans in the area to be held in his local temple. In all there were some 1,000 guests from 36 villages, on whom he spent a total of some 6,000 rupees.[31] The food was of course prepared by Brahmans, since pollution beliefs prevent a cook being of a lower caste; on the other hand, the Brahman sub-castes are differentiated between and among themselves, and while most of the Brahmans in this village derived their revenues as landlords before the reforms vested such land in their tenants, others undertook more menial roles, looking after temples and providing services for members of their *varṇa*, that is, for the richer or more learned Brahmans.

Such temple meals were served in ceremonial ways. The normal meal was dished up on the large metal *thali* with upturned rim, complete with smaller bowls for the more liquid food such as *kaḍhi* ('curry'). The food was eaten with the right hand, as among the Arabs and throughout Africa, the left hand being reserved for more polluting tasks.[32] Temple meals however were served on palm leaf plates and in cups of the same material, made by those Brahmans whose duty it was to look after the place of worship.[33]

One aspect of the food-cycle that the Indian material brings out so clearly is the disposal of the uneaten food, whether touched or untouched. Among the LoDagaa untouched porridge was placed in a pot of bitter water to be fed next day to the children. In Gujerat we were not allowed to use left-over rice on the following day, nor could we persuade the indigent Brahman widow who helped us to take the left-overs away for her own family. Left-over food, especially food that has been touched (*jutha*) is polluting. But the higher the original eater, the less polluting the left-overs, and the wider the range of possible consumers. When the domestic Vaishnava deity had 'eaten' food, the left-overs remain unsullied **for humans (Khare 1976a: 39)**. There is a sense in which sacrifice itself can be regarded as the left-overs of the gods. In a similar way the remains of the food of one's guru can be eaten, so that in these cases the general notion of pollution by saliva is modified by and dependent upon the network of social relations. The same is true of cooking itself; food prepared or presented by members of higher castes can always be eaten. It is the relation of food to rank, ritual rank, that places the cooking area next in the spatial hierarchy to the area of worship itself. Consequently great stress is placed on purity, and the kitchen has to be cleansed after use. 'All eating places within the domestic structure must be purified or cleaned after every cooking – eating cycle, since the aftermath of eating is always polluting under the orthodox Hindu scheme' (pp. 39–40).

But as we have seen, not all practices and beliefs about food in Lucknow or elsewhere were organised according to the 'orthodox Hindu scheme'. In any case, the very severity of such injunctions means that not only the lower castes but others too have difficulty in fulfilling its terms; they elaborate alternative norms that are not simply examples of 'aborted Sanskritization'. The most radical departures from these norms often occurred at the highest political levels, at the great courts of the Maharajahs, where, at least in North India, the rulers imported the practices of Islamic culture, later modified by the advent of the British. It is to the aspect of hierarchy in these two cuisines, the Islamic and the British, that I now want to turn.

The cuisine of the Middle East derives from that of Mesopotamia, of Assyria and later from that of the Persian Empire, dating from 550 B.C.,the earliest empire to envelop the whole region. Macedonian Greeks, Romans and Parthians struggled for dominance in the area, and during the period of the Sassanid Empire of Persia, from the third to the seventh centuries A.D., the culture of food saw major developments. In the latter part of this period, the empire expanded and the extravagance of the court reflected this imperial grandeur. Meat was marinaded in yoghurt flavoured with spices, many different kinds of almond pastry were prepared, jams were made with quinces and other fruits, dates stuffed with almonds and walnuts. Regional dishes were gathered from all parts of the empire, and there was a distinct cuisine for the rich. One recipe, for example, was even known as the 'king's dish' and consisted of hot and cold meats, rice jelly, stuffed vine leaves, marinaded chicken and a sweet date purée.[34] Such haute cuisine contrasted sharply with the food of the rural areas.

The Arabs themselves possessed a limited culinary tradition based on Bedouin and peasant food. The successors of Mohammed, the Umayyads, set up their capital in Damascus, which later moved to Baghdad under the Abbassids.

After a century of high moral standards, strict living and restraint, the Abbassid Arabs, dazzled by the aristocratic brilliance of the Persians they had conquered, adopted their traditions of chivalry and good living, thus perpetuating the glories of the Persian past, as well as that of their Greek and Roman predecessors. This became a period of Persian ascendancy and cosmopolitan culture. ... It was then (from the end of the eighth to the tenth century) that cooking reached the height of magnificence. A creative culinary genius flourished at the banquets of the Caliphs of Baghdad, which became proverbial for their variety and lavishness (Roden 1968: 21).

Food items were included in the luxuries that came to Baghdad from China, India, Scandinavia, Egypt, Syria and Russia. Spices were widely used in the recipes of the rich, some of whom were even catered for by Indian cooks (Ahsan 1979: 155).

This luxury survived, despite the decline of Abbassid power, at least until the thirteenth century. At the same time dishes from all over the Muslim world were incorporated in their cuisine. 'All the best dishes were put into the common culinary pool, and trade between the countries of the Arab Empire made it possible for ingredients grown in one country to become available in others' (Roden 1968: 24). Later on, in the seventeenth century, the capital of Islam shifted to Istanbul, the Ottoman capital, which became the home of Middle Eastern cuisine, after a period in the medieval times when Egyptian cooking had enjoyed the highest reputation (Ahsan 1979: 155). Meat was a staple mainly of the affluent, especially mutton and chicken, beef being regarded as inferior, while the poor had to be content with fish (p. 78). Foods of the rich were more spiced, their bread more refined, being made of white wheat flour rather than of millet or rice. A great variety of breads was made, some to be eaten with special dishes, for it was one of the basic foods. Rice was less important than at a later period and milk less important than in earlier Bedouin times. But many species of vegetable and fruit were used, especially by the rich. Some of the fruit was made into the innumerable sweet dishes (*ḥalwa*) of the well-to-do, using honey as well as sugar-cane from India. Some was made into the non-alcoholic drinks provided for convivial parties and sold in the market, though the rich avoided those favoured by the poor, especially if they were blackish in colour. Yet more was preserved by drying in the sun or by crystallisation in honey or sugar, a technique learned from Rome. Meat, fish and vegetables were preserved not only by drying but also by using salt, vinegar and other condiments. Ice imported from the mountains was extensively used by the rich for preservation as well as for cooling various drinks.

Such a development of the simples repertoire of Arab cooking clearly entailed differentiation into a 'court' and 'peasant' cuisine, the former accompanied by an elaboration of table manners, and the whole crystallised around the formal divisions of rank, giving rise to the kind of distinct sub-cultures illustrated in *Le Livre des Avares* of al-Jāḥiẓ, who was born in Basra in the eight century. The relative homogeneity of the nomadic desert Bedouin has been replaced by the sumptuary differentiation of their cousins settled in the cities.

You chide me with fastening a large basket holding costly fruits and choice dates (to protect them from covetousness), against a gluttonous slave, a greedy child, an abject slave and a stupid wife. But as far as I know, in the rules of politeness, in the organisation of command, in the customs of chiefs and in the conduct of lords as far as precious foods, rare drinks, costly clothing and of mounts of noble race, and fine and delicate objects of all kinds are concerned there is no question of treating in the same way the chief and his subordinate, the master and his slave; neither are they placed in the same position in an assembly, they are not addressed in the same way nor are they received with the same marks of politeness.[35]

The contrast was not only with the Bedouin past (and present) of Arab society. The cuisine of the rich contrasted with that of the urban poor and of the peasant farmers. More significantly, from one standpoint it contrasted with the voluntary poverty of the sufis and ascetics for whom fasting was part of the way of life. Some sufis ate no meat; others gave up bread (Ahsan 1979: 135). As in India and in Europe, the absolute rejection of certain foods and the temporary rejection of all, was one of the paths to holiness and grace.

The development of an elaborated cuisine was both formalised and extended by being put into written form. The literature on Arab cooking was largely a development of the Abbassid period, about the tenth century, a result of the Muslim conquest of Iran. In the thirteenth century, al-Baghdādī can speak of having consulted 'a great number of books devoted to the art of cooking in which were mentioned some foreign dishes'. Of these early works only three, including al-Baghdādī's, have been traced, though reference to many others exist (Ahsan 1979: 76); the *Wuṣla* of ad-'Adīm, partly translated by Rodinson, is slightly later, and only the work of Warrāq, *Kitāb al- Tabīkh wa Iṣlāḥ* dates from the Abbassid period itself. The manuscript, which discusses the beneficial and harmful properties of food as well as other culinary matters, is clearly the work of a writer who had access to the actual recipe-books of the caliphs of the time.

These books referred to the cuisine of the court, a court that had developed patterns of conspicuous consumption, based upon their Roman, Greek and Persian predecessors. They were composed not by cooks, but by great personages who concentrated upon their favourite recipes, omitting any reference to ordinary dishes. The books themselves were divided into a number of chapters which offered a formal classification of food. For example, the thirteenth-century manual, the *Kitāb al-Tabīkh* of al-Baghdādī, translated into English by A.J. Arberry, offers the following breakdown: (i) sour dishes, (ii) simple dishes, (iii) fried dishes and dried dishes, (iv) dishes of meat and flour, etc.

As Rodinson notes, in works like the *Wuṣla* and *Kitāb al-Ṭabīkh*, we are dealing with cooking for aristocrats. The ingredients are frequently expensive, involving goods that are in short supply, meat as distinct from beans, rarities like rice and sugar, as well as employing valuable spices that come from afar, from China, India and East Africa. The base is local cooking; fat is made from the much-prized tail of the sheep. But the higher cuisine has adopted exotic elements 'enriching the whole by greater complexity and refinement' (Rodinson 1949: 147). In this way Bedouin cooking was transformed not only by contact with the courtly culture of Iran but also by influences from Egypt, the Maghreb, Byzantium, the Crusades as well as from the Turks. It is a cosmopolitan cooking, using products that come from distant places and introducing foreign recipes, both characteristic markers of conspicuous consumption in the culinary field.

Not only are the ingredients expensive and the recipes widely drawn, but the cooking is one of great complexity. 'A series of operations follow one another; in turn, they roast, boil (often several times) and fry, they add elements prepared separately; sauce, balls of meat minced with vegetables and other ingredients' (Rodinson 1949: 153). The simple is despised as pertaining to the lower orders (*al-sūqa*) or the crowd (*al-'āmma*). As in the case of the court of Lucknow, such complexity extends from ingredients and cooking to decoration and presentation, which could reach extreme proportions; for example, the *Wuṣla* describes the preparation of an omelette inside a bottle. Equally the process of eating itself is surrounded by the heavy weight of table manners and etiquette demanded by court life, and later by bourgeois living. This subject, *ādāb al-mā'ida*, took an elaborate written form and, although many works are lost, a manual survives from the thirteenth century (Ahsan 1979: 157).

An important part of these table manners consists of washing at table before the meal, and afterwards in a side room. Among the masses, all food was placed on the table at once, but among the rich of the Abbassid period a menu would announce what was available. While food was normally eaten with the fingers of the right hand, the spoon was popular among the upper classes who also employed knife and napkin. But it was the consumption of food out of common bowl, after washing and praising God, that led to a particular stress on table manners. A man of taste should encourage his neighbour to eat first and avoid offending the assembled company in any particular, making no noise or mess, taking small portions, not reaching out in front. Jāḥiẓ recommends as a table companion one who does not pick marrow from the bone or grab at the egg lying on top of the vegetables or make for the choice morsels (Ahsan 1979: 160).

The complexity of cuisine requires as well as money the availability and differentiation of domestic labour, labour that has often been removed from the female sex (the harem is reserved for the pleasures of the bed) and allocated to the male. That labour, sometimes provided by slaves, is then sub-divided into a variety of tasks surrounding the acquisition of raw food, the preparation of dishes, and the serving of food for the great banquets of the princes and the lesser meals of the bourgeoisie.

The end of the Abbasid civilisation meant a change in the numbers and level of cookbooks, which now fall into the hands of the academic and merchant middle class.

It is no longer the game of princes, the distraction of the well-bred courtier, who edits these books, gaining in this way a reputation as an arbiter of taste and elegance. It has become the job of obscure scholars, the epicurians of their day, who are keen to preserve for themselves the recipes of dishes that have pleased them, so they can have them made by their servants when they want them, in other words, simple notebooks of recipes for household use, like the section on cooking of the *Ménagier de Paris* (Rodinson 1949: 104).

So in a general way, the literature on Arab cooking presents us with a microcosm of Arab history. The conquest of Persia was followed by the introduction of Sassanian culture, the decline of the Abbassids by a falling-off in culinary texts. With the growing influence of the West, cookbooks attempted to introduce their readers to the ways of the Occident. The growth of nationalism led to praise being lavished on Arab cooking for its positive qualities which have to be preserved from contamination by European imports. 'Let us take the example ', writes Basima Zaki Ibrahim, 'of the Japanese nation which ... has never departed, either in its cooking or in its table, from its ancient traditions and customs.'[36]

Here, as elsewhere, the early literature on cooking is closely related to that on dietetic medicine. Works in Arabic again drew upon Graeco-Roman predecessors.[37] Medical men were employed by the court watching over the table of princes and constantly consulted by them about their food (Rodinson 1949: 110). In effect they were employed to prevent attacks by poisoners or sorcerers as well as to attend to their masters' general health by regulating the input of food. Most of the great doctors wrote on the theme of hygiene and nourishment. One such work, *The Book of Food* by the Jewish doctor, Ishaq (L'Ysacus in medieval Latin), who worked in the Tunisian city of Kairouan in the tenth century, was translated into Latin by Constantin the African and was used as a dietetic manual at the school of Salerno until the seventeenth century. One could say, writes Rodinson, that until very recently Western Europe has followed the rules of Arab dietetics, themselves inherited from Greek doctors.

Imaginative literature, both verse and prose, also took the art of cooking as its subject and displayed something of the same two-edged quality that we have encountered in China and India. Mas 'udi mentions a poetical contest organised by the Caliph al-Mustakfi in the tenth century. A member of the company recited a poem by Ishāq ibn Ibrāhīm of Mosul describing a certain dish known as *sanbūsaj* (*sanbūsak*) in the following terms:

> If thou would'st know what food gives most delight,
> Best let me tell, for none hath subtler sight.
> Take first the finest meat, red, soft to touch,
> And mince it with the fat, not over much;
> Then add an onion, cut in circles clean,
> A cabbage, very fresh, exceeding green,
> And season well with cinnamon and rue;
> Of coriander add a handful, too,
> And after that of cloves the very least,
> Of finest ginger, and of pepper best,
> A hand of cummin, murri just to taste,
> Two handfuls of Palmyra salt; but haste,
> Good master haste to grind them small and strong.
> Then lay and light a blazing fire along;
> Put all in the pot, and water pour
> Upon it from above, and cover o'er.
> But, when the water vanished is from sight
> And when the burning flames have dried it quite,
> Then, as thou wilt, in pastry wrap it round,
> And fasten well the edges, firm and sound;
> Or, if it please thee better, take some dough,
> Conveniently soft, and rubbed just so,
> Then with the rolling pin let it be spread
> And with the nails its edges docketed.
> Pour in the frying-pan the choicest oil
> And in that liquor let it finely broil.
> Last, ladle out into a thin tureen
> Where appetizing mustard smeared hath been,
> And eat with pleasure, mustarded about,
> This tastiest food for hurried diner-out.[38]

But these expressions of amateurs of the high cuisine do not monopolise the field of culinary literature. These is also a counter-current, almost a counter-culture, that adopts a more critical, sometimes puritanical, even revolutionary tone. In an Egyptian manuscript from the fifteenth century we find an interesting description of a battle, which is at the same time a meal and a social conflict, between King Mutton and King Honey. The first had a powerful following mainly among the meats; he hears talk of a rival, King Honey, whom the poor have elected as their king and who rules over the vegetables, fruits, fish, sweets and milk. Battle is joined between the two forces, leading to the defeat of King Honey who was betrayed by the treachery of his followers.

The 'delectable war', as Finkel points out, is highly suggestive of a banquet and 'the manner in which the hosts advance represents the order of the courses' (1932: 131), while the final attack of the aromatic plants alludes to the Oriental custom of burning incense and scenting flowers at the end of a sumptuous meal.

But there is another aspect to the conflict between meat and vegetables, for it is a 'class war'. On the cognitive level there was always a conflict in Islam between the simplicity of the desert and the luxury of the town, a sentiment that is clearly expressed in the famous *Prolegomena* of Ibn Khaldūn. The adoption of Persian behaviour and the abandonment of Bedouin ways were targets for reformist scholars, bred on the Koran and reared in ascetic practices. As with other world religions, the egalitarian precepts of the original movement remained a potential source of danger to later institutional developments because they were permanently encapsulated in the Holy Scriptures and threatened to upset the division of society into rich and poor, each with their own way of life. In imaginative literature this opposition took more complex forms. In his edition of the poem, Finkel shows how the two kingdoms of food correspond to different social classes. Meat is the food of the rich, the rest the food of the poor. And he cites a seventeenth-century work by Sirbini, the aim of which is to ridicule the stupidity and bad manners of the peasants and persuade them to adopt the meat dishes of the upper class. Once again Eurasian society is marked by a hierarchical cuisine whose literary forms express the tension between the styles of life of rich and poor, some admiring the achievements of the *haute cuisine*, others sympathetic to the morality of denial, of poverty, of the simple life.

Finally I turn to Western Europe, and specifically to Britain. It has been suggested by Braudel that between 1350 and 1550 the diet of the European peasant may not have been too different from that of the nobility (1973: 128), that the stress on their difference may have been more literary than factual. If so, the period was exceptional and would run counter to the general hypothesis. But in any case one cannot dismiss the court feasts simply as 'the luxury of greed' (p. 127) since it was the ability to indulge this greed at such a luxurious level, in so ostentatious a way, that marked the rich from the poor. It is often true that in the course of this conspicuous consumption 'quantity prevailed over quality', at least as compared with later times. Braudel goes on to make the wider claim that there was 'no sophisticated cooking in Europe before the fifteenth century' (p. 127). Indeed, he sees 'elaborate cooking' as virtually confined to the Chinese from the fifth century,[39] to the Muslims in the eleventh and twelfth, and in the West only to the Italian achievement which was followed from the sixteenth century onwards by France, 'the place where the presentation and the ceremonial of those profane festivals of gourmandising and *bon ton* were perfected' (p. 125). While one can certainly argue, as Freeman does for China, that sophisticated cuisines of a particular type only developed in these few societies, there is surely an important and wider sense in which all the major Eurasian societies developed a sumptuary cuisine, a hierarchical cooking, though it may not have been a 'sophisticated' one. In fourteenth-century England, Geoffrey Chaucer himself describes internal differences in a way that gives 'gastronomic distinction to the moral qualities of the social classes' (Cosman 1976: 105), contrasting the well-provisioned order of the noble banquet with the crude guzzling of the middle class and the simple dignity of farmhouse fare. He presents us too with vivid portraits of the well-mannered Prioress, the careful Physician, the gourmand Franklin – offering a picture of medieval food-ways that is marked by hierarchical distinction and is most unlikely to be purely 'literary'.

Indeed, as Braudel notes, the period following the Black Death which he was discussing is hardly typical as far as the consumption of food is concerned. The underpopulated hectares of Western Europe allowed the rather profligate use of resources that a mass carnivorous diet requires; China and other regions of the Old World fed more people on much less land because they cultivated more intensely. And in Western Europe, which was highly carnivorous compared with other areas of the world, England was especially devoted to the eating of meat (Mead 1931: 79). Despite its relative abundance it was not equally available to all, either before the Black Death or after. For fourteenth-century Provence, Stouff observed that while meat was more plentiful than in modern times, its distribution was above all 'très inégales selon les diverses couches sociales' (1970: 276). From 1600 onwards meat was much more typical of rich than of poor diets. According to Bernard's analysis of peasant consumption in eighteenth-century Gévaudan, the basis was cereals, especially rye and barley, eaten mainly in the form of bread. There were also vegetables, butter, cheese and pork, this last from the 'family pig' killed between December and March at the 'liturgy' of the *cochonailles* which brought together friends and neighbours.[40] Even during the 'fat cows', Bernard comments, there were insufficient amounts of calories, fats and certain vitamins, deficiencies in animal protein, and all in all 'a monotonous diet based almost exclusively on bread' (1975: 40). Though there were periods of plenty, there were shortages by season and by year; even during the normal year great feasts were held at the end of harvest, yet periodic famines could cause much hardship on top of a generally deficient diet.

Views about the adequacy of diet are sometimes related to cultural preconceptions. The idea of meat as the most important element of human diet is held by many European historians, and accords well with the values of their own past that were practised by the rich and held as ideals by the poor. Aristocratic values of the fifteenth century are epitomised in John Russel's *The Boke of Nurture* which provides a menu for 'a dynere of flesche' (as well as one entirely of fish) in three courses, the last of which includes almond cream, curlews and snipes, quails and sparrows, as well as freshwater cryfish (*crevise*) (Furnivall 1868: 49–50). The same focus on meat is seen in the controversy over the peasants' pig (Hémardinquer 1979 [1970]; Braudel 1973 [1967]), and Braudel's discussion of the carnivorous nature of the diet in terms of 'Europe's priveleged position' (1973: 133) suggests that meat-eating is a critical factor in the development of the civilisation of the stomach. But the world's finest, most elaborate cuisine, that of China, was created on the basis of a much more sparing use of animal flesh, both at the top and at the bottom of the social scale. In one survey in the 1920s, 3.2 per cent of the food expenditure of Chinese workers went on meat, 80 per cent on cereals. While we cannot say with Braudel that 'meat was extremely rare' (1973: 133) it was certainly not a major element in the diet of peasants and workers. Yet their food, while simple, was well prepared. One Scottish observer in the 1850s who was checking the wages of local tea-pickers, found that 'the poorest classes in China seem to understand the art of preparing their food much better than the same classes at home', where 'the harvest labourer's breakfast consisted of porridge and milk, his dinner of bread and beer, and porridge and milk again for supper' (Fortune, 1857: 42–3, quoted Spence 1977: 267). In both societies the labourer's diet of the time included little meat. But the Scottish workers never shared in a developed cuisine, even at the modest level of their Chinese colleagues. Only the upper classes were in a position to adopt a cuisine largely from outside.

In medieval England the difference between rich and poor was important first of all at the dietary level. As Mead remarks, 'the poor ate to live, while in too many cases the rich lived to eat' (1931: 9). The same differentiation occurred at the level of manners and ceremony (Cosman 1976; Mead 1931). We see this class component in British cooking very clearly in the early written works on the subject which obviously record the upper rather than the lower cuisine. The first cookbook from Britain is the twelfth-century volume by Alexander Neckham, an Augustinian canon who was a native of St Albans (1157–1217) and later a teacher at the University of Paris. Two features mark this work. While it purports to be a guide to young housekeepers, 'we soon perceive that the author has in view the arrangements indispensable for a family of high rank and pretensions'.[41] Neckham, as Hazlitt says, prescribes for the great folks. Secondly, the work rarely uses any English terms for cooking, Latin and Norman-French being the languages employed. It was of course particularly in the context of the cuisine of the ruling classes that French predominated, and this fact that emerges in cooking as well as in language has influenced English in a number of important ways. Not merely are high-status cooking terms derived from Norman French (a process of borrowing that has continued over the centuries and culminates in the Franglais of the high-status *menu*), but there is the oft-noted but nonetheless remarkable fact to which we earlier referred, that the words for live animals are usually of Anglo-Saxon origin (e.g. cow, calf, deer, sheep, pig), whereas the corresponding terms for the meat on the table are of French derivation (e.g. beef, veal, venison, mutton, pork). The point was already made by Walter Scott in his tale of the conflict between the Saxon peasant and the Norman lord that he developed at the beginning of *Ivanhoe*.

'And swine is good Saxon', said the Jester; 'but how call you the sow when she is flayed, and drawn, and quartered and hung up by the heels, like a traitor?' 'Pork', answered the swineherd. 'I am very glad every fool knows that too,' said Wamba, 'and pork, I think, is good Norman-French; and so when the brute lives, and is in the charge of a Saxon slave, she goes by her Saxon name, but becomes a Norman, and is called pork when she is carried to the Castle-hall to feast among the nobles; what dost thou think of this, friend Gurth, ha?'

The solicited answer was phrased in terms of class conflict: 'The finest and the fattest is for their board; the loveliest is for their couch.'[42] It was a theme of conflict over cuisine as a facet of class that we have found in each of the main cultures of Eurasia.

Other major works on early English cooking also prescribe for the ruling classes. A vellum roll called *Forme of Cury*, supposedly written by the cook of Richard II, as well as *The Noble Book of Cookery*, cater for and describe royal and aristocratic entertainments. Another important volume was *The Book of St Albans* (1486), one of the first printed works from a monastic press that developed out of the earlier scriptorium. Here we find a curious and elaborate catalogue of the terms used in dressing and carving. These 'goodly terms of carving' became a standard set that was repeated in many cookery books up to the end of the seventeenth

century. Their fascination for contemporaries is clear from the fact that
they appeared in a number of the early printed books of Caxton and
Wynkyn de Worde, the following version being taken from the latter's
Boke of Keruynge (1508).

> Breke that dere
> lesche the brawne
> rere that goose
> lyfte that swanne
> sauce that capon
> spoyle that henne
> fruche that chekyn
> unbrace that malarde
> unlace that conye
> dysmembre that heron
> dysplay that crane
> dysfygure that pecocke
> unjoynt that bytture (bittern)
> untache that curlewe
> alaye that fesande
> wynge that partryche
> wynge that quayle
> mynce that plouer
> thye that pygyon
> border that pasty
> thye that woodcocke
> thye all manner of small byrdes
> tymbre that syre
> tyere that egge
> chynne that samon
> strynge that lampraye
> splatte that pyke
> sauce that place
> sauce that tenche
> splaye that breme
> syde that haddocke
> tuske that berbell
> syne that cheuen
> traunche that sturgyon
> tayme that crabbe
> culpon that troute
> trassene that ele
> undertraunche that purpos
> barbe that lobster.[43]

I describe the list as curious because it seems to have only a limited
connection with the general practices or terminology of the kitchen.

Rather it provides an example of the proliferation of a specialist vocabulary in a hierarchical situation. For whatever roots the categorisation may have in the peasant context or in the more general lexicon of daily use, it has been greatly elaborated and formalised, possibly by lower-class professional cooks, possibly by upper-class carvers, who were preparing food for aristocratic tables.

The terms themselves often refer to dressing rather than to carving meat. One writer considers they were intended as a kind of mnemonic for the cook and the carver (Hodgkin 1911: 53). But such pragmatic uses seem to have been accompanied, perhaps initiated, by more 'aesthetic' ones. The same author comments that 'the differentiation in terms of the same action when applied to different varieties of flesh, fowl, or fish, was a kind of kitchen heraldry and one wonders whether the original list may not may have been compiled originally as a *jeu d'esprit*, or skit upon the heraldry run riot of the period' (Hodgkin 1911: 53). Many words were of French derivation, 'traunche' from *trancher*, 'tayme' from *entamer*, showing that their origin and use was to be found in the households of the rich. At the same time, the element of play is clearly present in this as in some other schema consisting of categories of acts or objects, schema that develop the overlapping, polysemic usages of everyday speech into an elaborate yet simplified system of patterned correspondences. The result is less a guide to understanding than a display of esoteric verbal ingenuity of a kind that is dependent not only on specialist activity associated with the leisure class but in some degree upon the use of the written and especially the printed word. The last suggestion is made for two reasons. First, graphic modes of representation encourage the development of such systemisation; paradoxically, 'primitive classification' flourishes in early literate societies. Secondly, the advent of printing promoted the widespread circulation of schematic forms of various types – calendars, recipes, herbals, and so on. Its arrival made less difference to the creative process (for writing had already made the breakthrough in this respect) than to the communicative one. Large numbers of copies of the same item could be produced by the machine more cheaply, more accurately and more willingly than by the scribe. The cost of labour had been the major factor in the production of all forms of scribal work (Clancy 1979), and the mechanisation of writing was a breakthrough of immense importance in the field of human communication.

The carving at the table of a lord (as distinct from cooking in his kitchen), which this list brings out, played a very prominent part in the life of the princely courts where the office of carver was 'not reckonned as the lowest but among the most honourable'.[44] As Elias points out, stressing the carnivorous nature of the culture of the upper class of medieval society, the dead animal or large parts of it were often brought whole to the table. 'Not only whole fish and whole birds (sometimes with their feathers) but also whole rabbits, lambs, and quarters of veal appear on the table, not to mention the larger venison or the pigs and oxen on the spit' (1978: 118). The animal was then carved on the table, often by the sons of lesser noblemen sent to the establishments of their superiors to act as pages and to learn the ways of 'courtesy'. Meat and its dismemberment played a great part in the cooking of this warrior aristocracy, whose pastime was the hunt but who left the management of the domestic livestock to their subjects. Even in the seventeenth century the calculations for the diet of a North German court showed its resident members to consume two pounds of meat a day in addition to large quantities of venison, birds and fish. The description of late medieval feasts presented in the works of Mead (1931) and Cosman (1976) recall a fourteenth-century Chinese view of the Northerners, the Mongols, as people who 'pay great attention to carving and cutting (their food)'. As Mote comments, 'Nothing could have been more remote from Chinese cuisine and table custom than the sight of the eaters carving their meat with their own daggers' (1977: 207). Such a situation did not encourage the formation of an elaborate cuisine but it was certainly marked by considerable differences between rich and poor.

In Europe this carnivorous diet of the rich stood in direct contrast not only to that of the poor but also that of the holy. On the one hand there were the restrictions on the consumption of meat practised continuously in some monasteries, on the other the temporary abstinence of everybody for weekly and annual fasts. The monastic restrictions varied from order to order and from time to time; the long history of the Church was not always marked by ascetic denial. Nevertheless, a constant theme of its ideology, especially as expressed by St Augustine, was an aversion to 'gluttony' as one of the seven deadly sins. *Gula* had corrupted the world and many theologians attributed Adam's loss of Eden not to pride but to gluttony. 'While the Nobleman cultivated tastes and appetites as proof of education, political power, and economic supremacy, the Christian moralists saw in elaborate foods and eating ceremonials a way the devil acquired disciples' (Cosman 1976: 117).

While the constraint on the 'religious' was 'ideological', that on the peasant was caused by scarcity. 'If the peasant reared cattle, it was largely for the privileged, the nobility, and the burghers.'[45] Despite the earlier lack of an elaborated cuisine, despite some periods of plenty, the differentiation between classes was so great that it becomes difficult to speak of one culture of cooking, especially in England where the ruling class, in secular as in clerical life, imposed themselves by conquest on a population speaking a very different language.

There was perhaps an even greater gap in manners, of the table and elsewhere. More than a hundred years ago Furnivall drew attention to the collection of manuals for the instruction of young pages and others in the ways of the court, of which the lessons in carving may have been one variety. Works such as the *Babees Book* and Russell's *Boke of Nurture* are aimed at the court; the list of contents is sufficient to show for whom it was intended:

> The Panter or Butler. His duties...
> The Botery
> How to lay the table-cloth, etc.
> How to wrap up bread stately...
> How to manage at table
> Symple condicions (or rules for good behaviour
>   for every servant)
> The connynge of kervynge, etc. (Furnivall 1868)

The aim is to inculcate a code of manners that is specifically contrasted with that of the rustic; there is 'town – country' distinction that is also a kind of class distinction, though as in Restoration times the latter category may include aristocrats who have spent their days in the country, away from the civilising influence of court life. In any case what we see is a hierarchical differentiation of manners, including table manners, which make some of the most profound discriminators of stratified styles of life. Etiquette of this kind (not putting half-eaten meat back in the bowl, wiping one's nose on one's sleeve) is not superficial, a matter for the surface rather than the depths; refined ways of acting are so internalised as to make alternative behaviour truly 'disgusting', 'revolting', 'nauseous', turning them into some of the most highly charged and deeply felt of intra-social differences, so that 'rustic' behaviour is not merely quaint but barbarous. And it is obviously not only interclass but interethnic; the use of sleeve seems dirty to handkerchief users everywhere, and the handkerchief unhygienic to the consumers of tissues. The failure to employ a knife or an egg-cup in the specified situations places Anglo-American unions under a strain; the eating of peas with a knife has had men banished from the officers' mess. For these failures to meet one's own standards are not trivia to those who have internalised those customs in their childhood.

Since its preparation and consumption had such important implications for hierarchy, food tended to be the subject of competition between those of similar status as well as the subject of regulation between those of different rank. Equality of rank is a relative matter. But the presence of the status implications led to the opposing pulls of competitive display and statutory control. For within the system of fixed ranks, status could be raised or lowered by acting in ways that were seen as appropriate to another rank; the phrase 'to eat humble pie' implies being forced to take a lower position than one has assumed. The barons were unwilling to be outdone by the king, while the lesser nobility strove to emulate the hospitality of the barons, until finally Edward II in the ninth year of his reign (1283), issued a proclamation to restrain 'the outrageous and excessive multitude of meats and dishes which the great men of the kingdom used in their castles, and by persons of inferior rank imitating their example beyond what their stations required'.[46] As a result, the number of permitted courses was limited by decree, and sumptuary laws were issued to control the disbursal of food and drink. For the challenge involved in competitive feasting was not merely a symbolic operation; followers who formed the core of a man's political support were attracted by the lavishness of his table; as among the Swat Pathans (Barth 1959: 81) and in many other parts of the world, hospitality was a primary tool of politics.

Partly through ordinance from above and partly through the more general pressure towards the bureaucratisation of culture through the spread of writing, the system of governance for great households was reduced to a number of stated rules, drawn up in the form of Household Books, which regulated the charges and expenses of the establishment as well as the status of the various officers.[47]

A good part of these books is taken up with the ritual and ceremony of eating. In the earlier medieval period men widely separated in rank, the lord and his retainers, took their meals in common in the great hall of the castle or the manor. Something of the general pattern is preserved in the dining halls of Oxbridge colleges, though the common hall indictates neither equality of status nor equality of commons. In the hall with which I am most familiar, the spatial layout places high table opposite to the kitchen end and next to the chapel, raised a step above the level of the floor where the tables are set transversely rather than lengthwise. In formal terms the arrangement appears as follows:

HIGH	LOW
Chapel	Kitchen
Up	Down
Sideways	Longways

In medieval England as in contemporary Cambridge, a contrast was drawn between feasts and ordinary meals. On feast days and at banquets celebrating the installation of a new office-holder (spiritual as well as temporal), the profusion of food, drink and ceremony could be enormous. The meals often lasted for many hours, and their complexity and length announced the status of the giver and sometimes that of the receiver.

At feasts as on ordinary days, the differences in rank were emphasised in differences in food and in service. The high table was always served first. Then the food was carried to the next table in rank, known as the 'reward' because it was rewarded or supplied from the high table. Less valued parts of meat were served at the lower end of the table; the entrails, 'noumbles' or 'umbles' of the deer were offered only to the lower ranks, giving rise, as we have seen, to the expression, 'to eat humble pie'.[48]

Despite the differentiation, the very fact of commensality stressed certain bonds between those sitting above and below the salt, though the cleavages were also represented. On a national scale the great accession banquets had a somewhat similar function. 'When the guests below the salt had seen the ways of greatness, they departed to fulfill their several callings. These were political demonstrations with a clear and (for the age) not irrational object' (Hazlitt 1886: 47). The political aspects of such semi-public commensalism were obvious not only in the entertainments of ambassadors from abroad but of subjects and followers from within.

Banquets of this kind clearly required a high degree of organisation, and the creation of a specialised staff of household retainers was necessary even for the daily running of the royal household. The Sewer, for example, supervised the serving of each dish and ensured that all were first 'assayed' or tested against the possibility of poison or sorcery before the food reached the mouth of the nobility. The whole process of cooking, and more particularly eating, is closely linked with sorcery (bad) and medicine (good), with disease and health. As in most stratified societies, including those 'non-hierarchical' states of the African type, the holders of authority were always vulnerable to covert attack both by natural and by supernatural means. Consequently, protective measures were constantly being taken on their behalf. In England the assay was carried out by specialist tasters in a highly ritualised way. 'Each "cornet" of bread was dipped thrice in the dish under assay, and the sever flourished it thrice over his head before putting it to the lips of the two chief officers of the kitchen.'[49] In the king's household such offices were performed by the lesser nobility, who acted as his Carver, Server and Cupbearer; in other European monarchies it was the offspring of such lords who acted as pages and as children of honour.

These household roles became increasingly elaborate, resulting in a whole hierarchy of offices of the 'King's Mouth' which covered the work done not only in the kitchen but in the bakery, the pantry, the cellar, the buttery, the spicery, the catery, the saucery, the lardery, the chaundry, the pitcher-house, the napery, the poltery, the confectionary, the ewery and the wafery. Each office save the spicery was in charge of a sergeant and usually included a 'Yeoman of the King's Mouth'.[50]

By the sixteenth century great houses no longer kept open house throughout the year. The aristocracy, and even royalty, now started to retire for periods to one of their more distant properties where they 'kept secret house'. Hierarchical commensality disappeared in favour of a greater privatisation and a greater specialisation in styles of cooking.

Changes in food were paralleled by changes in manners, especially table manners. Instruction books already provided the rules for proper conduct. In the twelfth and thirteenth centuries it was learned ecclesiastics who set down in Latin precepts for correct behaviour in their particular order (Elias 1978: 60). From the thirteenth century we find books written in the vernacular languages, coming from the courts of the warrior nobility, and devoted to establishing the rules of courtesy, of *courtoisie*, of courteous, 'civilised' behaviour. The earliest are from Provence; the first in Germany were written by Italians. England in the fifteenth century saw the appearance of John Russell's *The Boke of Nurture*. But this was followed by works addressed to a different audience and to a more 'mannered' one.

The general development of civilisation (in the terminology of Norbert Elias), the slow adoption of good manners (in that of Fernand Braudel), meant learning ways of acting that in some sense individualised, privatised and restrained the behaviour first of the upper strata and then more generally. The individualisation was most obvious at the table. On the common trencher people cut meat with their own or with the common knife, then ate it with their fingers. Wine was often drunk from a single cup. The use of the individual spoon, knife and goblet did not become common till the sixteenth century (Braudel 1973: 138), with individual forks appearing in Italy at roughly the same period. The elaborate place settings and the use of porcelain and metal objects for the table provided each person with his own, so that a man no longer had to share with others, to draw from the common plate or pot, to use the same instruments. The privatisation is most marked in changes in sleeping arrangements, where gradually the idea of sleeping in the same room, let alone touching a stranger in the same bed, became anathema. The restraint appears in the content of books on manners where the young are counselled against seizing the first piece of meat; reticence at table meant not using the table cloth for cleansing oneself, and at the same time concealing 'natural' functions. While the ideology of purity is rarely explicit, the forms of behaviour advocated are not dissimilar to those widespread in India where care is taken to avoiding pollution by saliva, as in taking the food chewed by others. These forms of individualisation, privatisation and restraint are associated with the untouchability, not so much of a caste (though 'dirty' occupations were undoubtedly polluting), but of all other individuals outside the domestic group, and specifically beyond the conjugal pair whose union created the household and whose body fluids were necessarily intermingled.

The change of manners represents firstly the differentiation of higher from lower groups in hierarchical societies, in contrast to the rather similar ways of acting and eating among the intermarrying groups of the hieratic states of most of Africa. Secondly, it represents the diffusion of these restrained ways of acting throughout the society. But what is surprising is the fact that these differences in ways of acting are not simply arbitrary. Common elements exist between Europe and India as well as between the instructions for good behaviour current in Abbassid times. Again, some of the early Chinese table manners sound very much like the late medieval ones recorded by Russell (Furnivall 1868; Elias 1978; *Li Chi*, trans. Legge 1885). 'Do not make a noise in eating, do not crunch bones with the teeth; do not put back fish you have been eating; do not throw the bones to the dogs; do not snatch (at what you want)' (Chang 1977: 38). The instructions emphasise differences in rank and represent the 'norm'of upper-class Chou gentlemen. But they are not culturally specific; there is a measure of commonality among the hierarchical cultures whose standards become more generally adopted as the ways of 'civilised' behaviour.

In Europe the hierarchy of food and manners had its religious as well as its secular side, the two never entirely either supporting or undermining the other. Here I refer to the opposition between the secular and religious cuisine. For as in India, the path to holiness involved abstinence from sexuality and from food. Benedictine monks not only observed the rule of celibacy and performed the usual fasts and prohibitions that marked the Christian year, they also abstained from eating the flesh of animals.

Chapters 39 and 40 of the rule drawn up by St Benedict for monastic communities in central Italy during the first half of the sixth century specify the number of meals, the nature of the commodities and the size of the rations for the various intervals of the liturgical calendar. The eating of the meat of quadrupeds was completely forbidden except in cases of physical infirmity. The infirmary had not only its special dining room but separate kitchen where flesh was prepared not only for the sick but also for those monks who were undergoing regular bleeding for their health. Before the relaxation of discipline in the fifteenth century, earlier in some Benedictine houses, meat was transferred from the special kitchen to the flesh-frater or misericord (*misericordia*, i.e. indulgence). The permanent obligation of monks was the weekly obligation of the laity, to abstain from flesh on Fridays. This religious prescription led to a heavy consumption of fish, especially the salted variety (Stouff 1970: 276). In Abbassid Baghdad, Christians seem to have taken fish as their main food, raising the price on the market by their 'excessive demand' on certain days of the week which Muslims consequently tended to avoid (Ahsan 1979: 86).

The dishes served in the ordinary refectory of the monastery consisted of 'herbs', 'roots' and legumes, deliberately reminiscent of the early days of desert monasticism, though the diet also included substantial quantities of bread and wine. As we have noted, the Christian Church expanded the area of Roman cultivation of wine and corn partly because of its insistence upon the use of those items in rituals. But the consumption of bread and wine was not a Christian custom alone; the practices spread under the colonisation of Rome, being regarded throughout the West as 'basic signs of cultural advance' (Duby 1974: 18). Although in a large part of Western Europe the climate was ill-suited to corn-growing and still less to viticulture, these typically Mediterranean forms of cultivation were spread by bishops and aristocrats so that they gradually established themselves in the barbarian world.

Just as abstinence was holy, so excess was sinful, whether of food or sex; gluttony and fornication figured prominently among the seven deadly sins. In this context excess meant not only having too much but going outside the accepted limits. This criterion comes out most clearly in comments on the behaviour of other nations rather than other individuals, for example in the remarks offered by Marco Polo in the account of his travels through Asia. He sees excess in food as a matter of eating meat, conceived as 'unclean', that Christians would not touch. The people of the monastery of Perick in North Sumatra are said to 'eat human flesh and every other sort of flesh, clean or unclean' (1958: 253). Equally, excess in sexuality is having many wives, offering one's wife to other people, or marrying within the degrees prohibited by the Catholic Church. The breaking of prohibitions on food and sex clearly run in parallel lines;[51] they defined the boundaries of the civilised, or rather of the *domesces*, the familiar.

Similar threads run through the much later, post–Restoration, search for an English (i.e. Anglo-Saxon) cuisine, revealing an ambiguous attitude to the culinary influences of 'the continent', a word that itself invokes the ascetic purity of the island race surrounded by water, in contrast to the indulgence and excess of its neighbours. Local cuisine should be clear and straightforward. It is the elaborateness of the foreigner that is suspect, in cuisine as in manners, a sentiment expressed by Warner in his *Antiquitates Culinariae* (1791):

145

Notwithstanding the partiality of our countrymen to French cookery yet that mode of *disguising* meat in *this* kingdom (except perhaps in the hottest part of the hottest season of the year) is an absurdity. It is, *here*, the art of *spoiling good meat*. ... In the South of France ...it is the art of making *bad meat eatable*. (p. 125)

But the author expresses himself even more roundly in dealing with the Latin past where gluttony and depravity (presumably sexual) are once again close bedfellows:

The annals of the empire, are almost the annals of gluttony. The life of Tiberius, is little better than an unvaried scene of the most disgusting, and unnatural vices. He seems, in his retreat at Capreae, to have pushed human depravity, nearly to its utmost limits. Delicacy is unwilling to draw aside the veil, which time has thrown over his abominable impurities; it will be sufficient to remark, that it was customary with him to consume whole nights, in eating and drinking; and Suetonius gives us an instance, of his having spent a night, and two days, at the festal table, without ever leaving it. (1791: iv)

One persistent form of excess that foreigners practise is the breaking of taboos, implicit or explicit. The French addiction to the legs of frogs, the Chinese and their dogs are less potent foci of difference than the Muslim slaughter of cows to the Hindu or the European and Chinese devotion to pork for Muslim and Jew. But food and its taboos, even its characteristic dishes, are a way of defining one's neighbours, inside and outside the country – Italians with their spaghetti and ice cream, Germans with wurst, sauerkraut and lager. Clearly such differences take on a more dangerous significance when they are linked to profound ideological commitments and when the groups concerned are living side by side. Fantasy takes over, as when Jews in Europe in the Middle Ages were accused of the sacrifice of Christian children. Of more intractable significance are those fears based upon actual practices. The killing of the sacred cow, the consumption of dirty pork, these deeply internalised practices and avoidances not only define religious affiliation but serve to set off intercommunal riots of frightening proportions, not only in India but in Yunnan, Indonesia and in other parts where world religions come closely into contact one with another.

Widely applied to what other nations or religions eat, the concept of excess defines xenophobic attitudes. Less widely applied to what our own countrymen may extravagantly undertake (as in the gastronomic film, *La Grande Bouffe*, for the feast in itself borders on excess[52]), the moral criticism may extend to the nature of society itself. For an important element in differentiation, whether of authority or of cooking, is its tendency to breed the opposite. The tension which arises from marked differences of 'degree' and can take the more specific form of 'class conflict', the disorder in the 'society of orders', is related at one level to what Gluckman has analysed as 'the frailty of authority'.[53] In one form or other this feature marks societies where a segment has acquired, on a relatively permanent basis, more than is allowed by 'natural justice' or 'reciprocity', concepts used so freely and so vaguely by social scientists but essential to the analysis of human action. Luxury is a focus for discontent, particularly in regimes where the ideology (or one among the ideologies) is egalitarian, where the 'premise of inequality' (to use the phrase from Maquet's description of pre-colonial Ruanda) is challenged by other assumptions about the distribution of resources. In the Christian Church, as in others, the divergence between the egalitarian ideology, born of just such a challenge, and the hierarchical practices emerging in an established, property-holding corporation (though existing outside the organisation as well as within) gave rise to critical attitudes that fuelled the newer movements for reform and reformation. The fact that the original ideological statement, whether in the New Testament or the *Ancren Riwle*, had been embodied in writing meant that it lived on in the present as a persistent reminder of the extent of man's failure to institute God's rule on earth, for such statements constituted a particular expression of the way that 'natural justice' was perceived at that time and for that group or organisation.

This divergence in attitudes that lay at the heart of stratified societies is sometimes embodied in specific relationships. Certain roles, usually in the religious sphere, are restricted to those who practise abstinence. In one sense such persons as the Hindu *sanyasi*, the Benedictine monk, the Muslim sufi, the Buddhist priest act for all, or for one side of us all. Another form taken by the ambivalence and contradictions embedded in the value systems of hierarchical societies is when some individuals, philosophers or priests, explicitly condemn the luxury of the *haute cuisine* as the work of the devil, as a sin against God. In the last analysis the role of the holy man and the acts of the individual reformer can be seen as linked to the open resentment and covert tension that arises between groups in a hierarchical system. Indeed the opposed attitudes may be present not only as external but as internal contradictions; located in the one and the same individual, they give rise to ambivalence.

Since differences in cuisine parallel class distinctions, egalitarian and revolutionary regimes tend, at least in the initial phases, to do away with the division between the *haute* and the *basse cuisine*. After the fall of the English monarchy in 1648, there was a distinct change in culinary attitudes. Cromwell's tastes were simpler than earlier rulers. The remains of what feasts took place were distributed to the poor, a sop to conscience that was already the practice of churchmen. After the Restoration in 1660 the culture and cuisine of France came to have a dominant influence on the aristocracy, some of whom had lived there in exile. This culture soon proved attractive to the growing bourgeoisie – witness the increasing number of cookbooks in the early eighteenth century as the effects of printing on the kitchen began to make themselves widely felt. The diffusion of manuals on cooking and household management, much in demand from the burgeoning middle class, was made possible by the earlier development of print and the mechanical reproduction of the text which considerably lowered the cost of books. Not that the printed cookbook was altogether new, but it achieved a new audience, the middle class. 'The advent of the printing press', wrote Vehling,

changed the situation. With Platina, about 1474, an avalanche of cookery literature started. The secrets of Scappi, '*cuoco secreto*' to the pope, were 'scooped' by an enterprising Venetian printer in 1570. The guilds of French mustard makers and sauce cooks (precursors of modern food firms and manufacturers of ready-made condiments) were a powerful tribe of secret mongers in the middle ages. English gastronomic literature of the 16th, 17th and even the 18th century is crowded with 'closets opened', 'secrets let out' and other alluring titles purporting to regale the prospective reader in profitable and appetizing secrets of all sorts. Kitchen secrets became commercial articles (Vehling 1936: 29–30).

The act of becoming a commercial article at the hands of the printer could entail impoverishment, certainly when industrial cooking made its mark, in partial contrast to the earlier written elaboration of the high cuisine. Many good cooks in the peasant tradition were very wary of the written, because the formalisation did away with the personal element. Magaridou from the Auvergne was afraid the recipes of her grandmother might 'abîmer en les écrivant' (Robaglia 1935: 34). Magaridou herself had a horror of the cookbook though she produced a special one herself. 'The grocer gave me a cookbook which resembled the arithmetic of the teacher of Coren. You might call them addition without problems and think in reading them of a blank picture.

The book does not say: think a little about the things you are preparing, imagine the cauliflower in the garden in all its beauty, you can no longer let it burn!' (p. 36).

The first printed work on gastronomy by Battista Platina, native of Cremona, was called *De honesta voluptate*. Before the end of the sixteenth century many editions appeared, with translations in Italian, French and German. But it was not long before the middle classes of Western Europe produced their own guides to better living. In France, for example, Menon's *La Cuisinière bourgeoise* became a bestseller in the eighteenth and nineteenth centuries.

In Restoration England the attitude of the new dispensation is well brought out in the title of a small volume, 'The Court and Kitchen of

Elizabeth, commonly called Joan Cromwel, the wife of the late usurper, truly described and represented' (1664), which was designed to throw ridicule on the parsimony of the leading household of the land. Nevertheless the contrast persisted between a 'puritanical' approach to food characteristic of the *low* church, of the *petit* bourgeoisie and of revolutionary groups of the one hand, and the *haute cuisine* (and high life) of the aristocratic, mercantile, political, religious or academic establishment on the other.

At this level the revolutionary potential of food is not a matter of starvation, of famine, of food riots, but of the differences in access to luxury foods, associated with those in power as opposed to the fighters in the *maquis* or to other holders of puritanical values. A striking example of this opposition, in this case between a new and old regime, both with revolutionary claims, is the reaction of the Yugoslav partisan and politician, M. Djilas, to Stalin's Russia.

We became inured to all sorts of things in the Soviet Union. Nevertheless, as children of the Party and revolution who had acquired faith in themselves and the faith of the people through ascetic purity, we could not help being shocked at the drinking party that was held for us on the eve of our departure from the front in Marshal Koniev's headquarters, in a village in Bessarabia. Girls who were too pretty and too extravagantly made up to be waitresses brought in vast quantities of the choicest victuals – caviar, smoked salmon and trout, fresh cucumbers and pickled aubergine, boiled hams, cold roast pigs, hot meat pies and piquant cheeses, borsch, sizzling steaks and finally cakes a foot thick and platters of tropical fruit under which the tables began to sag (1962: 50–1).

It was these great dinners thrown by Stalin that caused Tito to inveigh against Russian drinking.[54]

A more recent example of the same revolutionary puritanism emerges in the report of a meeting in 1959 where Mao Tse-tung belaboured his colleagues for their laziness and love of luxury, quoting in his support the words of a Han poet: 'When one travels in a sedan chair, the body begins to decay. Women with pearly teeth and false eyebrows are the axes that cut down the body's vitality. Delicious meats and fatty foods are the 'medicines' that corrode the intestines'.[55] In both these cases sexual and culinary indulgence are seen as twin aspects of excess. The same themes emerged time and time again in the Chinese Cultural Revolution, with the closure of restaurants and brothels. With the arrival of the North Vietnamese in the Ville-Ho-Chi-Minh, formerly Saigon,[56] a similar, newly established regime closed the night clubs, seen as symbols of the American presence and of bourgeois decadence. At the same time the contrast between the new regime and the old, between puritanism and epicurism, between equality and hierarchy, appeared in their attitudes to food. A North Vietnamese colonel told the following story of the surrender of the Government of the South: 'In the president's office,' added Colonel Tin, there was still a dinner menu in a drawer. The dinner was never held. This evening they will dine on the rations of the army in action; some rice and tinned meat which the Revolutionary Government will give them.'[57]

Revolutionary situations of this kind are rare. But the contradictory attitudes, the opposition between groups, the class conflict, the ambivalence of individuals, are persistent features of societies that are hierarchically differentiated in their styles of life. Why then does the culture of cooking not change more frequently than it appears to do? Why are food-ways often seen as the most conservative aspects of culture?

Contrary to many assumptions, Indian food-ways have been described by Khare as being more subject to change than is marriage. The author is primarily considering the changes resulting from urbanisation, from the migration of a group of people into a radically different social and physical environment, which involved a complete change in their mode of livelihood and in their relations to the means of gaining their living. Even these dramatic transformations of social relations affect the level of transactions and the rituals of preparation and consumption rather than the cuisine in the more restricted sense. So his observations do not altogether contradict the view that behaviour surrounding food and the table persist over long periods in the face of radical changes in social life, and can therefore be seen as throwing some special light on the culture of a particular group or nation.

It would be a mistake to exaggerate the continuities in the culture of food; the change in the English cuisine over the last twenty years has been considerable. On the other hand, the changes in sexual mores have been more far-reaching over that same period. A striking example from the past is Scotland at the time of the Reformation which saw the rapid and radical transformation of sexual morals, indeed of many facets of that society. The earlier laxity of the Scottish church had been notorious; in 1456 the incumbent of a chaplaincy in Linlithgow was required to find security that he would neither pawn the property of the town kirk nor maintain for his enjoyment 'a continual concubine' (Smout 1972: 50). In the mid-sixteenth century monasteries and nunneries were far from celibate; no less than two legitimised children in seven were the bastards of priests. It was no surprise that the godly discipline enforced by the reformed kirk directed its attention primarily to sexual offences. In 1566 nearly 70 per cent of the cases that came before the Canongate session of the church court in Edinburgh had to with sex. Even the ancient custom of hand-fasting was punished by a public appearance on the stool of repentance. Whatever the effect (and even in the nineteenth century it was still normal, as in some other parts of Britain, for the labourer's first child to be born, or at least conceived, out of wedlock), the outward attitude of society changed 'from one of great permissiveness before 1560... to one of rigorous and inquisitorial disapproval in the seventeenth century'. Offenders were more furtive, the middle class more respectable.[58]

On the other hand, the Scottish cuisine changed hardly at all during this same period, still dominated as it was by the use of oatmeal and the northern preference for the boiled rather than the roast (Allen 1968: 23). The reasons for the greater continuity in culinary than in sexual mores are not far to seek. Before the advent of bulk transport, the elements of the cuisine were more closely linked to the local economy, to the availability of produce. Oats characterised the upland zones of the north and west of England, while wheat marked the lowlands of the south and east. So too in France, the cooking of the north was based on butter, that of the south on oil. The supply of food for the daily meal had to bear a close relationship to what the local ecosystem would support. In some ways, food choices are more rigidly circumscribed than sexual mores, at least until the coming of bulk transport and factory food.

However, even in pre-industrial societies a cuisine is certainly not determined by the ingredients alone. Continuity has other components which emerge more clearly when one considers the consumption of food; the nature and order of meals and courses (Halliday 1961; Douglas 1971), and the etiquette of eating, that is table manners, are much less dependent upon the technology and upon the components of cooking, though they are clearly not independent of the status system nor yet of the organisation of social life at the domestic level. These 'rituals of family living' (Bossard and Boll 1950; Goody 1961) are marked by formality and continuity. But these features are not adequately explained by a simple reference to ritual or to culture, nor yet by invoking a determinism based on homologies at the level of deep structure; for all these types of statement smack of circularity. The conservative nature of these actions is partly due to the fact that they are learnt by direct experience, at an early age, at home, in the domestic group. As a consequence, their staying power is great.

In their struggle to explain social facts, social scientists are constantly urged on by their *exigence d'ordre* to bring together disparate observations into some larger whole. This desire to see behaviour as 'fitting', 'interlocking', 'structured' or 'homologous', is an understandable aim that has done much to promote the advancement of human knowledge. At the same time, it may well lead to a premature determinism by allowing insufficient autonomy to the various spheres of human action: the system, the structure, the organisation dominates. Each part is then seen to be equally important in revealing the inner workings of that structure.

I have argued against such assumptions and in favour of a certain degree of institutional autonomy, the kind of autonomy that structural and neo-Marxists have been trying to assert in another domain (Althusser 1966; Danilova 1968). In this case the relative conservatism of specific dishes could be a reflection of their relative lack of entailment with the rest of the socio-cultural system. It would then be the autonomy of certain aspects of cooking that gave it a very special importance for individuals in situations of social change, especially of rapid, revolutionary change. The continuity of borsch may provide some thread of living to those passing through the years following the October Revolution, just as the hamburger clearly states to many an American that he is home and dry. Oatmeal may have bridged the gap between Catholic freedom and Puritan restraint. The persistence of these elements is not inconsistent with radical change in others. The antiquity of the English predilection for fried bacon (Wilson 1973) has been accompanied by great shifts in other aspects of cooking. Modern taste is so different from that of four or five hundred years ago, according to Mead, that 'scarcely one of the favourite dishes served at feasts would now be found eatable' (1931: 53). Nothing was left in its natural state; oysters were sprinkled with sugar; 'inharmonious elements' were piled on the same platter; high cooking was heavily spiced; the sweet is not separated from the sour (p. 75). Since the sixteenth century, he remarks, the art of cooking has undergone a complete revolution (p. 118), though there may well have been greater continuity at the level of the daily meal, especially in rural areas.

What changes took place were related to the changing nature of social stratification in England, and especially to the increasing dominance of the middle class. Their concern with status was greatly aided by the use of printed books, manuals of domestic behaviour including the ubiquitous cookbook. We have seen how these manuals helped them to breach the hierarchical organisation of cuisine, since the 'secrets' of rich households were now revealed and sumptuary laws prohibiting imitation were no longer effective. The opposition between high and low took on a different shape, more closely related to expenditure than to birth.

But the real revolution in the daily food of England occurred as the results of the events and inventions of the nineteenth century. The industrialisation of production was accompanied by the industrialisation of food, which led to the 'complete revolution' associated with an industrial cuisine. Originally middle-class, it extended rapidly with the expanding economy leading to the 'bourgeoisification' of the whole culture of food, accomplished through the vigorous support of the mass media. This process of change was dependent upon the mass importation not simply of luxuries but of staples. That is to say, it depended upon the development of overseas production by means of colonial expansion and the advent of bulk transport to make that produce available. Finally, it depended upon the invention of improved means of preserving food, of developing the 'smoking' pole of the triangle of cooking. The development of industrial cooking and its impact on the food of the Third World that supplied many of the necessary ingredients, form the subject of the two chapters that follow. As far as northern Ghana, and Africa more generally, are concerned, the nature of that impact is related to the largely egalitarian nature of the culture of food even in societies that were stratified politically.

vv

Industrial food: towards the development of a world cuisine

The British diet, claims the modern 'Platine', went straight 'from medieval barbarity to industrial decadence'. With the general sentiment one has some sympathy. But as we have seen, medieval barbarity meant culinary differentiation, if not into something as grand as a sophisticated cuisine such as the French established in building on firm Italian foundations, at least into systems of supply, preparation, cooking, serving and consumption of food that resolutely set aside the high from the low. And 'industrial decadence', whatever its consequences for the *haute cuisine* (larks' tongues are not promising ingredients for a mass cuisine, canned food is not always the best basis for a gourmet meal), has enormously improved, in quantity, quality and variety the diet (and usually the cuisine) of the urban working populations of the western world.[1] It is also making a significant impact on the rest of the world, initially on the productive processes, some of which have become geared to supplying those ingredients on a mass scale, and more recently on consumption itself, since the products of the industrial cuisine and of industrialised agriculture are now critical elements in the food supply of the Third World.

But before we consider the impact on the particular corner of the world on which we are concentrating, we need first to look at the world context in which those changes took place, at the rise of an industrial cuisine in the West. The immediate factors that made this possible were developments in four basic areas: (1) preserving; (2) mechanisation; (3) retailing (and wholesaling), and (4) transport. As we have seen, the preservation of food was a feature even of relatively simple economies like those of northern Ghana. The drying of fish and meat enabled animal protein to be more widely distributed in time and space; the drying of vegetables such as ocro prolonged their use into the dry season when soup ingredients were scarce. The preservation of meat and vegetables, by drying, by pickling, by salting and in some regions by the use of ice, was characteristic of the domestic economy in early Europe.[2] With the developments in navigation that allowed the great sea voyages of the fifteenth century, the use of long-life foods became a matter of major importance; the navies and armies of Europe required considerable quantities of such products to feed their personnel. Werner Sombart has written of the revolution in salting at the end of the fifteenth century that permitted the feeding of sailors at sea. In the Mediterranean, salted fish and the ship's biscuit were already long-established (Braudel 1973: 132); in the Atlantic, much use was made of salted beef which came mainly from Ireland. The enormous catches of cod that arrived from Newfoundland by the end of the fifteenth century were mostly salted. Salt was much used by peasants to preserve food during the winter months.[3] Butter and vegetables were also preserved with salt, and until recently the French peasant placed part of the 'family pig' in the salting tub, while the rest was made into sausages. But the importance of salt was not only dietary.[4] It was the hunger for salt, both for preserving, which became more common in eighteenth-century France, and for eating, that lay behind the peasant uprisings against the *gabelle*, the salt tax. Such taxes were an important source of revenue in Europe as in Asia, both to the merchants and to the governments; it was against such fiscal impositions, as well as against the alien government imposing them, that Gandhi led the famous march to the sea in British India.

Salting, of course, is only one method of preserving food. It is possible to pickle in vinegar as well as salt, and the production of vinegar was an important aspect of early industrial activity. Sugar was used to preserve fruit in forms such as marmalade and jam, as well as being used for coating ham and other meats. Spreading first from India and then from the eastern Mediterranean at the time of the Crusades, cane-sugar played an increasingly important part in the diets of Western Europe, a demand that led to the establishment of many of the slave plantations of the New World. Imports of sugar increased rapidly in the eighteenth century. It was the fact that supplies of cane-sugar were cut off from continental Europe during the Napoleonic wars that led to the fundamental invention embodied in the canning process, as well as to the use of the beet as a source of sugar; at the same time chicory developed as a substitute for the second of the trio of 'junk foods', as Mintz has called them, that is, coffee (the third being tea). It was these 'proletarian hunger-killers', to use another of Mintz's forceful phrases, that became such central elements of working-class diet in the nineteenth century and 'played a crucial role in the linked contribution that Caribbean slaves, Indian peasants, and European urban proletarians were able to make to the growth of western civilization' (Mintz 1979: 60).

It was this general context of colonialism, overseas trade and long-lasting foods that saw the development of the great British Biscuit Industry. Its product owed much to the ship's biscuit which was known there at least as early as Shakespearean times and was manufactured by small bakeries situated around the many harbours of the kingdom. 'Hard-tack' was essentially a substitute for bread (brown or white, depending on class, as had been the case since Roman times), which with ale, cheese and meat, was a basic feature of the diet of the common man (Drummond and Wilbraham 1958: 218). In the course of the eighteenth century the victualling authorities in certain of the king's dockyards such as Portsmouth set up their own large-scale bakeries 'creating a human assembly line that economised each workman's movements to the utmost' (Corley 1976: 14). Despite these organisational developments, the fluctuation of demand caused by the various wars meant that dockyard production had to be supplemented by the work of contractors. The situation changed in 1833 when Thomas Grant of the Victualling Office invented steam machinery to mechanise certain of the processes, reducing labour costs, increasing output and improving the quality of the biscuits.

'Fancy biscuits' like 'hard-tack' also had a long history, being employed for medicinal purposes as well as for the table, especially at festivals. The earliest proprietory brands were probably the Bath Oliver, invented by Dr William Oliver (1695–1764) and the Abernethy, called after a doctor of that name (1764–1831). All these biscuits were initially made by hand, but mechanisation was applied to their manufacture not long after the technological changes had taken place in the dockyards. In the late 1830s a Quaker miller and baker of Carlisle, named Carr, designed machinery for cutting out and stamping biscuits. In 1841 George Palmer, another Quaker, went into partnership with his cousin Thomas Huntley who made biscuits in Reading.

The business that developed into Huntley and Palmers had been founded at a bakery in that town in 1822. Huntley's shop was opposite the Crown Hotel, a posting inn on the main London – Bath road. He had the idea of sending his delivery boy to sell biscuits to the waiting passengers. Their quality led customers to demand Huntley's produce from their grocers at home, opening up the market from a purely local one. So Huntley persuaded his son, who had been apprenticed to a Reading ironmonger and kept a shop nearby, to make tins and tinned boxes in order to keep the biscuits fresh. He also employed a traveller to collect orders for Abernethy, Oliver and other biscuits in the south of England, which he dispatched mainly by the canal system. When Palmer joined the firm, he immediately investigated the application of steam power to mixing the dough, to rolling and cutting, and to providing the oven with a continuous feed. These inventions subsequently led to the development of a whole secondary industry of specialised manufacturers of machinery for the trade, a development that helped to fuel the Industrial Revolution.

Industrial food

The sales of biscuits made rapid headway. The manufactured brands, Carrs, Huntley and Palmers, later Peek Freans, were distributed throughout the nation. In 1859, these firms sold 6 million lbs of their products. Changing eating habits in the shape of earlier breakfasts and later dinners led to a further increase in consumption, and by the late 1870s the figure had risen to 37 million lbs a year. Huntley and Palmers had become one of the forty most important companies in Britain, and within fifty years their biscuits were distributed not only throughout the nation but throughout the world. As with the early canning industry, much of the production of biscuits had first of all been directed to the needs of travellers, explorers and the armed forces. Such produce sustained sailors, traders and colonial officers overseas; only later did industrial production impinge upon the internal market in England or upon the local market overseas, eventually becoming part of the daily diet of the population.

PRESERVING: CANNING

The creation of a long-lasting cereal product, the biscuit, long pre-dated the Industrial Revolution, though its production and distribution were radically transformed by the course of those changes, making the biscuit an important element in the development of the industrial cuisine. But that cuisine was based in a large degree on two processes, the discovery of the techniques of canning and of artificial freezing. The preserving of food in containers again dates back a long way, but the canning on which modern industry depends was invented by Nicolas Appert in response to an appeal of the Directoire in 1795 for contributions to solving the problems created by the war situation in France. During the Napoleonic wars France was cut off from its overseas supplies, and this separation stimulated the search for substitutes. At the same time the recruitment of a mass army of citizens raised in a very radical way the problem of supplying food for a large, mobile and non-productive element in the society; in 1811 Napoleon invaded Russia with over a million men. So the aim of the appeal was partly military, though the citation to Appert when he received the award refers to the advantages of the new invention for sea voyages, hospitals and the domestic economy (Bitting 1937).

This invention of 'canning', what the English call bottling, was based on earlier practices and earlier devices, such as the 'digester', a sort of pressure cooker, invented by Denis Papin in London in 1681, which provided John Evelyn, the diarist, with a 'philosophical supper' (Cutting 1955: 5; Teuteberg in E. and R. Forster 1975: 88). A contemporary account of Appert's book in the *Edinburgh Review* (1814, vol. 45), calls the process 'neither novel in principle, nor scarcely in any point of

157

practice' (Bitting 1937: 38), and declares that 'our fair country women...
unless they have alike forgotten the example and precepts of their
ancestors... must... be more or less acquainted with the methods'
(p. 39). Nevertheless the author on to recognise the importance of
Appert's contribution, especially as the ladies of 1814, having been
relieved of various household tasks by the Industrial Revolution, tend to
know too little about such things.

Appert had been a chef, and he worked out his new methods at his
business near Paris. It was in 1804 that a series of public tests were made
on his produce at Brest, and in the same year he opened his bottling
factory at Massy, near Paris. Five years later he was awarded the prize of
12,000 francs by the committee that included Guy-Lussac and Parmentier, on condition that he deliver a description of the process, in 200
copies, printed at his own expense. This description he published in 1810
and proclaimed the use of his method of bottling as a general aid to
domestic life. Entitled 'Le livre de tous les ménages...', the book gave
instructions for bottling pot-au-feu, consommé, bouillon or pectoral
jelly, fillet of beef, partridge, fresh eggs, milk, vegetables (including
tomatoes or love apples, spinach, sorrel and petit pois), fruit and herbs.
'No single discovery', declared Bitting, 'has contributed more to modern
food manufacture nor to the general welfare of mankind' (1920: 13).

Nor did Appert stop there. Investing his prize money in production
and research, he founded the house of Appert in 1812, produced bouillon
cubes two years later and experimented with a number of other ideas,
turning eventually to the use of the tin can to supplement that of the glass
jar.

In England, where as much interest had been displayed in Appert's
discoveries as in his own country, the tin can had been in use for some
years. An English translation of Appert's book appeared in 1811, a
second edition in 1812, and an American edition in the same year.
Already in 1807 T. Saddington had been awarded a premium by the
London Society for Arts for his work on bottling, and he probably learnt
of Appert's process during his travels abroad. In 1810 Peter Durand and
de Heine took out patents on the process, but in the former case it was
adapted for preserving 'food in vessells made of tin and other metals'.
The potentialities of these inventions aroused the interest of Bryan
Donkin who was a partner in the firm of John Hall, founder of the
Dartford Iron Works in 1785. Whether he acquired either of the earlier
patents is not known, but he appreciated the potential value of Appert's
discovery for his firm.[5] After various experiments, Donkin, in association with Hall and Gamble, set up a factory for canning foods in metal
containers in Blue Anchor Road, Bermondsey. The Navy immediately
purchased supplies of 'preserved provisions' to form part of their medical

stores. These were used for numerous expeditions, by Ross in his voyage to the Far North in 1814, by the Russian von Kotzebue to the North-West Passage in 1815, by Parry to the Arctic in the same year. In 1831 Admiralty Regulations decreed that all ships should carry such provisions as part of their 'medical comforts' (Drummond and Wilbrahm 1958: 319). This was the prelude to their more general spread into the domestic economy which was still hindered by their great expense compared with other foods.

Glass containers continued to be used for most purposes and had a history dating back many years. At the end of the seventeenth century there were 37 glass-houses in London making only bottles, approximately three million a year, which were used mainly as containers for wine and medicine. The chemist Joseph Priestly gave the industry a further boost when early in the eighteenth century, he discovered how to make artificial mineral water which led to a flourishing new industry. By the end of the century, the Swiss, Jacob Schweppe, had set up a factory in London (Wright 1975: 46). But it was with Appert's invention that the glass container came into wide use for preserved foods.

From England the process spread to the United States, where bottles rather than cans were used. William Underwood, who had served his apprenticeship in pickling and preserving with a London house, left for New Orleans in 1817. By 1819 he had made his way to Boston, and in the following year he and one C. Mitchell founded a factory for bottling fruit which by 1821 was shipping goods to South America. Damsons, quinces, currants and cranberries were the main items preserved at the beginning, but the major part of the business had to do with pickles, ketchups, sauces, jellies and jams.

In England these preserved foods did not reach the shops until 1830 and were slow in selling because of the high price. In America too the local trade was initially poor, and most of Underwood's produce went abroad to India, Batavia, Hong Kong, Gibraltar, Manila, the West Indies and South America.[6] Much of it was marketed under an English label to counter the prejudice against American goods (Butterick, 1925). In 1828 Underwood was shipping preserved milk to South America and in 1835, having imported the seed from England, he started to bottle tomatoes, partly for export to Europe.[7] Up to this time the fruit was little known in the States and indeed was regarded as poisonous, even though it had been domesticated in the New World and taken from Mexico to Europe.[8]

In America the local trade developed with the shift from glass to the cheaper metal containers and with the immense boost to sales given by the Civil War (1861–5). Once again the demands of the army were of major significance. But the point of take-off had now been reached for society as a whole. At about the same time as Underwood started his factory in Boston, another English immigrant, Thomas Kensett, and his father-in-law, Ezra Doggett, set up a cannery in New York for salmon, lobsters and oysters. In 1825 Kensett took out a patent for tin cans but they did not become widely used until 1839.

Many of the pioneer factories in the States started with fish as the primary product, and fruit and vegetables as incidental (A. and K. Bitting, 1916:14). In Europe the canning of sardines, that is, young pilchards, began in Nantes in the early 1820s. By 1836 Joseph Colin was producing 100,000 cans, and the industry spread along the coast of Brittany. But it was not until 1870 that a rapid expansion began. By 1880 50 million tins of sardines were being packed annually on the west coast of France, three million of which were exported to Britain. The world of industrial food had begun.

The canning of the other major object of fish packaging, the salmon, began about the same time in Aberdeen on a small scale. Others in Scotland followed, in an attempt to save the long haul of salmon, frozen and smoked, to the London market. The first large-scale salmon cannery was established at Cork, in the south of Ireland, in 1849 by Crosse and Blackwell. It was with the development of canneries on the Pacific coast in 1864 that large-scale production began in America.

The canning of meat was especially important for the army, being developed not only in the American Civil War but also by the Anglo-French forces in the Crimea. It continued to be of great military significance, and in the First World War the Germany Army were producing eight million cans of meat per month. The process was less important for the domestic market, especially after the advent of refrigeration techniques in the latter part of the nineteenth century, when frozen produce became widely available and was preferred by the consumers.

Condensed milk was another major product of the canning industry. In Britain Grimwade took out a patent for evaporated milk in 1847 and was supplying some to expeditions at an early date. In 1855 he took out another patent for powdered milk which could be reconstituted with water. A great improvement in milk processing was made possible by Borden's work in the United States. Borden, who had been stimulated by the needs of migrants in the Gold Rush to market pemmican and meat biscuits, applied for his patent in 1853 and his process was used for production not only in America but also by the Anglo-Swiss Company, later Nestlé's. Condensed milk became a major item of diet in Britain, and in 1924 over two million hundredweight of the product was imported, more than the total imports of tinned fruit and the combined imports of beef and fish.

Food was also processed by other techniques than canning, and some of the results played a prominent part in the new cuisine. Meat extract was developed by the Frenchmen, Proust and Parmentier, and after 1830 meat bouillon was boiled down to a stock soup, dried and sold as 'bouillon bars' in pharmacies and for use on ships. Large-scale production became possible in 1857 as the result of Liebig's research on muscle meat, and in the following years factories were built in Fray Bentos, Uruguay, to process meat into a brown powder for shipping to the growing urban populations of Europe. Soon the process of manufacturing meat foods spread to Australia, New Zealand, Argentina and North America with the result that the soups and gravies of the English kitchen became dominated by the dehydrated products of the international meat industry.

PRESERVING: FREEZING

While the canning of food was the most significant step in the development of an industrial cuisine, other processes of preservation also played an important part, especially the artificial freezing of foodstuffs. In cold climates the technique had been practised since prehistoric times, and natural ice continued to be used until very recently. In the early nineteenth century the Russians were packing chickens in snow for consumption as occasion required, and frozen veal was being sent from Archangel to St Petersburg. In Scotland ice-houses had long been attached to richer homes, and the practice spread into the food trades. By the beginning of the nineteenth century every salmon fishery in Scotland was provided with an ice-house. The fish were packed in long boxes with pounded ice and dispatched to the London market (Bitting 1937: 29).[9]

In America natural ice was also packed in 'refrigerators' from the beginning of the nineteenth century. Indeed, ice gathered from the Boston ponds became big business. Beginning in 1806 with the West Indies, Frederic Tudor developed a world-wide operation, which between 1836 and 1850 extended to every large port in South America and the Far East; within thirty years ice had become one of the great trading interests of the city of Boston, and one French source claimed that in 1847 the Asian trade of one house was almost equal in value to the whole of the Bordeaux wine harvest (Prentice 1950: 114ff.).

The demand of Asian countries for Boston ice had a history in the local usage of Chinese society where in pre-imperial times the feudal nobility had the prerogative of storing ice to keep sacrificial objects fresh. In later imperial times eunuchs supervised the cutting of blocks of ice from rivers and ponds, packing it in clean store and keeping it in trenches. The use of ice was not limited to the imperial house, though it helped to supply the court with fresh food. Mote remarks that 'refrigerated shipping seems to have been "taken for granted" in Ming times, long before we hear of such a development in Europe' (1977: 215).[10]

About the time of the development in the Boston trade, ice became widely used in America for transporting food on the railroad. It was in 1851 that the first refrigerated rail car brought butter from Ogdensburg, New York, to Boston, Massachusetts. Of greater significance was the ability to transport frozen meat from the Chicago stockyards to the urban centres of the East, an enterprise associated with the names of Armour and Swift, and providing a parallel development to the international shipment of meat to Europe from America and Australia.

With the development of rail transport around the middle of the century, fresh sea fish began to make its regular appearance in inland markets in England, leading to a decline in the popularity of salted and picked herrings, which had long been a staple food. Fish from rivers and dew ponds had long been available, sometimes being marketed alive by the fishmonger in tanks. Live fish were carried by the wives of sea-fishermen to towns as far inland as Coventry, being transported in brine on pack-horses (Davis 1966: 15). But the expense of such products meant that they were not available to the majority of the population, a situation that rail transport helped to change. Meanwhile in America a great deal of herring had been frozen by exposure since 1846, 'providing the masses with a cheap and wholesome food' (Cutting 1955: 296).

In cooler climes and for longer distances the extensive use of refrigeration depended upon the development of artificial rather than natural ice. The newly exploited pastures of Australia and America produced an abundance of livestock, but the problem lay in getting meat to the industrial consumers. Shipping cattle live to Europe presented great difficulties until the length of the voyage had been reduced. Nevertheless American livestock was imported into Europe in appreciable numbers by the early 1870s. The Australian voyage was much longer and, although meat was now canned, its quality left much to be desired. In 1850, James Harrison, a Scottish immigrant to Australia, designed the first practical ice-making machine, using the evaporation and subsequent compression of ether. Ten years later, the French engineer Carré produced a much more efficient machine based on ammonia gas. But the problem of transporting Australian frozen meat to Europe was not solved until 1880 when the S.S. *Strathleven* brought a cargo from Melbourne to London. Meanwhile similar experiments were being carried on in other countries, and frozen meat reached the London market, probably from the United States, as early as 1872. In France, the engineer Charles Tellier had been working on the same problems since

1868, and after several unsuccessful attempts, the S.S. *Frigorifique* brought a cargo of meat from Argentina to Rouen in 1876. These developments led to a rapid diminution in the amounts of canned and salted meat being imported from those countries, just as the use of natural ice in Britain had earlier led to a decrease in the amount of salted and pickled fish.

Not only diet but cooking too responded in significant ways to technological changes. While domestic refrigeration had to wait until the following century, in the later part of the nineteenth century such machines were used in the new catering trades. It was these developments in freezing techniques that enabled Lyons tea-shops to serve their popular cucumber sandwiches all the year round. Started by the successful operators of a tobacco business in 1887, these shops followed the rise of the coffee public houses of the 1870's which had been organised by the temperance societies as an alternative to the pub. Out of these coffee houses developed two sizeable catering concerns, the first multiples of their kind, Lockharts and Pierce & Plenty. The growth of the commercial catering business was the counterpart of the decline of the domestic servant; in 1851 905,000 women in Britain were employed as domestic servants, plus 128,000 servant girls on farms; by the 1961 Census, there were no more than 103,000 resident domestic servants in England and Wales.[11]

Many of the other developments surrounding food in the nineteenth century had little to do with preservation *per se*, but rather with branding, packaging, advertising and marketing. In 1868 Fleischmann provided a standardised yeast for the American market; Heinz bottled horse-radish sauce in 1869. In England sauces, based on vinegar, featured early on in the commercial food business; their production was stimulated by the cheaper spices brought back by the East India Company in Elizabethan times, and the demand was later increased by the return of families from abroad. The well-known Worcester sauce, for example, was produced by the analytical chemists Lea and Perrins, who went into partnership in 1823 to run a pharmacy that also dealt in toiletries, cosmetics and groceries. They began to market their own medicinal products, and their first catalogue listed more than three hundred items, such as Essence of Sarsaparilla for scurvy and Taraxacum (dandelion coffee) for liver complaints. These products were soon in great demand from the new industrial towns of the Birmingham area as well as from abroad; travellers set off with a Lea and Perrins' medical chest, and this publicity led to orders from all over the world. However it was the invention of the sauce which exemplifies the rapid growth of prepared foods, the shift of focus from kitchen to factory, as well as the influence of overseas trade and overseas colonisation.

Mr. Lea & Mr. Perrins were perfecting their medicines, hair lotions and marrow pomades when Marcus, Lord Sandys visited the shop in Worcester. Late Governor of Bengal, he had retired to his country estate at nearby Ombersley Court, and would be obliged if they would make up one of his favourite Indian sauces. They obliged. Having already arranged their own supplies of spices and dried fruits, from Asia and the Americas, they had the ingredients to hand. Scrupulously following his lordship's recipe, they made the required quantity, plus some for themselves. One taste was enough. The sauce was ghastly: an unpalatable, red hot, fire water. His lordship was entirely satisfied. The remainder however was consigned to a cellar below the shop, and there it stayed until the annual spring-cleaning and stocktaking.

It was on the point of being poured away when Mr. Lea amd Mr. Perrins detected its appetising aroma. Tasting it once again they discovered it had matured into a rare and piquant sauce. The sauce was saved, more was made. Customers were persuaded to try the new Worcestershire Sauce, and did not need more persuasion: the sauce was an instant success. Sales rose. In 1842, Lea & Perrins sold 636 bottles. In 1845, a manufactory was set up in Bank Street, Worcester. Ten years later the yearly sales were up to 30,000 bottles of Worcestershire Sauce. Travellers covered Great Britain and there were agencies in Australia and the United States (Wright 1975: 31).

The product still adorns the tables of cafés, restaurants and dining rooms the world over.

Another item of processed food which has substantially changed eating habits in many parts of the world, including the new bourgeoisie of Ghana, is the breakfast cereal. Initially these foods were developed in the United States to meet the needs of vegetarian groups like the Seventh Day Adventists, who were experimenting with cereal-based foods at Battle Creek, Michigan, in the 1850s. Dr John Kellogg was director of the 'medical boarding house' at Battle Creek where he carried out research in the 'dietary problem' and in the development of so-called 'natural foods' (Deutch 1961). It was in the 1860s that he produced 'Granola', the first ready-cooked cereal food, made from a mixture of oatmeal, wheat and maize baked in a slow oven until thoroughly dextrinised (Collins 1976: 31). It was his brother who later became the promoter of these foods.

The 1890s saw the invention of most of the basic types of pre-cooked cereal and manufacturing process – flaking, toasting, puffing and extrusion: Shredded Wheat appeared in 1892, and in 1898 Grape Nuts, invented by Charles W. Post, an ex-patient of Kellogg's who also produced Post Toasties. It was Post who pioneered the use of advertising techniques employed by the makers of patent medicines to market his products, 'selling health foods to well people'. Ever since this market has been heavily dependent upon massive publicity campaigns. After the First World War the American foods spread to Britain, where as elsewhere in the world the market is still dominated by more or less the same products. Pushing aside porridge and other breakfast foods, they owed their success to their ease of preparation, especially important for breakfast in households whose members are all working outside the home; but their widespread use was also due to the vigorous sales campaigns, later directed primarily towards children, to the general shift to lighter meals consistent with the changing nature of 'work', and to rising real incomes which made it possible for people to buy 'health' foods and so transform them into utility foods.[12]

MECHANISATION AND TRANSPORT

The use of machines in the production of industrial food has already been noted in the case of the biscuit industry. But it was equally important in the whole canning industry at three levels, in the mechanisation of the production of the food, especially in agriculture, in the mechanisation of the preparation of the food, cleansing, peeling, podding, etc., and in the mechanisation of the canning itself.

When canned goods first reached the shops about 1830, they made little impact on domestic consumption on account of their price, even with the cheaper metal containers. A skilled man could fill only 50 or 60 cans a day; the cans themselves were made from rolled sheets of wrought iron; their lids were fitted by placing a sheet of metal across the top and then hammering it down at the sides, after which it was soldered on. The early cans were so heavy that they sometimes had to be fitted with rings to lift them, and they could only be opened with a hammer and chisel. During the course of the second half of the nineteenth century these obstacles were gradually overcome; in 1849 came a machine for pressing out the tops and bottoms, then a substitute for the soldering iron, and in 1876 the Howe machine produced a continuous stream of cans for sealing so that two men with assistants could produce 1,500 cans a day (Cummings 1941: 68). The methods of canning themselves improved in 1861 when the addition of calcium chloride to the water increased its temperature and cut down the boiling time required from five hours to thirty minutes, a time that was further reduced by the invention of the autoclave (a closed kettle). The other bottle-neck lay in the preparation of the food itself, a phase that also gradually became dominated by new machinery – washers, graders, peelers, corn huskers and cutters, bean snippers and filling machines. Once again a whole series of subsidiary industries arose to meet the new requirements.

It should be stressed that the manufacture of many processed and packaged foods did not require great advances in techniques of preservation but rather the adaptation of simple machinery for producing standard goods on a large scale. This happened not only with biscuits but with pasta. Possibly coming from China through Germany, this 'typical' Italian dish was adopted in the fourteenth century.[13] It spread across the Atlantic with the influx of Italian immigrants late in the nineteenth century, and in 1890 it was manufactured on a large scale by Foulds, wrapped in a sanitary package and advertised as 'Cleanly made by Americans'. Mechanisation permitted the domestication and purification of foreign foods.

Not only production but distribution too was mechanised, involving a similar massive use of energy. The mechanisation of the process of distribution depended upon the development of a system of transport that could shift the very large quantities of goods involved in the ready-made market; in the United States this amounted to some 700 million cases of canned goods a year in the 1960s, each case including an average of 24 cans. The distribution of processed foods to a mass market was dependent upon the railway boom which in Britain marked the beginning of the second phase of industrialisation (roughly 1840–95). Following the little mania of 1835–7 came the big railway mania of 1845–7; during this period, from 1830, over 6,000 miles of railway were constructed in Britain (Hobsbawm 1968: 88). Here was an opportunity for investment, for employment and for the export of capital goods which laid the basis of working-class prosperity in the third quarter of the century, permitted the growth of the mass markets for preserved and processed foods, and built up the volume of imports from the Colonial (now the Third) World.

Critical to the growth of the overseas trade was the development of large cargo ships capable of transporting the raw materials to the metropolitan country in exchange for the mass export of manufactured goods. These various processes of mechanisation and transportation were essential to the preservation and distribution of food on a mass scale, and so to the industrialisation of the domestic diet of the new proletariat. But more immediately relevant to the domestic level were the social changes that took place in the organisation of the actual distribution of food to the household, since a whole series of agents now intervened between the producer and the consumer.

RETAILING

The changes in the English retailing trade were marked by two phases. The first was the shift from open market to closed shop which began in Elizabethan times, although the move to retail shops in the food trade was strongly resisted by many urban authorities. The second retail revolution occurred in the nineteenth century and was associated with industrialisation rather than with urbanisation itself; indeed it affected food and cooking in both town and country.

In medieval England market-places were areas for exchanging the products of the nearby countryside with those made by local craftsmen. Great efforts were made by the authorities to prevent the intervention of any middle men, except in the long-distance trades where their services could not be avoided. Shops for buying food scarcely existed; the town authorities forced the food trade into the street market for the purposes of control.[14] Frequent regulations were made against 'forestalling' the market by buying goods outside it, against 'regrating' those goods, that is, selling them at a higher price, and against 'engrossing', or hoarding. At the same time an attempt was made to control the quality and the price;[15] control lay partly in the hands of the occupational associations and partly in the hands of the collective authority of the corporation. In Chester, butchers and bakers were made to take a public oath that the food they supply to their fellow-citizens shall be wholesome and fair in price.[16] Such regulations also included rules about the use of standard weights and measures, instructing men 'not to sell by aime of hand'.

It was impossible completely to control the marketing of food, even at this time. In addition to 'foreigner' or 'stranger' markets (i.e. those catering for country folk) there was a certain amount of hawking. But the move to establishing food shops only developed with the growth of suburban London, the main markets being too far away for their inhabitants. By this time the cornchandler and a few other traders were beginning to act as wholesalers with fixed premises. Nevertheless it was well into the eighteenth century before the big open markets ceased to be the normal place to buy food (Davis 1966: 74).

Apart from the shift from market to shop, little had changed in London as late as 1777, when the country was on the threshold of the great changes in the processing and sale of food that industrialisation brought. In that year, James Fitch, the son of an Essex farmer who, like others in a period of depression following the great agricultural changes of the earlier part of the century, came to London to enter the food trade.

The only retailers allowed to trade were those who had been apprenticed to a freeman of the City, and who, on completion of their apprenticeship, had themselves taken up the freedom of a City Company or Guild. The Lord Mayor and his Court were still virtual dictators of trade within the City walls and for up to seven miles outside. Price control was exercised from the Guildhall, and it was an offence of offer goods for sale other than in the markets. No one was allowed to own more than one shop selling poultry, butter or eggs (Keevil 1972: 2).

Control was exercised by the great City companies, and freeman engaged in selling produce had to belong to the appropriate Livery

Company, Butchers', Poulterers', Bakers', Fruiterers' or Grocers'.

It was the last of these, the grocers, who were the key to later developments. Originally one of the minor food trades, grocery overtook all the others. For many years grocers were associated with the import of foreign goods. In the fifteenth century they had been general merchants dealing in most goods except fresh food and clothing. But in London they gradually concentrated on the non-perishable items of food arriving in increasing quantities from the Mediterranean, the Far East and the New World. The English (London) Company of Grocers was made up of merchants dealing in spices, dried fruit and similar commodities which they imported or bought in bulk ('gross', *grossier* in French is a wholesaler), and sold in small quantities. Later they added tea, coffee, cocoa and sugar, all of them initially 'luxury' goods.[17] One of the most important commodities was sugar, first imported at a high price from Arabia and India but then brought in much more cheaply first from the Canaries and then from the Caribbean, one of the 'junk foods' that were key components of colonial plantations and working-class diets.

The grocer was distinguished from the provision merchant who dealt in butter, cheese and bacon, and the distinction obtained until very recently in the larger shops where there was a 'provision' counter dealing in these items; the British housewife herself referred to these central foods as 'provisions' and to the dry goods as 'groceries'.

It was the grocer dealing in dry, imported goods who led the second retailing revolution. Authors such as Davis (1966) and Jefferys (1954) have considered this great development in retailing (as distinct from wholesaling) to lie in the growth of multiples, of shops that were organised in branches along national lines. Since this growth was based upon the rise of working-class incomes, it is not surprising that the first such organisation was that of the Rochdale Pioneers whose cooperative was begun in 1844 – not the first of its kind but the first commercial success. In 1856, at the request of loyal customers, it opened the first of its many branches. At the same time the cooperative experimented in vertical integration by starting the Wholesale Society in 1855 which moved from purchase and distribution directly into production. It was not until some time later that private firms entered into the same field.[18] Indeed, the great boom came in the last twenty years of the century, when Coop membership rose from half a million in 1881 to three million in 1914.

One of the first trades to develop a network of chain stores was footwear which had 300 shops in 1875, rising to 2,600 in 1900. Butchers started later, with 10 shops in 1880 and 2,000 in 1900, while grocery branches jumped from 27 to 3,444 over the same period (Hobsbawm 1968: 131). In 1872 Thomas Lipton started his grocery shop in Glasgow;

twenty-six years later there were 245 branches scattered all over the kingdom. Selling a limited number of cheaper goods, the new multiples in turn influenced the trade of the old-fashioned grocer who now had to deal with the appearance of 'an entirely new style of commodity in the form of manufactured foods' (Davis 1966: 284) – tinned goods, jams, powders for custards, grains and so forth. Just as imported goods became cheaper with the new developments in transport, so too manufactured goods and items packaged before sale came to dominate the market. These products were generally branded goods, 'sold' before sale by national advertising.

Advertising in the modern sense was a critical factor in these developments and had begun with printing itself; already in 1479 Caxton printed an advertisement for books from his press. The first newspaper advertisement appeared in 1625, and by the mid-eighteenth century Dr Johnson was complaining of their ubiquity. But the major development of the business came in the nineteenth century with the advent of the wholesale trade which itself derived from the industrialisation of production, as well as with the coming of the mass newspaper dependent upon the rotary press. Large-scale manufacture brought with it an increased gap between producer and consumer so that some new way of communication was required. During the fifty years from 1853 the quantity of soap bought in Britain increased fourfold, with the main companies, Levers', Pears', and Hudson's, competing by means of national advertising campaigns of which the use of Sir John Millais' painting 'Bubbles' was the most famous example. In America, N.W. Ayer and Son, Inc., the first modern agency, was founded in Philadelphia in 1869, acting as an intermediary between producer and media, and making possible the more complex advertising campaigns which not only enables products to reach a wider market but which to some extent create that market, as in the case of breakfast cereals.

The role of advertising in promoting the Hovis loaf is an interesting example of this process. This patent bread has been the product leader in brown bread since 1890 when it had probably been adapted from a loaf invented by an American vegetarian, Graham, in the 1840s. The problem was to overcome the popular prejudice, in existence since Roman times at least, in favour of white bread.[19]

In the early years the goal was to acquire a sound reputation with a public that was sceptical of patent foods and wary of adulteration. Thus early advertisements made considerable play of royal patronage, of awards and diplomas for quality and purity, and of the need to beware of cheap imitations (Collins 1976: 30).

The relics of the system of royal patronage and international diplomas employed by the industry remain with us to this day. They were essential parts of the initial legitimation of processed foods, just as the advertisement and the grocery trade were essential aspects of their distribution.

This whole process led to a considerable degree of homogenisation of food consumption and was dependent upon the effective increase in demand from the 'working class', which now had no direct access to foodstuffs, to primary production. Because of this mass demand, mass importation and mass manufacture, grocery, formerly one of the minor food trades, became by far the most important. 'The vast majority of consumers of all income groups drink the same brands of tea, and smoke the same cigarettes, and their children eat the same cornflakes just as they wear the same clothes and watch the same television sets' (Davis 1966: 84). Differences in income, class and status have to manifest themselves in other ways.

While some historians see the second retailing revolution as developing with the growth of the multiples, Blackman would place it earlier in the century when processed foods and mass imports began to make an impact on the market as a result of changes in technology that were linked with the new demands of the industrial workers. Cheaper West Indian sugar and less expensive Indian teas became essential items in the improved diets of the working class (when they were employed) in the latter half of the nineteenth century. In the 1860s grocers added other new lines, processed foods, including cornflours, baking powders and dried soups, such as Symingtons'. As we have seen, many of these 'processed' foods were not the results of changing techniques of food preservation so much as the advent of national instead of local products, such as soap or 'patented' branded foods consisting of established items broken down, packaged and sold through public advertising campaigns. Blackman notes that at this time one grocer in Sheffield was buying dried peas, oatmeal and groats from Symingtons' Steam Mills at Market Harborough, and mustard, cocoa, chicory and other commodities from forty different firms including starch and blue from J. & J. Coleman's, the mustard manufacturers who had a dramatic rise from the time in 1854 when they purchased a windmill in Lincolnshire, before moving to Norwich. In the United States too the national canning industry took off in the mid-1860s when Blue Label canned foods, founded in 1858, started advertising nationally, though items like Borden's condensed milk (1857), Burham and Morrill's sweet corn (c. 1850), Burnett's vanilla essence (1847) and various brands of soap were already available.

By 1880 a grocer in Hull was buying Wotherspoon's cornflour, Brown and Polson's brand of the same commodity, Symingtons' pea flour, Goodall's custard and egg powders, several brands of tinned milk, including Nestlé's, tinned fruit, Crosse & Blackwell jams, and many other items which are still household names. It was the technical revolution of mass-producing and semi-processing foodstuffs in common use together with the increased volume of trade in tea and sugar that now brought the grocer into focus as 'the most important food trader for regular family purchases' (Blackman 1976: 151).

ADULTERATION UNDER THE NEW DISPENSATION

Complaints against the adulteration of food are as old as the sale of foodstuffs itself. In Athens protests about the quality of wine led to the appointment of inspectors to control its quality. In Rome wines from Gaul were already accused of adulteration, and local bakers were said to add 'white earth' to their bread.[20]

Adulteration is a feature of the growth of urban society, or rather of urban or rural society that is divorced from primary production. The agro-towns of West Africa were not so divorced, while even many of the rural inhabitants of modern England have little or nothing to do with the land. With the growth of a distinct town life in England in the centuries after the Norman Conquest, an increasing number of merchants, artisans and shopkeepers had to rely on others for their supply of food, and it was these non-food producers who were the targets (and sometimes the perpetrators) of adulteration. The quality and price of bread and ale was controlled as early as 1266 and continued to be so for more than five hundred years.

It was that 'most revolutionary social change' of the first half of the nineteenth century, the rapid growth of towns, and especially the industrial towns of the midlands and north of England (Burnett 1966: 28), which was based on the development of manufacturing industry in the previous century, that made the adulteration of food a major social problem. Protests against impure food had already taken a literary form by the middle of the eighteenth century and were mainly aimed at millers, bakers and brewers. In 1757 'My Friend', a physician, published a work entitled *Poison Detected*; the next year saw the appearance of *Lying Detected* by Emanuel Collins, attacking the general trend of this literature, as well as a work by Henry Jackson entitled *An Essay on Bread... to which is added an Appendix; explaining the vile practices committed in adulterating wines, cider etc.* In a later period of scarcity and high prices, we find *The Crying Frauds of London Markets, proving their Deadly Influence upon the Two Pillars of Life, Bread and Porter*, by the author of the *Cutting Butcher's Appeal* (1795). But it was the work of Frederick Accum in 1820, *A Treatise on Adulterations of Food and Culinary*

Poisons, etc., that had the greatest influence on the public since he was a respected analytical chemist and a professor at the Surrey Institution. He gave widespread publicity both to the methods adopted and to named individuals until he had to flee to Berlin, possibly as a result of 'a deliberate conspiracy of vested interests' (Burnett 1966: 77).

The adulteration of food continued to be a problem for the industrialisation of cooking, particularly in these early days. While Accum's departure from the country led to a temporary neglect of his work, the fight continued. The main analytic contribution was a series of reports made by Dr Hassall between 1851 and 1855, published collectively in the latter year. Hassall recounts that within months of coming to live in London in 1850 he saw that 'there was something wrong in the state of most of the articles of consumption commonly sold' (1855:xxxvii). So he examined a range of items sold at grocers' shops (coffee, cocoa, mustard, sauces, preserved goods, prepared flour) as well as butter, bread, beer and gin. Some passed the test; many failed. To take a typical example, 22 out of 50 samples of arrow root were adulterated; one variety advertised on the label as

Walker's

Arrow-root

sold in packages, '2d the quarter pound', elicited the comment (most were equally lapidary) 'Consists entirely of potato-flour' (1855: 41). Much of the produce was packaged in the stores in which it was sold. Some had been wrapped and even produced elsewhere, being labelled with the maker's name. These names were publicised by Hassall so that the brand became a mark of quality, or lack of it. Names like Frys and Cadbury's already appear in the cocoa trade (pp. 264–5), Crosse & Blackwell and Fortnum & Mason's in the sauce trade, J. & J. Coleman for mustard (p. 131). Each of these well-known firms was indicted for selling adulterated products and no doubt took steps to improve the quality. On the other hand a positive recommendation for a branded product was clearly an important aspect of publicity as well as of quality control, as for example in Hassall's conclusion: 'That Borden's Patent Meat Biscuit was in a perfectly sound state, and that there is much reason to regard it as a valuable article of diet in the provisioning of ships, garrisons, etc.' (1855: xx). Firms soon began to employ the label as a certification.

Vicker's Genuine Russian Isinglass for invalids and culinary use.... Purchasers who are desirous of protecting themselves from the *adulteration* which is now extensively practised are recommended to ask for 'Vicker's Genuine Russian Isinglass', in *sealed packets*.

The samples that were tested by Hassall sometimes indicate the foreign provenance of their constituents or recipes. India had an obvious influence on the appearance of chutneys as well as on the fact that three varieties of 'King of Oude' Sauce were on the market as well as an 'India Soy', consisting of burnt treacle. Hassall tested seven tomato sauces, six of which were adulterated, including two from France, one of which was from Maille ('very much of the red earth', he comments).

The combined contribution of public medical testing, branded goods and widespread advertising brought adulteration under control at the same time as creating a national cuisine, at least as far as processed ingredients and prepared foods were concerned. At the same time the pattern of the grocery trade changed radically. For now the shopkeeper was no longer the one who selected and certified the product; that was done by the producer and packager, by the name and the advertisement. Regional tastes continued to be important, as Allen (1968) has pointed out. But these comprised only a small component of a largely nationalised, even internationalised, repertoire.

Given these developments in retailing, the move towards self-service, even automatic service, was the next major step. Consumer services become of less and less importance; small special shops tend to vanish while large general stores prosper. But not altogether. In some European countries the tendency is less marked. So it is in rural areas where the owner-managed general store persists. In towns, smaller shops often specialise in new products, in second-hand and antique goods, filling the spatial interstices created by the supermarkets, the department stores and the discount houses, while market stalls arise in unexpected places to sell objects of craft manufacture or local produce. But in general the larger stores offer lower prices, wider choices and the impersonality of selection that a socially mobile population often appears to prefer.

The effect of these changes on the diet and cuisine was enormous. A great deal of domestic work was now done before the food ever entered the kitchen. Many foods were already partly or fully processed, and even sold in a ready-to-eat form. Consequently not only have the ingredients become standardised but a number of the dishes as well, at least in many homes in England and America where only the festive occasion, either in the house or at the restaurant, requires the food to make some claim to be 'home-made'. While Ghana is far from attaining this extreme condition, the industrialisation of food has begun to affect the country not only as a supplier (essentially of cocoa) but also as a consumer. Within a relatively short space of time tinned sardines, condensed milk, tomato paste and cartons of lump sugar have become standard features of the small markets throughout Anglophone West Africa. A drain on the limited resources of foreign exchange, the demand for which is continously expanding while cocoa production remains static, the absence of these items causes hardship and complaint; these industrial foods of the West have now become incorporated in the meals of the Third World.

6

The impact of the world system

In precisely what way has the Third World been affected? To answer this question let us return to the region which we know in some detail. It is not one that has been directly involved in the production of cash crops or minerals for overseas, although it has supplied much of the labour and received little of the wealth arising out of these activities. Because of the marginal position of much of the savannah country in recent developments in West Africa, the patterns of life described in an earlier chapter still exist among the bulk of the inhabitants of northern Ghana today.

At the same time the growth of the nation state has led to the emergence of an elite involved in administrative, professional, political and military activities, an elite that constitutes a 'new class'. Although this class is spoken of as the bourgeoisie or middle class it is in fact the ruling class, and it seems curious to refer to an emergent middle class when locally at least there is no one else on top. The immediate basis of their recruitment is education. The first echelon of schoolchildren were sometimes the offspring of chiefs, traditional and government-appointed, who were enjoined to send representatives to the newly establised schools. In other cases the school children had less noble genealogies, having been pressed into service in the place of chiefs' sons. In recent years recruitment has come from a wider range of families, though the early elite has usually succeeded in training their own children for positions similar to those they occupy, introducing a strong hereditary element into an ostensibly meritocratic system.

The strength of this elite did not initially rest on any privileged position regarding the system of primary production: the ownership of landed property did not figure prominently in its system of support. But the situation is changing rapidly. Since 1968 the effects of the Green Revolution have been felt even in the savannah regions of northern Ghana, with its relatively poor soil, limited water and restricted techniques. For the extensive cultivation of rice in valley bottoms by means of the tractor and the combine harvester, using improved varieties of high yielding grain, has become a common feature of the area. Whereas the elite had earlier tended to keep out of agricultural production, many of them have now joined the men of commerce, the traditional chiefs and other entrepreneurial farmers in the cultivation of rice for sale. This new system of production has been accompanied by a shift in the nature of land tenure, in the relations of farmers to the land. In order to gain access to the necessary capital, members of the elite have to borrow money from the banks, either government or private. To get such a loan a man needs greater evidence and security of tenure than the indigenous system could give to anyone, certainly to any one man. The whole process of registration, to which some would-be entrepreneurs have resorted, meant a sudden individualisation of land tenure, a setting aside of lineage, village and familial rights in favour of 'individual ownership', a revolution in rural life (Goody 1980).

What is the influence of this process of class formation, at present in its early stages, on the patterns of consumption?

It was the demands for the ingredients of processed food products from overseas that played an important part in the development of the economies of West Africa. Beginning in the 1830s, exports of gold, ivory, kola and slaves took second place to the sale of palm-oil and after the end of the century, of cocoa. Palm-oil was required for soap and then for the new food processing industries of Europe; the shift of cocoa and chocolate from a luxury to an item of everyday use meant a huge increase in the demand for produce that now had to be cultivated, not simply gathered.

As with sugar it was the changing class demands for foods, associated with the development of an urban work-force, of large-scale transport, of food preservation techniques and the changes in distribution (i.e. in shopping) that created the conditions for the mass export of produce from West Africa. By providing new foods for the people of Europe, these countries acquired the exchange capacity needed for imports of manufactured goods. Some of these were capital goods, many were items of consumption. Gradually the Industrial Revolution began to change the food habits of even the rural areas of West Africa by providing cheap sugar, bottled beer, and above all the products of the canning industry, sardines, tomato paste and milk, all of which began to take their place as the staples for an important element in the population, especially the employed and the mobile.

It is here in the domestic domain that we see most clearly the impact of the cultural patterns of the industrial nations upon local styles of life. The houses of government employees (and a large percentage of non-traditional housing is built and furnished by the State) are constructed according to plans that are found throughout the western world. Often they are built of cement blocks, with pitched roofs and verandas. In towns of any size, piped water and electricity have become prime necessities, involving a heavy expenditure of resources to maintain an intermittent supply and to allow the import of the household equipment – refrigerators, radios, cookers – to which this source of power gives access. For getting from place to place a car is seen as a necessity for all senior officers and as the goal of all junior ones; being 'carful' again involves the import of high-cost equipment and of the energy to run it.

Apart from imported household equipment, the house is fitted out with furniture made in Ghana but designed along the lines of a suburban dwelling in Europe. The drawing room is provided with armchairs, side tables, a buffet and in the best bungalows and Rest Houses (the descendants of the round thatched houses of mud which were built by the early District Officers) the floors are even carpeted. Curtains adorn the windows, cushions the chairs, ashtrays the tables. At one side of the room is a dining table surrounded by high-backed chairs, laid out at meal times in the impeccable manner of a small hotel, complete with cutlery, china and sometimes a tablecloth. The gear of western modes of consumption is part and parcel of daily living, at least at this level.

Yet neither the cuisine nor the table manners of the West have entirely taken over from local custom. While individual members of the elite are perfectly adept in eating according to the western pattern, nevertheless at home, and increasingly in public, they prefer their natal ways. Porridge appears very regularly on the table, accompanied more frequently by meat soup but just as often served with a relish made from okra, ground-nuts, tomatoes or vegetable leaves. One is tempted to express surprise at the lack of variety; a man can eat nothing but porridge (*saab*) every day if it can be arranged, and this is sometimes true even of those who have been resident in Europe for a long period and have been forced to use some local substitutes. But such fidelity is less surprising when one contemplates the regularity with which the meat loaf, macaroni cheese or the hamburger appear upon the tables of the Anglo-Saxons, not to mention the unchanging character of breakfast menus, whether in France, Holland, Germany or Scotland. What is different in Africa is the vitual absence of alternative or differentiated recipes, either for feasts or for class.

Traditional food demands traditional treatment. By preference, porridge is often eaten with the fingers rather than with the mediating instruments common in the West. In restaurants and hotels throughout the world, western cutlery has come to dominate the table, with the partial exception of the Chinese and Japanese who had their own mediators between fingers and food, between plate and palate. In northern Ghana, as elsewhere in Africa, the apparatus of consumption was limited to the bowl, apart from the occasional use of a wooden spoon. The eater scoops up a portion of porridge between the thumb and

177

fingers of the right hand, dips it into another bowl of relish and rapidly slips the two into his mouth. Such is still the common practice, accompanied by a careful washing of the hands before and after eating, a procedure that has perhaps become more deliberate in recent years but was always a feature of Islamic culture in the region. Both cuisine and table manners are positively valued as part of traditional ways; they are seen as linked to the maternal language itself, another basic component of the domestic domain, English being the language of the world outside.

While cuisine and manners have remained substantially intact at the domestic level, except for some changes discussed below, at the public level this is not the case. For formal occasions, defined in the context of the new life, people will repair to restaurants, the more elaborate of which will offer 'European cuisine' though some will serve Ghanaian food as well. Formal occasions require formal food, which tends to be defined as European. But it is the drink rather than the food that testifies to the external influence of industrial societies and the internal growth of differentiation. Bottled beer has conquered the elite market, though there is an upper echelon that prefers whisky and cognac; on the other hand the bulk of the rural population outside Muslim areas sticks to the locally brewed beer. In other words the progression: local drinks/bottled beer/spirits characterises the hierarchy: rural workers/lower elite/ upper elite, though even the latter drink mainly beer, while locally brewed spirits (*akpetashi*) are now spreading into all the country districts.

Beer is brewed and bottled in Ghana. As in other African countries, the brewing of beer was one of the first manufacturing processes to become established, just as it had already played an important part in the early industrial developments in Europe. Mathias writes of a new age of industrial brewing beginning in London in 1720 with the introduction of 'porter'. Already in the period 1578–85 there were 26 Common Brewers in London as well as the ubiquitous publican brewer, and they were the most important non-domestic users of coal; a century later London had 194 Common Brewers, none of them very large at this time but all of them operating on a commercial scale, selling beer to publicans within a radius of four to six miles which, with land transport, was the economic limit to the marketing area (Mathias 1959: xvii). One critical factor in this development of the industry was the change from ale to beer; the earlier introduction of hops from the Low Countries had added not only taste but acted as a preservative, a necessary element in the industrial product that had to travel and keep. The second factor was the development of 'porter', a heavier beer which Mathias argues was the only one suited to 'mass production' at that particular time. It was certainly the manufacturers of porter rather than of ale who became the large brewing firms at the end of the eighteenth century. Their growth depended upon developments in the trade that took place from 1720 onwards and were introduced by the 'power loom brewers', as Charles Barclay called them, who industrialised even before the major transformation of the textile industry in the 'First Industrial Revolution' (1750–1840).

In Ghana too it was beer, together with mining, that led the way. But since a number of the ingredients had to be imported – barley, malt, hops, even bottles – shortages were always occuring because the demand was constantly expanding and apparently insatiable. Under these conditions the gaining of control over these consumer products is a central feature in the local community; to have both the licence and the ability to purchase beer from the factory is a source of power as well as profit. For just as the locally brewed beer remains an essential ingredient of every social gathering among the rural LoDagaa, so today bottled beer fulfils the same function among the elite. 'Christmas without beer'! exclaimed one of my friends recently, offering an implicit but far-reaching criticism of the economy of Ghana and the military regime which partially controlled it. Some days later another friend walked some five miles to a market in Upper Volta in order to drink a bottle of beer at five cedis, one pound at the official rate of exhcange.

The new dispensation, arising out of the contact with industrial societies, has meant other significant changes of diet. For many years even the smallest markets sold canned food imported from outside. Foremost among these imports have been tins of sardines and of tomato purée. Animal protein has always been scarce and expensive to buy; so too has fish, except in some favoured locations near the coast. Sardines provide an easy means of making a rich and tasty soup, sometimes mixed with meat and often with tomatoes. Tomatoes grow well in West Africa, having been brought from America by European ships along with many others crops that have since become staples: maize, cassava, ground-nuts, squash. But they are seasonal products and hence available for only part of the year. It is the industrial process of canning that has made them available cheaply and without regard to season, that has done for meat and vegetables what the earlier methods of storing grain, beans and yams, in the granary, pot or stack, had long ago done for the staple foods; they were preserved at least through the annual cycle of production so that mankind was no longer dependent, as so often in hunting and gathering societies, on the continuous search for food for immediate consumption.

Today tins of sardines and tomato paste are no longer as ubiquitous as they have been in the recent past. As imported foods they depend very much on the state of the national economy; as early as the mid-1960s they were sometimes in short supply. In 1979 they were virtually unobtainable despite the heavy demand. This demand for canned food arises for some of the same reasons as in Europe; not only is it relatively cheap but it also provides a convenience food that makes it attractive to drivers, labourers and others who are temporarily without the domestic services of their own women and fear the services of strange ones.[1] For travellers in particular are worried about the possibility of being 'poisoned' by the food provided by persons outside their own domestic group; canned food is safe from tampering.

The demands for these foods led to efforts to process meat, fish, fruit and vegetables locally. In these attempts food, as in many other countries, had been preceded by drink. The production of beer was one of the earliest factory processes to be set up in Ghana. That was a private concern. After the Second World War a government canning industry began to process fruit and fish. In northern Ghana industrial activity is practically confined to the two plants built near Bolgatanga out of public funds for canning corned beef and tomatoes. Problems of supply, spares and management have impeded these various attempts to industrialise the processing of food. Only beer and now spirits have achieved any notable success, and the country still has to call upon external sources for much of what it consumes, or would like to consume.[2]

There has been greater success, perhaps because its production rests firmly in the hands of small local bakers, with bread. Bread and ale had been one of the mainstays of the diet of many Europeans of earlier times, but its spread is more surprising in a country where no wheat or similar grains are grown. In Europe, we noted, the northern extension of bread from the Mediterranean was associated with its use by the conquering Romans and by the missionising Christians, who sacralised this high-status food through its use in the Mass.

Give us this day our daily bread.

In Ghana the same two factors were at work. Not all European foods have had such an enthusiastic reception at the grass-roots, and one reason, as with sardines, has been its utility as a food for travellers, ready-baked, and easily transported, a food that does not render one at the mercy of the strange woman at the pot, the fear of poison, the terror of sorcery.

It is women who bake the bread that one can now buy at each small village on the roads where lorries stop for refreshment, for passengers or for loads. Two elements were necessary to start up this craft. First, wheat had to be imported, since the local grains are no good for bread, though elsewhere people make pancakes and flapjacks from millet and maize. Secondly, the methods of cooking had to be transformed by the introduction of the oven, an enclosed space with heat applied either outside by a fire or inside by embers. Ovens were of course characteristic of the Bronze Age civilisations of the Near East where they were used not only for cooking but for baking clay, for bricks, for tablets and for pots. In Africa pots were fired by building a fire on top, while bricks were dried in the sun. With the baking of bread, ovens now appeared in every small town for the first time.

More recently the baking of bread has moved from individual craft into small-scale industry. The industry began with large-scale plants established by foreign capital and then by the state. More recently it has been individual entrepreneurs, backed by bank or state loans, who have bought electric ovens so they can make bread in greater quantities than the kerbside baker.[3] The change in scale has once again led to a shift from women's work to men's.[4]

The changing situation on the culinary front is more marked in the urban areas of the south where the food of the new members of parliament, university teachers, military officers and businessmen now includes the regular addition of items such as tinned milk, tea, sugar, breakfast cereals, etc. One element in these metropolitan areas has to do with the cross-national communication that occurs in hotels, universities, businesses and government offices. Just as there is in effect an international standardisation of time, and especially of festival time (so that in northern Ghana Christmas is becoming a 'holiday', with closed offices and family reunions, for Christian, Muslim and pagan alike), so too a standardisation of food and table manners provides the language for communicating at meals, a sort of culinary Esperanto.

The changes in private, as distinct from public, diet affect children more than adults, and it is often for them that canned milk, breakfast cereals and similar commodities are seen as necessities. In Accra birthday parties for the children of the upper bourgeoisie can be very elaborate, complete with pastries and iced cakes – all the paraphernalia of a rather formal affair in a London suburb, but representing a much greater expenditure of money, time and effort, and including alcoholic drinks for the adults.

The fact that the shift in patterns of consumption centres particularly on children is partly a result of the weight given to 'child care' in the new educational system. But it also reflects a direct investment in the next generation, an effort to maintain and advance the standards of attainment that is characteristic of a group whose status depends upon its educational achievements; the birthday party represents a claim to status for the future generation as well as for the present, a status that has to be achieved in competition with others. Hence the magnitude of the investment. But investment is inevitably selective. The relatively undifferentiated treatment of the children of kin (one's classificatory 'children' terminologically) that marks indigenous society has not altogether disappeared; help is certainly offered to and sought by kinsfolk, especially in the realms of education and employment. Nevertheless the willingness to invest in children other than one's own is less in evidence, or else motivated by more pragmatic considerations. The children of kin now reside in the house as 'servants' rather than as equals. In the plan of the house itself, the servants' quarters tend to get separated from the living area after the colonial pattern. And classificatory 'children' tend now to be called 'nephews' and 'nieces', just as for them your brothers and sisters become their 'aunts' and 'uncles' rather than their 'mothers' and 'fathers'.[5] The unit of consumption tends to shift from the 'joint household' to the 'nuclear family'. At the same time there is an increase in the joint activities of husband and wife, at least as far as the financial affairs of the elite are concerned (Oppong 1974). The couple themselves are drawn together at the expense of being pulled away from collateral kin on both sides, stressing the ties not so much of affinity as of conjugality, the dyad of husband and wife. Indeed it is this process of differentiation that is sometimes described as 'the emergence of the nuclear family'. However the nuclear family did not emerge at a particular point in time – it has always been with us. On the other hand the sharpness of its boundaries has changed over time; there has been an increase in the degree of its separation from wider kin, which has been seen by many as a move in the direction of 'individualism'. This is the process we are witnessing among today's elite, and it is related to the differentiation between man and man.

The process is visible not only in consumption but also in patterns of marriage; indeed the two are related. For those individuals whose activity depends upon maintaining the connections of an economic, political or religious kind between village and town, polygynous marriage offers a way of linking together the two areas of activity, a wife in both places being the means of so doing (Fortes 1954; Clignet 1970; E. Goody 1973). But for those educated at schools who use the literate technology as a ladder of social mobility, for those who convert to Christianity and for those who adopt the Western menage, the possibility of polygyny is often excluded. Literate wives, that is, wives of the *same* rather than different backgrounds from the husband, become desirable, often imperative, at some stage in a man's career. And such wives usually insist upon monogamy. Marriage itself may become differentiated, with a husband keeping not only a legitimate spouse but also an 'outside wife', a concubine whose rights are fewer though her rewards may be greater (Harrell-Bond 1975). This differentiation of sexual partners is characteristic of European marriage rather than traditional African institutions (Goody 1976) but it is becoming increasingly widespread. Divorce provides yet another alternative. As Gibbal points out for Abidjan, social climbers simply abandon their illiterate spouses in favour of more suitable wives (1971: 197). For literacy in itself has a divisive effect on these cultures, indeed upon all cultures, since it imposes not only a dichotomy between literate and illiterate but also a ladder of achievement that discriminates between those with greater and lesser qualifications in this sphere. It is one measure of 'difference', among others, that permeates all cultures with writing.

The tendency is not simply for literate to marry literate but for like to marry like in other ways, leading to the 'destructuration' of traditional societies and to a new strategy for the social group. 'Witness the marriages between the children of the ruling class and the almost unsurmountable obstacles that townsmen, new and old, meet when they want to marry the daughter of a "big man"'.[6] Even lower down the hierarchy, parents have very precise ideas about the choice of a partner.

Children are free to choose a partner from another ethnic group but on the other hand they will be restricted by the social origin and socio-economic level of their future spouse. In this way the development of marriage practices in the towns is one of the best indices of the emergence of class society (Gibbal 1971: 197).

Thus with the advent of literacy, as well as with the increasing differentiation of belief, property and training that comes with 'modernisation', the children of different groups of the towns marry among themselves. Sub-cultures emerge; marriage goes inwards; the processes are complementary.

The direction of these changes is not determined by the world system alone. The nature of the indigenous societies is of prime importance; so too is the nature of the particular colonial encounter. In the pattern of children's birthday parties in Accra we have a clear example of the influence of a particular colonial regime upon local practice; similar parties were given by members of different ethnic groups as well as by expatriate wives. Despite the brevity of the contact, colonial regimes have had a surprisingly strong influence on some aspects of the behaviour, especially upon the food preferences, of the inhabitants of their respective territories. The first experience that spelt out the intensity of this influence came early in my first visit to northern Ghana (then the Gold Coast) when a football match had been arranged between the district team and one from the adjacent area of Upper Volta. At the time one was a British and the other a French colony. The team from the Gold Coast returned home amazed at the diet of salads they had been offered and were even more astounded at the modes of greeting adopted by their fellow-tribesmen across the boundary. On a number of occasions I have been witness to the discomfort of Ghanaians at seeing men greet one another with a kiss, despite its biblical roots, or at their difficulty in getting beer in a country flowing with wine. The sight of fellow-Africans eating a very elaborate lunch complete with wine and cheese flown in from Paris gives rise not only to a feeling that their opposite numbers have been subject to more penetrating colonial or neo-colonial pressures but to some of the same sentiments that the English at times experience in the face of the 'continent' – especially in the face of those parts of Europe that neither suffered nor enjoyed that thorough spring-cleaning of cultures carried out by the Reformation. The tastes displayed on these more formal occasions smack to both of luxury, even of excess.

The Africans concerned have not given up their indigenous form of cooking, certainly in northern Ghana, despite the modification in patterns of consumption that we have mentioned. Dependence on local crops and local cooks, combined with the continuing constraint of maternal care and kinship responsibilities, would hardly allow this to happen. But their tolerance for the strange has been largely determined by the foreigners they got. Just as they employ the English language for the new politics, religion and education, so too they use a variety of English cooking in formal contexts, without abandoning the use of their maternal tongue and their maternal recipes in other situations. This emergence of a culinary as well as a linguistic diglossia gives rise to a situation that we see as relatively stable, not simply a point in a continuing progress from one monolingual situation to the next. For the diglossia is part of an emergent system of socio-cultural stratification, a true hierarchy. For just as we have a progression at the level of the consumption of drinks (Table 1), and to a lesser extent of food, so too the other phases of the process of production and distribution display recurrent differences of the same kind, that are crudely summed up in Table 2. Crudely, because any diagrammatic representation of this kind tends to make contrasts out of continua and to disregard overlapping in favour of breaks, to set up permanent as against contextualised

Table 1　*The progression of drinks*

	Lower	Middle	Upper
Rural	Millet beer		
	Palm wine	Bottled	+Whisky
		beer	Cognac
Urban	+Home-brewed		
	sprits		

Table 2   *The differentiation of styles of life*

		Lower	Middle	Upper
Production		Wives assist on farm (rural), in market (urban)	Wives trade	Professional and trading wives
Distribution	(raw)	Granary (rural) Market (urban)	Market/store	Store
	(cooked)	Market	Local restaurant	Hotel
	(personnel)	Women	Women/men	Men
Preparation (kitchen)	(hearth)	Stones	Wood stove	Electric stove
	(containers)	Earthenware pots	Metal pans	
	(personnel)	Wives, plus kin (rural)	Wives plus 'housemaids'	Servants/cooks
Consumption (table)	(instruments)	Fingers	Fingers, spoon	Cutlery
	(containers)	Bowl	Plate	China plus tablecloth
	(place)	Floor	Table	Table
	(personnel)	Eat with same sex, men served by wives		Eat heterosexually, served by male stewards or waiters

distinctions. With this caveat the table can still serve a limited purpose in the struggle to formulate and communicate.

It was not, of course, in the sphere of food alone that the methods of industrial production made their mark on northern Ghana. In other ways too the importation of cheaper products has had far-reaching effects upon patterns of consumption in a wider sense, leading to the abandonment of local techniques in favour of reliance on the productive activity of others. The radical effects of cheap iron have been mentioned earlier. It was the same with cloth, the most important item of local manufacture in the indigenous market system.[7] In his account of pre-colonial trade Binger (1892) notes how Hausa cloth was cheaper than local products even a thousand miles away from its point of origin.

Those local products from regional centres competed against one another in a more restricted way. But yet more expensive cloths for the use of the greater courts and richer merchants of West Africa were imported across the Sahara from the Mediterranean coast, possibly even from Gujerat in India which had a flourishing export trade long before the 'expansion of Europe' – in the Middle East, in Egypt, in Indonesia and China and on the east coast of Africa.[8] The opening up of a direct route to India encouraged the import of textiles but it was essentially the cheap manufactured product of England and France, often imitating the designs and textures of the more expensive Indian goods, that swept the market from the 1840s onwards and began to make cotton goods available to a wider section of the population. In recent years such goods have become necessities in all but the most resistant tribal areas. Local factories have begun to produce the type of cloth required, but as in other spheres, the demand has increased much more rapidly than the supply of locally manufactured goods, which in any case requires large inputs of raw materials, plant and skills from overseas.

Soap and unguents are two other ingredients where all levels of the population have quickly come to depend upon the results of industrial production. So too with lighting fires where matches are now irreplaceable. In all these areas the previous technology has been virtually forgotten in a matter of fifty years. When I was in Ghana at the end of 1978, it was impossible to buy soap, or indeed virtually any industrial commodity, in the normal way, i.e. in a store or stall. Even the soap produced in Ghanaian factories had disappeared off the shelves of stores and out of the market stalls. One could occasionally find a bar at the house of a friend, for in this so-called *kalabule* economy of illicit exchange (Goody 1980), stocks of items were acquired by individuals who then sold them at higher prices in order to cope with the massive rate of inflation, the low wages and the dire shortage of commodities. Local soap produced according to traditional methods could be found in the market but it was poor in quality mainly because that technology had fallen into desuetude.

With hoes, the basic instruments of production, the situation was even worse. Not only had they disappeared from the market, but earlier knowledge of smelting iron had been lost altogether. No one was willing to revive the simple and laborious methods that had been practised until the beginning of this century. All that was on sale in the market-place were the sad remnants of old hoe blades worn thin after years of hard use. For new hoes one had to go *kalabule,* or else cross the international border to fetch back, at inordinate prices, the new hoes that had been so profitably smuggled there by those into whose hands the subsidised Ghanaian imports had fallen.

The impact of the world system

The important point is that these manufactured goods have so wide a distribution that society's dependence upon them is now very great. Imported iron, cloth and sardines are no longer 'prestige goods' or 'valuables', the *de luxe* items that Binger found in the Salaga market in 1888; they are commodities of mass commerce, staples of the local store and market, widely diffused among the population though clearly not everyone has equal access. Their adoption has been so rapid and so extensive that local craft production has virtually disappeared, except for some weaving. What happened was a case not so much of 'underdevelopment' as of 'de-evolution', the replacement of local handicraft production by goods manufactured abroad. Even when manufacture took place locally, the industrial processes were dependent upon access to raw materials and plant that had to be brought in from outside.

It is the nature of the mass importation of cloth, oil, soap and similar commodities that societies become dependent, and in some ways interdependent, on the world outside. Political regimes then become vulnerable to the consequences of external changes in the price of distribution of these goods. For such changes affect the domestic economy in a direct and very telling fashion, since they bear upon the materials of the daily meal, the evening drink, the clothes we wear, the tools we use.

It is easy to contrast, with sentimental undertones, the self-sufficiency of earlier communities with the dependency generated by the impact of industrial production, a process that has affected food as much as anything else. But it would be a mistake to imagine that pre-colonial societies in Africa were ever entirely self-sufficient, self-subsistent in any absolute sense. There already existed a division of labour, a division in the distribution of raw materials and skills, that involved exchange, not simply of the kinds referred to as reciprocity or transfers, but also trade, both local and long-distance. On the other hand, most towns were agro-towns in the sense that the vast majority of the inhabitants participated in primary food production, a very different situation from that described by Marco Polo for the huge cities of China with their immense markets and developed means of transport.

Industrialisation therefore had important effects on food which, while part of a world-wide process, were in some ways more far-reaching because of the extent of local self-sufficiency. I do not refer here to the changes associated with the 'Agricultural Revolution', nor yet to the later application of mechanisation to farming, for these processes played little part in northern Ghana until very recently. It was rather the shift to processed foods, the change in patterns of consumption resulting from the introduction of sardines and tomato paste, of bread and beer, into the diet of the country. This process is part and parcel of the changes taking place in the industrial nations where the bulk of the population is no longer directly involved in producing food, with the marginal exceptions of the working-class allotment or the kitchen garden of the middle classes. It is a shift that gives cooking a special quality in urban western society because it is partly disassociated from the preparation of food and totally separated from its production. The ingredients arrive already prepared, sometimes even ready-mixed. The flour is milled; the bread baked; the snails stuffed; the pie-crust frozen; the cheese and wine are ready for the table.

I would not wish to underplay the role of part-time production and the creation of the daily meal in industrial societies, nor that of the division of productive labour and the role of prepared food in pre-industrial ones. Little cooking is done in Hausa towns in Nigeria except in the evening, sometimes not even then. People send out to a woman in the neighbourhood who cooks food for sale (Schildkrout 1978: 128). In the Gonja town of Daboya, children in the weaving section were given a small sum of money each day to buy breakfast from a woman of that section, a practice that has been long established in other parts of northern Ghana.[9] The purchase of ready-cooked food became much more common with the growth of industrial food in those societies where husband and wife are both working (partly because of their high potentialities to consume) and where collective action (in the sense of getting together, either for consuming food or for entertainment) is minimal. When leisure activities are carried out within the domestic group itself, there is a trend towards convenience foods. Typical of this is the TV dinner, pioneered in the United States. Electronic communication involves the high consumption of goods, a heavy work-load, plus 'home entertainment'; except on festival occasions 'home cooking' becomes mainly a question of heating up.

The English equivalent of the TV dinner is that prototypical take-away dish, fish and chips, which does not even require the heating up providing it has been properly wrapped. This ready-made dish appears to be on its way out; perhaps its urban working-class origin is against it in this time of 'embourgeoisement', although the high prices of fish, fuel and labour have made their own contribution to its disappearance. The new equivalent which is higher status in content, produced by harder-working, lower-paid immigrants, is the Chinese take-away, which provides ready-made food of an only partially manufactured kind. New to this country, for in its own this way of supplying cooked food has a history going back to the Middle Ages.

These features of the urban food supply are not inventions of the post-war world. Nor is the industrialisation of food itself. As we have seen in the previous chapter, it was in the nineteenth century that many of our ancestors (or those without servants) gave up making gravy and took to Bisto. It was then that many stopped making jam and bought it at the local store.

Each transformation of the economy bearing on the productive and distributive processes has its influence on cooking. But none has been more radical in its effect than the process of industrialisation which has affected all types of modern society – socialist, capitalist, fascist, military and the whole range of 'mixed' forms. And it has affected distribution as well as production. The critical focus of distribution in the industrial economy is not the market-place, which in most advanced societies remains an ecological residue devoted to the unpacked, the uncanned, the raw. The focus is the store, the shop, the SUPER-market, the HYPER-MARKET, whether these be organised by company, cooperative or by traders.

It is difficult now to visualise a village without its shop, a town without the grocers, given all the essential food that they provide. If there is no butcher in the village, there is tinned meat in the shop. If no baker, then wrapped bread and biscuits. If no greengrocer, then cans, dried and frozen fruit and vegetables, and the whole array of imported 'necessities', tea, coffee, spices, around which the sale of basic food in the grocer's shop gradually accumulated.

The effect of this shift in production and distribution has been radical. For the trend of industrial food has been to reduce the differences within and between socio-cultural systems. Processed food is more or less the same in Ealing as in Edinburgh; the aim of the manufacturers is to get as wide and as standard a distribution as possible. Cornflakes make their appearance on Ghanaian breakfast tables; Coca Cola is available wherever the company has been able to make a profitable agreement. Because they profit from demand, such items are rarely directed at an elite or specialist market; the general aim is to cross class as well as regional boundaries. Which in turn postulates a distribution of effective purchasing power, some closing of the income gap, as between different elements in the society, and even between nations.

Nor do we underestimate the continuing regional differences, those chronicled for England by Allen (1968), those only too visible in France, let alone the ones marking the different 'Worlds' into which history and politics have divided the globe. Nevertheless the similarity of packaged foods, the range of drinks at airports, the identity of meals in international hotels, argues for a tendency towards the homogenisation of taste that accompanies the industrial processes of the world system. Nor is this only a matter of the elite. Packaged foods, like the sardines and tomato paste of Ghana, reach into ordinary homes. And now the electronic media provide an even more potent force that probes right into

189

the heart and hearth of the domestic group, influencing its preferences for food, its linguistic behaviour, its table manners. Much earlier, the mechanisation of writing meant that printed calendars and almanacs lent their weight in favour of standardisation, a process that was further stimulated by the spread of mass literacy and the industrialised production of printed material in the shape of the newspaper, carrying cooking hints, recipes and details of household management. But the close and continual contact with that combination of the oral and the visual modes embodied in the television set has reinforced this process in a most powerful manner, providing an immediate entry into the mores of different cultures, within one's own society and without. The manners of *each* group are displayed, for emulation or rejection, independently of domestic models. And the cuisine of Italy and America become as familiar as fish and chips or roast beef and Yorkshire pudding.

There is as yet little or no TV in northern Ghana. The cinemas are few and far between, the newspapers are in English and the radio not of great importance. But while the direct impact of the mass media on northern Ghana is less marked than on other parts of the Third World, the indirect effects are there. For this and other reasons the consequences of the impact of industrial food are beginning to make themselves felt, more noticeably than in areas that already had a strong culinary tradition enshrined in literate forms. The very perviousness of the oral tradition has opened the way for rapid change. Literacy is in some ways more conservative. It is these differences in the written and the oral that bring us back to the problems with which we started, the differences in the culture of cooking that are related to the modes of communication on the one hand and to the modes of production on the other.

7

Cooking and the domestic economy

In looking at the nature of cooking, and more generally at the mode of consumption and the way it is related to production, we have drawn a broad contrast, often implicitly, between the practices found even in the states and empires of Africa on the one hand, and those of the major societies of Europe and Asia on the other. This comparison was not undertaken as an exercise in taxonomy, let alone geography, but in order to throw some light on the social processes at work.

In looking at the cuisines of the Eurasian societies, we noted a set of specific characteristics:

1. The link between cuisine and 'class', with social groups being characterised by different styles of life.

2. The contradictions, tensions and conflicts connected with this differentiation. The various forms include the contradiction between ideologies of equality (which for St Francis were religious, for Djilas revolutionary and for Mencius philosophical) and ideologies of hierarchy (both in church and state), as well as the conflict, at the individual as well as the group level, between fasting acknowledged as 'good' and feasting as 'pleasurable'. In the case of the Yugoslav Djilas, the contradiction was exacerbated by the external situation, by the identification of luxury with the foreigner, or with foreign influence.

3. The increased range of ingredients and menus resulting from exchange, tribute and commerce, based on the continuing interplay between the *haute cuisine* and 'peasant' cooking, if only because the latter were the source of the basic foodstuffs.

4. The specialisation of the cuisine that restricted literacy encourages through the collection and publication of recipes.

5. The elaboration of the division of culinary labour, high-status tasks often getting transferred from women to men.

These five features mark off the pre-industrial states of Asia from those of Africa, the cuisine of the 'Asiatic' from the 'African' modes of production. In addition two further features represent differences in degree rather than in kind.

6. The close and long-standing link, so frequently the subject of

191

extended metaphor, between food and sex, between production and reproduction. The link appears not only at the level of these primary activities themselves but in the prohibitions or taboos that surround them, namely in the spheres of 'totemism' and 'incest' as well as in the concomitant prescriptions and preferences for food and for wives. It follows that the two activities central to the domestic domain, cooking and copulation, should be closely entwined, each one subject to specific prohibitions and preferences that in their turn define those important aspects of the socio-cultural system, marriage and eating.

7. The link between eating and health, the manipulation of consumption for bad (sorcery, poison) and good (medicines, antidotes), and sometimes for sex ('oysters is amorous') (Platine 1978c; Cosman 1976).

Two points deserve some further comment before we return to the major theme of differentiation. The link between literacy and the elaboration of the repertoire, not only in the sense of storage but also of programming, has been discussed in an earlier work (1977a: ch. 7) and was referred to again in the context of Arab cookery. But the terminology of culinary terms could also be affected by changes in the mode of communication, for in medieval England this was subject to a professional and, in the case of the 'Terms of Keruynge', to an 'aesthetic' elaboration. With the advent of print the cookbook, like other literary forms, opens up avenues of social mobility, for it is then possible to teach oneself the mores (the menus and the table manners) of higher-status groups by studying books on cooking, household management or 'etiquette', just as one could 'improve' agricultural practices or religious beliefs by diffusing texts or tracts to others.

But writing is not only an instrument of enlightenment, not only a tool for the extension of knowledge. Over most of the first five millenia of written cultures, from 3000 B.C. until today, societies were stratified by their access to literacy (or to literate specialists), so that writing could also be an instrument of oppression as well as of liberation. It was one method of alienating land from non-writers by means of courts and bureaucracies that necessarily privileged the use of written claims, written pledges, written testimonies, written wills, even written laws, setting these activities above the oral forms of the common man. Restricted literacy preferred the signature to the man himself, the letter of the law to the word of mouth. And so writing has been instrumental in preserving and often, as today in northern Ghana (Goody 1980), in creating, those inequalities in the rights of people to the means of production that in the past have led to social differentiation of a radical kind.

Cooking and the domestic economy

The other point that needs a further comment has to do with the sexual division of labour. Right back to the early Egyptian period, the great courts of Europe and the Mediterranean employed men as cooks. It was men who took over the female recipes of daily cooking and transformed them into the *haute cuisine* of the court. In other words the difference between high and low tended to be one between male and female. In Africa, on the other hand, women normally cooked at the courts of kings, and the menus showed little change from the recipes of ordinary life. Indeed these women were often cooking not in the role of household servants but in that of wives. Only with the colonial era did men enter the high-status role of cooking foreign foods for foreign rulers. Previously the sexual and culinary roles of women were not separated in the way they were in the European or Asian hierarchies. In the great Topkapi palace of the Ottoman rulers of the Turkish Empire, the seraglio or harem stands on the opposite side of the courtyard to the kitchen; the segregation of roles is reinforced by the whole architectural scheme.

The subsequent dissociation changes the role of women. The prehistorian, Gordon Childe, pointed out the contribution women made to the cultural developments of the Neolithic, many of which turned upon domestic activity and therefore upon the preparation of food. For the kitchen was the birthplace of many technical operations and apparatus – furnaces, gear for grinding and crushing, alcoholic fermentation, methods of preservation, and the extraction of liquids by pressure from seeds and fruit. But when these processes left the kitchen for specialist control they generally shifted from the hands of women to those of men.

In these various ways that I have listed the culinary traditions of these major cultures of Eurasia stand out in contrast to the practices of African societies, even those that had kings and courts. In Africa there was rarely any written corpus from which to draw; whereas in Eurasia the mere presence of collections of recipes widened the choice of the few, encouraged the flowering of difference and eased the introduction of the new. Even those sub-Saharan areas into which Islamic writing had spread remained little influenced by the culinary culture of the Middle East. Under Muslim tuition there was some elaboration in the merchant towns of the East African coast and in the courts and towns of northern Nigeria, another area that was in continual contact with the Mediterranean and the Near East along the sandy trade routes of the Sahara. Among the Hausa the uses of literacy were perhaps the most developed of anywhere in Black Africa; craft production, manufacture and trade were most advanced and social differences were most emphasised. So the

Hausa kingdoms, much influenced by the countries north of the desert, display an embryonic differentiation of styles of life among social groups that shows up in patterns of consumption.

These differences are the subject of the poem written early in the colonial period by al-Hājj 'Umar of Salaga on the subject of poverty, a concept that implies the opposite, riches, in the same way that slavery implies freedom. While a somewhat similar concept was found among tribal peoples such as the LoDagaa, here it is developed out of all recognition. Moreover, poverty appears in types of diet and of culinary tradition as well as in mere quantities. A translation of the unpublished poem is given in full not only because it points to differences in ways of domestic living that were based on access to wealth of one form or other, but also because it contains a partly satirical comment on the consequences of setting up a cultural hierarchy. Here again hierarchy develops its own internal contradictions which are acknowledged in the guarded criticisms of intellectuals. Guarded because the ambivalence of the comments reflects the position of the literati who in time-honoured manner are eating the cake and criticising the system at one and the same time. But this commentary is not only an expression of the internal contradictions of the emergent class structure of West Africa, for it looks over its shoulder at the traditions of early Islam with its egalitarian ideology – 'Do not wear silk or silk brocade,' 'And eat and drink and be not immoderate.' The criticism is a feature not of one but of all hierarchical systems, and bears so often on the linked activities of eating and sex.

POVERTY (TALAUCI)

by al-Hājj 'Umar, translated by I.A. Tahir[a]

In the name of God, The Merciful and The Compassionate. The blessings of God be upon our guide, Prophet Muhammed, His Relatives, His Companions, may they be blessed indeed. This is a poem in the Hausa language.

1. We begin in the name of God
   And our aim is to warn about poverty.

2. We shall list the marks of poverty
   And of wealth so you may learn about them.

3. Poverty is like a dark man with matted hair,
   Like a hunchback, like deformity and dirt,

4. Like scurvy, like mustiness and filth,
   With a body smell like rotten meat,

5. With a short neck, fat cheeks and a noseless face,
   Like the fruit of the bladder tree.

6. If he attacks a young man, he ages him,
   Deforms and contorts him into a hook.

7. If he attacks an old man,
   He makes him as thin as a whisp of straw.

8. He gets confused, bemused and senile,
   Wears rags and a mangy little hat.

9. By and by he is regarded as an old fool,
   He's insulted and called a man of real poverty.

10. If an honourable man becomes poor,
    He's looked upon as an evil man without honour to his name.

11. The poor man's words can never draw a crowd,
    His ideas must remain locked in his heart.

12. When he puts his case, even though it's valid and true,
    He's told, you lie, we refuse to listen.

13. The whole matter is distorted and confused
    Until he is made into a fool and a laughing stock.

14. Everybody looks upon the poor man as a child
    And calls him a mad bull.

15. He's called a man of no sense,
    He's called a big-for-nothing man.

16. On festivals no one puts him on the guest list;
    Only when it is all over they ask, Oh, where is so and so?

17. If he is included in a group to go visiting,
    He's never called but is later asked to follow on.

18. He stands out in a crowd
    With his threadbare trousers and cheap Zaria robe.

19. Even God Most High hates poverty,
    For The Rich One is one of His names.

20. Great men like Siddiku and Usmanu,
    Faruk and Haidara, they all hate poverty.

21. A young man who is poor is thought old
    And given the years of an aged eagle.

22. The poor man's anger is only a laughing matter.
    Who cares whether he's pleased or annoyed?

23. The poor man has no friend.
    Whoever will befriend the son of a trollop?

24. None but God loves the poor man,
    He who created him in his dire condition.

25. Every evil bedevils the poor man,
    If we speak the truth as people see it:

26. Dirty habits, stupidity and splitting the family,
    Bad language and showing off.

27. There is no evil like the poor man's
    In all this world, this we should know.

28. If he speaks pleasantly, he is asked
    Why be so bumptious?, for he is keen to cut a dash.

29. If he is quiet, he is called a loner
    Who harbours some ill-design in his heart.

30. Really, the poor man can never earn praise,
    For the moment he begins to speak they shout, 'Stop'.

31. We know you well, and in all you say
    You never utter anything worthy of agreement.

32. Even the poor man's kinsfolk run him down,
    Saying he is a relative of no worth.

33. The poor man's work is never praised
    By word of mouth or in the hearts of men.

34. If he is quick, they say, 'Oh, it's no good,
    He has cut corners just to show off to us.'

35. If he does it properly, they say he's slow,
    Delaying things he should have done the day before.

36. An amiable nature in the poor man is derided
    And to all and sundry he is as foolish as an ape.

37. If he is calm and restrained, they call him evil;
    His heart is as deep as an unfathomable well.

38. If poverty were but a real person,
    We would surely raise an army and lay siege to him.

39. Despite his evil nature, we would engage him in battle,
    Defeat him and put him in chains.

40. We would throw him down, bind and slay him,
    Then drag out his body for the vultures.

41. If it were a weed, we would pull it up,
    Dry it and burn the evil thing.

42. If it were water, we should never drink it;
    Even if called there, we would never go.

43. If we are shown the path of poverty,
    We won't follow it but rather (go the other way).[b]

44. The poor man's wives disgrace him;
    If he calls, they never reply.

45. If he brings home grain, his wife throws it away
    And says his corn is nothing but chaff.

46. If he tries his utmost to give her a treat,
    She says, 'Look, your meat is nothing but muscle.'

47. If he complains she says, 'There, there,
    You never speak the truth, now do you?'

48. If he gets annoyed and calls her to order,
    She retaliates with, 'Your mother's arse.'

49. She pulls his beard and tweaks his lips
    And exclaims 'You bastard, you stray dog.'

50. She calls him a simpleton, a faint heart
    Who curls up like a weed.

51. If he's hurt and strikes her,
    She gives him a blow with her pestle.

52. She cries, 'You're so miserable,
    You don't even own a goat.'

53. I see this question (of poverty)
    As a source of degradation in this world.

54. Pay attention and listen to this poem,
    For though I appear to jest, I am speaking the truth.

55. A father and a mother with no riches
    Are not really loved and trusted in the heart.

56. A father and his son, a mother and her daughter,
    Come to blows because of poverty.

57. A poor man's words never earn him praise;
    His honey is called the juice of sour fruit.[c]

58. If he brings firewood, he's told it's green,
    And his sweetmeats are adulterated with soot.

59. His daughter never looks beautiful;
    They say she's as stocky as a parrot.

60. Her head is bald, her cheeks are bloated,
    Her fat mouth is like the stump of a tree.

61. She is bow-legged, has no buttocks,
    And her hands are shaped like gourds.

62. She is dirty and reeks of body odour;
    When she passes, she smells like a sewer.

63. If she's beautiful, she's said to be brazen,
    Like a hussy who has no family.

64. Oh let's hate poverty with all our hearts,
    To live with poverty is impossibly difficult.

65. In times of famine the poor man's food
    Is the leaves of jute, the locus tree and *gasaya.*[d]

66. Cassava, *taura, gaude* and *tsada,*[e]
    And *dinya,*[f] *tafasa*[g] and *rujiya,*[h]

67. And *faru, gonda*[i]-and shea-fruit[j]
    And wild water melon,[k] real marks of poverty.

68. A poor woman is rejected in marriage
    And is decked out with all manner of faults,

69. A dirty slut who abandons the house,
    One who is bald and unkempt.

70. If a poor malam walks by,
    They say 'What brings this mad man here?'

71. They say his learning has touched his mind;
    And he's made to seem an imbecile and a laughing stock.

72. If he cites the authority of doctrine, he's ignored;
    And if he quotes the Koran extempore, they say:

73. 'His madness came on in the early morning.'
    And his neighbours add, 'No, it came on yesterday.'

74. If dark, his daughter is likened to a scorpion,
    And people wonder if she is a piece of burnt food.

75. If light-skinned, they say that's too bad,
    Such excessive whiteness belongs to an albino.

76. If she's short, they say she's ugly,
    Far too lumpy like a fat seed potato.

77. If she's tall, they say it's too much;
    Such excessive height, what an amazon!

78. You have heard of the marks of poverty.
    Pay heed, prepare yourselves to search for wealth.

79. Mount a caravan and go up to Fatoma,[l]
    Return through Bobo and on to Daboya.

80. Turn on to Jiji and then back to Duri,
    Proceed to Mossi and then to Harkiya.

81. Return to Salaga,^m go on to Kumasi,
    Turn to Gunfi and thence to Agaya.ⁿ

82. Kano isn't far, go beyond it
    To Wadai and come back to Zaria.

83. Touch on Kura to buy turbans of black cloth,
    Come back through Jega, Tadfu and on to Gaya.

84. Follow through Saye and come back through Mangu,
    Turn on to Dagomba and come to Kubya.

85. The search for wealth is binding^o upon us,
    If only to provide for our lives in this world.

86. Fasting, marrying, naming and the Beiram offering,^p
    Buying books, all these require wealth.

87. Giving *zakka*, offering alms and feeding orphans,
    Helping your neighbours, all these require wealth.

88. Oh God most High, keep us from want,
    From poverty, disease and hunger.

89. Now we want to list the marks of wealth;
    To hear them is so soothing to the heart.

90. The wealthy man is respected by people
    And sought after as a relation and friend.

91. If he talks, everybody gathers round,
    'Oh, you've spoken the truth and we all agree.'

92. Often the rich man invents a fantastic lie
    And people say, 'He's no fool, come and listen.'

93. If he's noisy and bumptious
    They say 'Oh he's such a sport, such lively company.'

94. They say he's so in tune with the world,
    He's so full of humorous anecdotes.

95. If he tells lie upon lie of an incredible kind,
    They're all touched up and made into truths.

96. He is the wisest, and oh, his sagacity,
    He has scarcely an equal in all the world.

97. The singers make him drunk with praise,
    His virtues are chanted all over town.

98. Come and see what a great man he is,
    As handsome as an enchanted spirit.

99. His father is so and so, his mother so and so,
    His grandfather so and so, that you should know.

100. His son is so and so, his daughter so and so,
     And his grandson so and so, go ask and find out.

101. He gives away the trousers as well as the robe,
     Together with money, grain and a young bull.

102. He gives away women's cloths and baskets of corn,.
     And all his gifts are offered with thanks on his part.

103. Whether it's true or it's a lie,
     They accept it all and repeat it to everyone.

104. The wealthy man is the only wise man.
     People exclaim, surely there's no one else like him.

105. If he's silent, moody and forbidding,
     They say he's discreet, honourable and truthful.

106. They say he doesn't speak out of turn.
     Such a discerning man, where is his equal?

107. His daughter is never ugly in anyone's eyes,
     They say she's as beautiful as a gazelle.

108. 'Look at those lovely buttocks and such beautiful teeth,
     Her neck is as long and graceful as a swan's.

109. She is tall and slender, her eyes white as milk
     And her skin is as lovely as a water buck's.'

110. They say, 'Oh, how many children she will have
     And how many bounties are sure to flow from her.'

111. She wears a *barage* slip and a *hadaya* cloth[q]
     And is bedecked in silver bangles and ankle rings.

112. Her hands are so soft for she never grinds corn,
     Pounds grain or sifts flour.

113. If she is very dark, they say that's good,
     For her blackness is the type that glistens and shines.

114. If she is very light, they say 'That's pleasingly
     White; she looks like an Arab girl.'

115. If she is dumpy, they say 'That's nothing,
     Look how becomingly she moves.

116. Her stature is just perfect and fits her
     Like the nose on a face and the navel on a belly.'

117. If she's very tall, they say 'That's becoming,
     Her height, long neck and beauty all combine.

118. Her height fits with a good figure,
     Her neck is beautifully arranged with gold jewelry.'

119. Of suitors she has up to ten;
    They say, with such a woman is the world taken by storm.

120. She has large breasts, no, waterpots;
    Her eyes are bright like a wood pigeon's.

121. When she marries, wealth is heaped up,'
    For she'll live like the daughter of a rich man.

122. Property, money and clothes in plenty
    Are carried round to show the town.

123. If a rich man dresses shabbily,
    They say he's a follower of the ascetic way.

124. They say he cares little for the things of the world,
    Seeking after God and scorning ostentation.

125. Should he be dressy, they say he's thankful to God,
    A man of taste and of so good a nature.

126. His wives respect him, you know,
    They obey and love him for his wealth.

127. They kneel down and give way to him,
    They avoid' him and hide their faces in deference.

128. If he commands them to stop this or that,
    Saying 'I do not like it', they reply, 'We obey.'

129. Whether he gives them anything or not,
    They are content as long as he amasses wealth.

130. A poor man may feed his wives
    Even better than a rich man.

131. It avails them nothing when it's gone,
    Like water poured into a sieve.

132. It's futile for a poor man to give gifts to women,
    For even if he does, it gets him nowhere.

133. When a man of learning comes into wealth,
    People say, 'Oh, he's a real sheikh, quite an expert.'

134. If he chants his lessons, they say, 'How lovely,
    Sweet as the sound of the *goge* violin.'

135. If he asks a favour of God, it is granted;
    His prayer is as swift and efficacious as an arrow.

136. What a great malam, what a well-kept house,
    A man of order, never succumbing to the caprices of his heart.

137. Men listen to his sayings and obey them,
    For surely he received them in a dream.

138. Even during a famine, the rich man's
    Diet remains the delicious *taliya*,[t]

139. And *kaki*[u] rice cake with rich gravy,
    Soft thick porridge mixed with rich gravy,

140. *Kuskus*[v] and *chacchaka*[w] mixed together
    And bathed in a rich juicy stew.

141. When you see a rich man's house,
    You know what wealth is, even before you're told.

142. The poor man's house is always unkempt,
    Dusty and littered, overgrown with thornbush.

143. His room is narrow and old-fashioned in design,
    Its interior caked with soot, webs and grime.

144. The marks of poverty are only one hundred and ten,
    Whoever wants to know them, let him ask around.

145. The marks of wealth are a thousand two hundred,
    Of this there can be no shadow of doubt.

146. If you observe the world, you'll know them;
    Even if you're not taught them, you'll learn.

147. The rich man has the king for a friend,
    Together with the learned and the old men with children.

148. Oh, calm yourselves from the harshness of this poem.
    The poor man I fancy is now annoyed.

149. This is where we end our sitting, for we want
    To finish this talk because of exhaustion.

150. Let us pray the Most High to give us wealth
    And keep us from that crippling scourge.

151. In the name of Muhammad the Most Exalted
    And of Moses, Jesus and of Armiya,

152. I thank God that I have finished
    This poem on the marks of wealth and poverty.

153. May blessings and honour be added
    Upon the Messenger Muhammad, the father of Rakiya.

154. I started it before noon on Wednesday
    And finished it on Thursday without difficulty.

155. A thousand years today since the Hijra
    And three hundred added to these, following close behind.

156. (This verse adds another few years but is not clear).

157. As for the month, it's the last Rab'iu[x]
   And eight days have passed since its beginning.

Notes:

   a. Manuscript IASAR/371, deposited in the library of the Institute of African studies, Legon, Ghana, written by al-Ḥājj 'Umar b. Abī-Bakr of Kano, Salaga and Kete-Krachi, c. 1923. See 'Writings in Gonja' by J. Goody and J. Wilks, in J. Goody (ed.) 1968. Translated by I.A. Tahir, December 1969.

   b. Word unclear.

   c. Tsamiya.

   d. A bush.

   e. Three wild fruits.

   f. A black berry.

   g. A bush.

   h. A wild tuber.

   i. Two wild fruits.

   j. kadanya.

   k. duma.

   l. Spelt Fartoma. Bobo Dioulasso is in Upper Volta, Daboya is a salt and weaving town in Gonja, nothern Ghana.

   m. Salaga was the great trading centre of Gonja.

   n. Or Gaya.

   o. wajib.

   p. Gifts made on the birthday of the Prophet.

   q. Both are expensive Hausa cloths.

   r. Gara: the property a bride takes along when she goes to her husband's home.

   s. In the special sense of the word, meaning 'respect'.

   t. A rich man's food, made from wheaten flour.

   u. A wheat savoury.

   v. A North African dish, *couscous.*

   w. Meat roasted on a skewer, a North African dish.

   x. i.e. Rab'iu Sani.

The poem is clearly a product of literate culture, with its emphasis on listing the attributes of abstract concepts, even enumerating them in a precise fashion (verse 144). And the literate culture is not so much an endogenous growth but an adjunct of Islam, prescribing the form of verse, the mode of address and farewell, and in some ways the content as well. The poem is part of a wider literary tradition. But it is also a product of a social system that was beginning to approach the hierarchical regimes of Europe and Asia, not only in the use of writing for administration and trade but also in its organisation of production, much of it by slaves, in agriculture, trade and manufacture. Just as economic activities differentiate, so too does food and clothing, rich clothes being appropriate for the wealthy. The daughters of the rich take property with them into marriage; the daughters of the poor hardly get the chance, and certainly not the choice, of marrying. While some of the content of the poem is undoubtedly 'literary', it does indicate the direction in which the society was developing under the influence of Islam, of manufacture and of trans-Saharan trade.

In general, African cultures, even the cultures of states, displayed greater cultural homogeneity, greater culinary uniformity (and indeed 'poverty') than the Eurasian ones we have already discussed. At the end of the seventeenth century the Dutch factor, Bosman, offers a general view of the state of affairs on the West Coast of Africa:

I have hinted with what sorry and how little Food the *Negroes* content their Children; which would hardly be possible if they fared deliciously themselves. But they are not guilty of this sort of Intemperance, but live rather too soberly, Two pence a day being sufficient to diet one of them. Their common Food is a Pot full of Millet boiled to the consistence of Bread, or instead of that Jambs and Potatoes; over which they pour a little Palm-Oyl, with a few boiled Herbs, to which they add a stinking Fish. This they esteem a nice Dish; for 'tis but seldom they can get the Fish and Herbs: As for Oxen, Sheep, Hens or other Flesh, they only buy that for Holy-days: Of which more in another place. The *Negroes* are not so sparing in their Diet because they don't desire better Food, of which we have sufficient Proof when they eat with us, for they are then sure to satiate themselves with the best at the Table at that rate, as if they were laying in for three days. Nor is it for want of Money that they live thus, but only out of pure sordid Covetousness.

I have been sometimes of Opinion that they thought all dear things unwholesome. The Diet I have described is that of the Commonalty; nor do the Rich fare much better: They allow themselves a little more Fish, and a few more Herbs. For an extraordinary Dish they take Fish, a handful of Corn, as much Dough and some Palm-Oyl, which they boil together in Water; and this rhey [*sic*] call *Mallaget*; and is, I can assure you a Lordly Entertainment amongst them; and, to speak truth, 'tis no very disagreeable Food to those who are used to it, and is very wholesome in this Country. (1705[1967]: 123–4).

Bosman's description fits with what seems to have existed further inland in pre-colonial times, and even today in those parts little influenced either by the new styles of life created by 'modernisation', or by the earlier modes of conspicuous consumption linked with the merchant cultures of the coast. For both among the centralised Gonja as well as among the tribal LoDagaa, the cooking of rural Africa continues to be simple and relatively undifferentiated. Adults tend to receive more than children, men than women, chiefs than commoners. Otherwise the similarities in eating are remarkable. Even in the great kingdom of Ashanti cooking seems to have been much the same in royal households.

Cooking and the domestic economy

Contrasting their form of status differentiation with that of European or coastal societies, Arhin notes that there was some difference in the food of different groups.

> The ownership of slaves enabled the king and chiefs to cultivate larger farms and there maintain a larger table than the rest who had access to the king's or chief's table. The meals of the king and chiefs were different from, and better than, those of the commoners: the former had 'soup of dried fish, fowls, beef or mutton... and ground nuts stewed in blood'; the soup of the latter was concocted of 'dried deer, monkeys flesh, and...the pelts of skins'. (1968: 37–8, quoting Bowdich 1819: 319)

However Bowdich, on whose observations Arhin bases his comments, goes on to remark:

> The higher class could not support their numerous followers, or the lower their large families, in the city, and therefore employed them in plantations, (in which small crooms were situated,) generally within two or three miles of the capital, where their labours not only feed themselves, but supply the wants of the chief, his family, and more immediate suite. (1819: 323)

Certainly we find some differences in the styles of life of the holders of high office, and to a lesser extent of their kin. Part of this difference has to do with the greater consumption of cloth and other scarce products. Often, however, it is a question of taboo. Taboos, avoidances, prohibitions, offer ways of distinguishing a group or an office which are alternatives to the transformation of behaviour into a distinct sub-culture. Or, from another angle, a sub-culture can be viewed as an extension of the field of prohibited and enjoined behaviour. But they are linked with different forms of social organisation, the hierarchic and the hieratic, which rest on different productive systems.

Certainly there was an elaboration of table manners in royal courts in Africa. As in fifteenth-century England, special individuals were employed to taste the king's food before he touched it. But the court remains, for the purposes of consumption, the domestic household writ large. One finds neither the elaboration of functionaries[1] nor the transfer of cooking and other household tasks from women's to men's work.[2] The household of the court reduplicates that of the commoner.

At the level of social groups, the culinary culture was relatively unitary. Individual distinctions there are for these holders of office, but there seems little by way of group differentiation leading to the formation of different types of cuisine. As we have seen in Gonja, at times of the great ceremonies much is made of the fact of eating out of a common pot, not always literally, but stating in a metaphorical way that the food, the cuisine, is one. And on these occasions it is eaten communally.

205

Cooking, cuisine and class

In all societies the intake of food, the eating itself, has some collective aspects, especially at festivals where the consumption of *larger* quantities and often of *special* foods takes place in a communal situation. But the household too involves communal eating. As the Prophet remarked, 'Eat together and do not eat separately, for the blessing is with the company' (*Saḥīḥ Bukhārī*, ed. Ali, 1951: 356). On the other hand, dealing with the excretion of what one has eaten is essentially a private process, and individual act. Public input, private output. Eating alone is the equivalent of shitting publicly. The privy (encapsulating the private) is for one; the dining room for the many.

To eat alone is in a way equivalent to marrying in. African kings may be required, for reasons of state, to eat on their own, just as they may be required to commit 'incest'. But normally they eat in company and are subject to few of the collective prohibitions that achieved their apogee in India, and that prevented upper levels of the hierarchy from dining with or marrying members of lower castes. Marrying-in and dining-in go together and both are associated with a deep concern with concepts of ranked purity (Yalman 1963), of difference (Pocock 1957) and of hierarchy (Dumont 1966).

The contrast should not be taken too far. Clearly there were some in-marrying strata in Africa, and it was precisely those that tended to elaborate different cuisines.[3] Such was the case in the kingdom of Ruanda where pastoral Tutsi ruled agricultural Hutu, the two differing greatly in the foods they prized and ate. The political situation was intricately linked to the domestic domain.

In most of Africa the link was of a different kind. Even in the courts of kings the kitchen personnel normally consist of wives, with some outside help from slaves and now from children, foster-children and housemaids. Wives came from many groups and strata in the society. Households were often polygynous and marriage frequently took place outside one's own descent or status group. Hence any differences in culture that existed would tend to get ironed out at the domestic level; recipes would be exchanged, manners merged, tasks shared, customs compared, and children raised by 'mothers' of differing origins.[4] This tendency to out-marriage, as others such as Tillion (1966) have observed, contrasts directly with many Middle Eastern, European or Asian societies where groups and sub-groups tend to in-marry, to protect their purity, to develop their differences; like tends to marry like. The cultural and political implications are profound; the theories of those who have seen in out-marriage the origin of human culture, the control of hostilities or the genesis of community, would lead us to expect heterogeneity for homogeneity, segregation for integration, opposition for cooperation. The terms are exaggerated. But even in African states,

206

we find that the tendency for strata to differentiate themselves culturally is muted by marriages across the internal boundaries. Equally, marriage across external boundaries was rare precisely because of the strong emphasis on cultural homogeneity, on the 'tribe' (or 'nation') rather than the 'class' (Goody 1969). Some have argued that the strength of African kingdoms lay in the identification of *le pouvoir* and *le sacré*. I would rather point to the advantages both for the rulers and the ruled of what Georg Simmel and, following him, Max Gluckman have called 'the web of group affiliations' or 'cross-cutting ties'.

The nature of the relations between the strata on which this policy depended, that is, the relations of production in the most general sense, was linked in turn to specific features of the mode of production. It is the nature of these features that must make us beware of applying in too facile a way concepts of socio-economic structure, of class or even of cooking that have been derived from the European scene. For we are faced here with basic differences related to the mode of agricultural exploitation, where the absence of advanced agriculture in the shape of either the plough or elaborate irrigation influences the nature not only of productive relations but of interaction on a much wider front.

Swidden agriculture, shifting cultivation, is typical of Africa and is well described in Audrey Richard's account of the Bemba of Zambia to which I have earlier referred. It is also found areas of the Eurasian continent where the investment in land (e.g. irrigation ditches and water tanks) or in mechanisation (e.g. the plough and trained oxen) was small. It is the kind of agriculture identified with the hoe, sometimes existing on the fringes of plough civilisations, as occasionally in Russia[5] and among the assarters of Europe, as well as more centrally among the South-East Asian cultivators such as the Mnong Gav of the high plateau of Vietnam, described by Georges Condominas (1957) under the attractive title of 'Nous avons mangé la forêt...'. It is the agriculture of the Kachin of Highland Burma as distinct from the immigrant Shans from China (Leach 1954).

The introduction of simple agriculture of this kind was an outcome of what Childe called the Neolithic Revolution. In the hunting societies of Australia, foods of course distinguished one clan from another; this one prohibited what another ate. But the differentiation was vertical rather than horizontal; taboos applied to a limited range of objects and they related to ingredients rather than to cooking. The main method of cooking in the Palaeolithic was roasting and smoking since boiling required some man-made receptacle. However cultures such as the Eskimo made little use of fire in the preparation of food, the major part of which was eaten raw. But other techniques of cooking were found. Food was steeped in water heated by hot stones to make it more palatable. Elsewhere other ways of food preserving and preparing food developed, such as drying in the sun, freezing, and so on.

The initial shift from the collection of food by means of hunting and gathering to its production by means of farming was accompanied by little horizontal differentiation either of classes or of cooking. The collection of vegetable foods as distinct from the killing of wild animals was often in the hands of women, and under simple agriculture they often seem to have made a major contribution to the growing of food crops, as well as developing the new forms of food preparation which the Neolithic technology of pottery permitted. Using the digging stick or hoe, the amount of land that each individual could cultivate was necessarily limited, which in turn restricted the total amount of foodstuffs that could be produced. By and large holdings were relatively equal, and land was not scarce. There were of course always pockets with higher densities. In some states land was cultivated by slaves but *per capita* productivity remained low, especially in the savannah areas. Consequently there were limited possibilities for developing different styles of life based upon primary production, and it is critical to note that the simpler, shifting cultivation of Africa did not lead to the growth of landlordism, of rent or of serfdom. The political lord was rarely the economic lord he was in Europe, not at least in relation to the basic agricultural resources. It has been argued that feudal systems are marked by the subdominant role of the economy as against the polity. The implications of the statement apply with yet greater force to the non-feudal kingdoms of Africa. Kwame Arhin has acutely observed that the important West African state of Ashanti belonged to a category of society where

the bases of differentiation have to be sought, not in differences of wealth, but in other sectors of social organization and values; for instance, as among the interlacustine Bantu or in the Northern Nigerian Emirates, in the...military/political organization of society. In these societies what M.G. Smith calls 'prestige distribution' is tied up with association with government and power. Upward or downward status mobility depends on the increasing favour or disfavour with the ruler incurred in service in his household or administration or on the battlefield. In contradistinction to the rule in industrialized societies, economic position depends on political status (1968: 34).

The point is well made, but the distinction has initially more to do with the nature of agricultural production than with industrialisation itself. For it was the move from extensive shifting cultivation by means of the hoe to the intensive forms of farming linked with irrigation and the plough that provided the possiblity of large-scale surplus and laid the socio-economic foundation for a cultural hierarchy. Significantly it was in Ancient Egypt that historical evidence for the emergence of a high and low cuisine first appears.

The intensification of agriculture had two effects relating to internal differentiation. First, the increased yields could maintain and were made possible by non-producers such as craftmen, priests, landlords and rulers generally. Secondly, the capacity to cultivate larger areas meant an increase in differences among the farmers themselves. Because of the greater efficiency of the plough and the energy expended by the draught animals, one man alone could now farm substantially more land than another. Not all was immediate gain. Animals require feeding, so that a proportion of the crop had to be kept aside for this purpose. And there are some situations where the plough is less useful than the hoe. Hill farms, swampy land, stony ground, frontier areas, all present difficulties for certain types of plough. Some historians of nineteenth-century Ukraine have claimed that there was a reversion from the deep to the shallow plough (see Smith 1959: 78). Increased population and smaller holdings might make it difficult to support the animals needed for the heavier plough, especially if there is less communal pasture available.[6]

However, where the growth in *per capita* production permits differences as well as an increase in consumption, we may expect the emergence of variations in styles of life. Insofar as these differences are related to agriculture, they are based upon continuing rights in the basic means of production, that is land. Other groups depend upon the benefits of bureaucratic or managerial activity, but these are less stable since they are based in part on individual achievement and hence liable to greater fluctuation from generation to generation. In order to maintain their livelihood and their way of life, the benefits deriving from land have to be passed on in some form to the children, both male and female. Daughters are usually provided for, directly or indirectly, by means of a dowry or by inheritance, while sons seek and are sought by marriage partners with the same or better prospects as they have themselves. In this way sub-cultures emerge and consolidate; difference permeates society.

One key aspect of this process is suggested by the words attributed to Muhammed: This [the plough] does not enter the house of a people but it brings ingloriousness with it'.[7] The implications of this passage are disputed, but one commentator remarks: 'The idea is that the farmer, attached to the glebe, has to submit to the exactions of the central authorities and, in particular, to pay the taxes which the nomad can escape by moving elsewhere. He becomes sedentary and has to live with his neighbours' (Tillion 1966: 191). The ability to produce a 'surplus' means the possibilty of it being taken away or voluntarily handed over.

For a man may now have to contribute part of his earnings to the national state, to the local nobility, or to both. Systems of rural taxation are indeed often directly linked to the plough, as in early Russia (Smith 1977: 30).

So agricultural development brings differentiation to the countryside, leading to another form of 'ingloriousness', the deprivation experienced by those people who have too little land, too few animals or no plough. Only by the elaborate process of regular redistribution,[8] said to have been a feature of the Russian *mir*, can one avoid the inequalities that the plough brings with it.[9] Even when the land has been equally redistributed by this means, there remains the inequality of the landlord in whose interest the equalisation may have been carried out. But redistribution is rare and elsewhere inheritance perpetuates these differences and modifies the corporate identity of 'tribe' and 'land'. For when women as well as men are endowed, to maintain their status, which sometimes involves the transfer of land as well as valuables, their marriages inevitably reshape the form of corporate capital. Despite the complex methods adopted to try and avoid dispersal, such as marrying cousins or exchanging fields, the corporation is threatened. In any case endowments vary according to parental resources, both for men and for women, so that 'individualism' prevails on another front. Muslim law, which is sometimes held to be anti-feminine in this respect, works in just this way, as Tillion clearly sees:

In effect, the Koran requires that the daughter received a part of the property of her parents, and that the husband gives his wife a sum of money when they marry, which she often offers to her father, converted into traditional gifts, or which she uses herself according to her liking (1966: 158).[10]

In such societies not only men but women too are differentiated, in marriage, in domestic arrangements, in culture and in cooking.

We have set up a contrast between African and Eurasian states and a comparison between African states and tribes. There is one junction point to look at, and perhaps 'test', the relationship between production and differentiation, between plough and cooking, namely Ethiopia, which lies geographically inside the African continent but culturally outside. For unlike the rest of the continent south of the Sahara, the plough dominates the agricultural life of many Amharic communities. The visitor from Black Africa is immediately struck by the neatly laid out fields that impose their pattern on the natural landscape, for the patterns of fields are closely linked to the use of the plough. 'Ploughing', writes Levine, is 'a year-round occupation.... The central position... in the world of the Amhara peasant is shown by the fact that the word for his vocation *irshā*, literally means 'ploughing' (1965: 59).

Cooking and the domestic economy

In the culture of 'class' the gap with the rest of Africa, West Africa at least, is equally apparent. In imperial times the visitor was impressed by the social distance observed on the streets of the capital of Addis Ababa, whether in dress, demeanour or approach. By contrast the gay, jostling crowds of West African cities show little respect for place or person. In Ethiopia, different ranks and sub-groups still wore their traditional dress; in West Africa today it would be difficult to distinguish people by this criterion except on ceremonial occasions. The rich, embroidered *kente* cloth of Ashanti became a kind of national dress of anyone wealthy enough to afford it, even among people originating in tribal areas where this or any type of cloth had never been used. More recently the northern smock has taken on a similar pan-Ghanaian role.

The respect that marks the relations between classes in Ethiopia is very clearly brought out in the remarks made by a Gondare student when he drew the contrast with other parts of Africa.

In the midst of my studies in Western Europe, I had the chance one summer to visit a number of West African countries and then to return home and spend some time in Gondar. I had not thought very highly of my people before that trip, and what I experienced was a great surprise. What I found – what we have, that I did not find in the African countries I visited – is a special sort of dignity of manner. (Levine 1965: 53)

The dignity the student observed is in part the respect intrinsic to an aristocratic society, one which arises out of the differentiation between stratified sub-cultures. In his study of the Amhara Levine speaks of a 'gentry sub-culture' that inculcates special skills and manners, and spares its children from the menial drudgery that is allocated instead to servants and retainers. Above all, he observes, the style of life of the nobility is coloured 'by a seemingly unlimited command of deference' (1965: 157). The assessment of deference and the evaluation of authority are not simple tasks. But the contrast does seem valid, even with African states; it relates to the problem raised by the Prophet's comment on the plough, for in those societies the authority of the bureaucratic state and the position of the landlord reach down into the fabric of domestic life itself in a way that seems qualitatively different from the equivalent relations in most other parts of Africa.

Leaving aside this dangerous area of conjecture on the comparative sociology of deference and authority, let us return to a more substantive area, that of cooking itself.

Until recent events overwhelmed the ancient kingdom, conspicuous consumption took the form of a surfeit of servants who performed a variety of household tasks and each of whom had to be fed from the table of the lord. The traveller d'Abbadie observed the situation in the previous century. 'A lord of even mediocre importance names his seneschal, his provost, his guards, a foreman of domestics, a chief baker, a butler, a square, and various captains and pages; then he sets up a hierarchy often in ridiculous disproportion to his position' (1868: 374–5). As in medieval England, the organisation of the noble household placed a great emphasis on provisioning, preparing and serving food. The table was a common one, but the cuisine was internally differentiated.

> What sauce, my lords, was on your plate?
> We had but peas; 'twas fish you ate.
>
> (Levine 1965: 255)

The implication is not only of difference in kind and quantity of raw materials but of cuisine too. The basic elements of *wat* (sauce or stew) and *injera* (bread) were not the same in noble as in commoner households. While the cuisine of the gentry sub-culture bears a general resemblance to that of the peasant Amhara, it lays more stress on exotics derived from the trade in high-cost spices, cloves from Zanzibar, cardamom, cinnamon and black pepper from China, India or Indonesia. With these ingredients the flavour of the food of the well-to-do bears a resemblance to that of South-East Asia,[11] certainly in contrast to that of West Africa which is largly dependent on salt and pepper alone.

The cuisine of Ethiopia does not seem to have been elaborated in literary works. The only text I know is of recent date, impregnated with the strong flavour of 'domestic science'. *The Empress Menan School Cook Book* (Addis Ababa, 1945) was composed from recipes submitted by students and staff of the school. While the total range of the recipes is not great, the sub-varieties of dish are considerable, much more so than in works from other parts of sub-Saharan Africa where much simpler cookbooks have begun to make their appearance for courses in 'home economics' ('domestic science'), for community education and for similar activities.[12]

One striking though debatable indication of the limited nature of African cooking in contrast to Eurasian, limited both in writing and in practice, emerges from the illustrated Time – Life series on 'Foods of the World' which includes books on France, Italy, India, China and so on. The African volume is interestingly different. Of the eight chapters, four deal with the cookery of South Africa, one with Portuguese Africa, and the sixth with the Highlands (formerly known as the 'White Highlands') of East Africa. A further chapter is devoted to 'The Ancient World of Ethiopia' which I see as falling within the area of differentiated cuisines. The remaining chapter covers the rest of Africa south of the Sahara, that is, the whole of non-colonial, non-Ethiopic Africa. Even here the author, Laurens van der Post, can find so little to say about indigenous cooking that he has broadened the scope and calls the chapter 'New Cuisines for New Nations'.

The shape of this book does more than reflect the views of its author, personal as those may be.[13] The New Nations are properly contrasted with Ancient Ethiopia from the standpoint of cooking, not because their history is any shorter but because they lacked the same kind of elaboration of courtly culture. Ethiopia was the only society that was based on both literacy and on the plough, and hence closer to the Eurasian model.

We have tried to distinguish the kind of cultural organisation, and specifically of cooking, of the pre-colonial African states and the major societies of Europe, Asia and the Middle East, what I have called hieratic as distinct from hierarchical societies.[14] Differences in socio-cultural organisation of these pre-industrial societies were related to the type of agriculture and in particular to the nature of the means of production, for example, the hoe, the plough and the tractor. Not that these factors were the only important ones, and developments in the means of communication were also stressed. But the general nature of the cuisine bears a close link to the basic productive processes, to the crops grown (oil/butter; wine/beer), to the productivity of agriculture and all that the 'surplus' implies, including the ensuing conflicts over the distribution of resources.

In stressing the link between the nature and distribution of resources and patterns of consumption, I have not tried to seek out a single factor to explain every feature of the culture of the kitchen, but rather to explore the extent this can account for differences in time and space. The method will not recommend itself to those who find it uncomfortable to work with more than one propositional frame. But such an approach should require no defence.

The subjects and methods of sociological enquiry make elemental binarism an unsatisfactory guide, even when the proferred 'theories' have some value in directing the enquiry in one direction rather than another. The analysis of cooking, for example, can never be a matter of ascertaining 'meaning' alone, if by that we imply meaning to the actor. Actors in any case never come singly, except as favoured 'informants'. A complex system of sub-cultures cannot be analysed in such simplistic, individualistic terms, especially when the culture of a ruling class may have an international rather than a national reference. Symbolic structures, as Mintz has reminded us, are not outside time; the boundaries of the meaning of an item of food may extend far beyond the context in which it is produced or consumed (1979: 71). An understanding of a set of activities needs to take into account the hermeneutic dimension wherever this is relevant, together with the various levels of cryptophoric meaning. But the sociological analysis of meaning must also take into account the social dimensions of the actors involved, a task that inevitably raises the problem of their roles and relations, their position in the hierarchy, their membership of one society as against another and their position in the world system. The concern with culture must not exclude the social; the analysis of relationships has to include an examination of the elements so related.

I am aware that too little attention has been paid to the ritual, symbolic and cosmological aspects of food. This neglect arises partly because of the work done on those aspects of the subject by many contemporary anthropologists, in Zahan's book on the Dogon, *La Viande et la graine* (1969), in the works of Lévi-Strauss on South American myth, in studies of witchcraft and *les mangeurs d'hommes*, the coven's meal of the victim and its relation to disease, in accounts of festival meals and of sacrifices to the gods, such as I have myself presented for the LoDagaa in *Death, Property and the Ancestors* (1962). Sacrifice itself can be interpreted as left-overs of the gods as well as an aspect of commensalism and communion. In France the classical scholars Detienne and Vernant have discussed *La Cuisine du sacrifice en pays grec* (1979), and the former has examined the role of aromatics in ritual in *Les Jardins d'Adonis* (1972). If I have not followed up these paths, it is only because a solution to my particular problem seemed to lie elsewhere, not because I wish to allocate a universal pre-eminence to the mode of production, let alone to the means of production.[15]

To claim that one has to see the ritual cuisine in the context of the domestic is, again, not to give universal primacy to the economic, any more than the reverse would privilege ideology, or myth in a similar way. To assess approaches to an enquiry in such either/or terms partakes of a kind of simplistic dualism that opposes the 'real' world out there to the things of the mind, that opposes norm (or ideal) behaviour to actual (or real). It is a duality that refers back to the body/mind division that is so widespread a feature of human cultures and provides such a useful (but from another standpoint, such a misleading) mechanism for 'the construction of the world'. It is a mechanism that lies behind concepts of witchcraft as well as visions of the gods, but has little relevance for the construction of social theory.

My attempt to put flesh on these very general remarks and to discuss a hypothesis, rather than a theory, in the framework of socio-cultural history, has led to some oversimplification. Because of the mode of discourse that social scientists and others are virtually bound to use, it is difficult enough not to deal in crude oppositions rather than in more subtle variables. In trying to show how African states differed from Eurasian ones, the differences have been overemphasised at times, encouraging a dichotomy where a continuum might have been more appropriate. This emphasis derives from the attempt to indicate the *systematic* nature of the differences between sets of societies. We are not dealing with a collection of disparate facts but with the connections within social systems, some of which allow for great autonomy and others for little. Cooking is closely related to production on the one hand and to class on the other. In a system of differentiated access to resources we tend to find a differentiated cuisine, often expressed and elaborated in a culinary literature. But the flowering of culture, the cultivation of taste, also has its oppressive aspects, not only from the standpoint of the have-nots but from that of the ascetic element which is an intrinsic part of the human condition. In terms of my own personal research and experience, what I have tried to do is to show why and how the repression exercised by the Gonja or Ashanti prince over his subjects differed from that of the Norman lords over my Saxon and Scottish ancestors, a difference that comes out not only in the small amount of tribute extorted from cultivators by African rulers, but also in the absence of anything we might call an *haute cuisine*.

Appendix

Terms, operations and cognition

The source of the data used for 'semantic' analysis of the kind undertaken by Lévi-Strauss and other scholars is not always clear. That is to say, there is no necessary assumption that notions such as 'culture' and 'nature' are always present as specific linguistic categories; even in the study of 'category systems' evidence for inclusion is drawn from a wider array of data, which clearly raises the question of the actor/observer status of the concepts.

Adrianne Lehrer has primarily been concerned with the analysis of lexemes. In her first study (1969) she used the set of English cooking terms to test two semantic theories, the field theory of Lyons and the componential theory of Katz and Fodor. A later paper (1972) extends the attempt to eight other peoples, including the French and the Yoruba, and takes into account the culinary triangle and triangle of recipes developed by Lévi-Strauss.

The first problem is the need to establish the notion and existence of a set. The argument is familiar. Speech has its own code for behaviour and things, e.g. verbs for actions, nouns for objects, etc., which provide the basic categories for most thought and most communication that human beings undertake. The words (morphemes or lexemes) used in sets of related activities (e.g. cooking) or objects (e.g. animals) may constitute formal sub-systems of the kind that have become familiar in the analysis of colours and of kinship. One major problem is that, while these sets of terms ('classificatory systems') form the bases of much anthropological enquiry, the investigators find it necessary to eliminate many 'metaphorical' or 'extended' meanings, such as the use of 'father' for God and the priest, the Mennonite employment of 'sister' for wife, or the usage of the name of an object (e.g. an orange or a violet) to indicate a colour.

This problem arises not only when we are dealing with a linguistic analysis of this kind but when we are using, as we usually have to, our own language for the generation, specification or elaboration of notions about other cultures, or about culture in general. For example, Lévi-Strauss naturally draws most of his analytical concepts from his own language. In doing so he not only utilises the core meanings of the 'basic culinary terms' but sometimes exploits the wider range of referential meanings, as when he points to the phrase *pot pourri* as indicating the rapprochement of the boiled to the rotten (1965: 22).

There can be no objection to introducing this 'extended' meaning, at least when one is studying a particular culture. Problems obviously arise in using a wider range of evidence in this way. If we admit its validity, then the horizons burst open. For example, in the analysis of 'roast' we should be allowed to recall the existence of *la rôtie*, the present of the young people of a village to the newly-weds on the morning after the ceremony when they have been discovered in their retreat. This 'roast' often took the form of onion soup served in a chamber-pot decorated with a variety of inscriptions (Rivière 1950; Van Gennep 1943: i, 111ff.).[1] Despite the container, this particular usage would appear to bring the boiled closer to the raw than the rotten, though its presence in that area jars with other associations. If we substitute the English 'cooked' for the French *cuit* (though the difference is of considerable significance in understanding the triangle as it is presented), one would want boiled, like roasted, firmly associated with the cooked rather than the raw; logically, the common factor of their treatment by fire (i.e. cooking) seems more important than the distinction between cooking in water and cooking in air.

The wedding 'roast' draws attention to the question of the level of analysis, whether it is of language or of operations. But of more immediate relevance is the problem of any form of componential analysis, that is, the nature and source of the analytic coordinates, e.g. nature/culture, air/water, endogenous/exogenous, and the lexemes on which they rest. A cursory examination of any cookbook will produce a much more elaborate list of culinary procedures than enter into academic discourse. On what principles do we discard some and retain others?

The problem of the range of data upon which the frame is based raises questions about the treatment it undergoes when fitted to a triangle of linguistic origin. In phonology, the vowel triangle is there not because it has been imported from another context; the form relates to the position of the vocal organs when making the sounds in question. No rationale is provided for constraining the general elements of cooking by such geometrical forms, whether triangles, squares or circles. Their analysis requires a more complex ordering than that provided by the triangle of recipes; their parameters and coordinates need first to be established outside the context of any particular form of cooking (whether French or Guyanese), so that the different operations and terminologies of specific societies can then be fitted to the general frame.

A related problem is the failure of an analysis of a classificatory system in the lexigraphic sense to exhaust the possibility of the linguistic coverage of a set of activities. One may refer to an object such as a lion as 'king of the forest' or to an action such as sexual intercourse by means of a periphrasis (as indeed I have just done) or by means of a phrase where there is no 'basic term', that is, single lexeme, as in *cuire au four*, 'cooking in the oven', for 'baking'. This fact itself may well be of sociological significance, though such complicating usages tend to get excluded in the analysis of 'terms'.

These limitations are important if one is tempted to draw extensive conclusions about a culture, or cultures in general, on the basis of the terms in a lexical set. Lehrer is aware of the problems and her conclusions take them into account. First, she sees the phonological model based on Jakobson's binary components as too restricting. Certain features of the operations resemble phonological ones in providing information on whether the valence is positive or negative: [– Water] means that water must not be used. But many components are not of this sort.

Secondly, with regard to the terms themselves, her cross-cultural study leads her to modify Lévi-Strauss's contention that there is a central distinction between *bouillir* and *rôtir* (which, as we have noted, has a somewhat different range of meanings from the English 'roast'); for, while all the languages in her sample distinguish between boiling and something else, 'this something else is not necessarily roasting' (1972: 167). When it comes to the relation between the oppositions, boiling/roasting and culture/nature, a subject on which Lévi-Strauss agrees that his data are ambiguous, she concludes that her material does nothing to confirm his associations (p. 169).

Thirdly, the only language that support the notion of a triangle in which 'smoking' is presented as the third and equal term is Jacaltec, an indigenous American society. 'Baking' is a more likely candidate for the third term, since some informants refused to recognise 'smoking' as a sub-class of cooking, presumably because the operation was directed at the preservation rather than at the immediate consumption of food, bringing it closer to operations like drying and pickling.

It is the case that several of the activities we think of as connected with the *preparation* of food have been associated in other, mainly earlier, societies with its *preservation* over time (and hence possibly with its transport over space). These methods included drying, smoking, curing, dry salting, preserving in syrup and pickling in brine. Most of these techniques were based upon desiccation, either by the application of heat or else by the use of salt. The extensive trade in salt was partly dependent upon its use for the preservation of food, and it was in this context that a good deal of 'cooking' also took place. The balance between the various processes might well depend upon the availability of alternative resources; where fuel was in short supply, as in the Middle East before the use of oil, then salting became more important than smoking.

Similar techniques for preservation were sometimes applied to the uneatable as well as to the consumable, a well-known case being the embalming of mummies by the Egyptians to preserve the human body as a fit receptacle for the returning soul. Because of the profound significance of this act, especially in the royal family, great expertise was devoted to the embalming process which involved a considerable knowledge not only of the relevant incantations but also of human anatomy and of the use of chemicals. While salt would have been equally useful as a desiccating agent, the rarer natron was deemed to be at once more sacred and more effective.

Returning to the characteristics of the three methods of cooking incorporated in the triangle, namely, roasting, smoking and boiling, Lehrer sees no particular reason for including the rapid/slow distinction of Lévi-Strauss (1965: 26); nor does she find any evidence to confirm the associations of raw/roasted, cooked/smoked, boiled/rotten which play such a central part in linking the culinary triangle with the triangle of recipes, as well as in his interpretative schemas of 'mythology'. Different languages, she reasonably asserts, make different correspondences.

Nevertheless her own analysis of cooking terms does not lead her entirely to reject the culinary triangle. But in the new version presented in Fig. 3 both content and form are modified. The whole basis of the analysis has shifted, as with Lévi-Strauss, from lexemes to 'practices', from the linguistic to the operational. And in this sphere the nature of the common factors, as she recognises, is clearly linked to materials and techniques, to the world outside rather than to the structure beneath.

The form has changed because, as with Lévi-Strauss, the two-

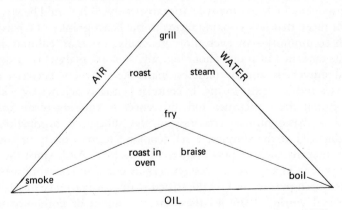

Fig. 3 *The tetrahedron of culinary operations* (after Lehrer 1972)

dimensional triangle has now become a three-dimensional tetrahedron, which provides 'a neat model of cooking practices, but it does not serve as an accurate model of how cultures are likely to categorize their own cooking practices, at least as revealed by the semantic structure of the lexical field' (p. 169). While it can be argued that cognitive structure is not wholly revealed by the semantic structure of the language, her enquiry was based upon the judgements of natural language speakers, and there seems little alternative to accepting their assessment of the situation, at least if one is interested in the emic rather than the etic level of analysis.

Lévi-Strauss, she concludes, is correct in arguing that it is possible to say things about cooking in general as distinct from cooking in a particular culture. It is possible to establish a relatively small set of components that will describe the oppositions of cooking terms in all languages (though each language will not use them all and they will not all be binary in form). But his error is to assume that we can have a 'neutral structure of cooking concepts that will be valid for all languages', for each language selects some components, combines them in diverse ways, arranges them in varied hierarchies and, finally, produces different (though not radically different) semantic structures.

I have presented Lehrer's detailed argument concerning cooking terms because it bears upon a central problem of any analysis that seeks to locate the source of regularity in the general features of the human mind, and to deal with variation at the level of 'transformation', different possibilities being realised by a kind of cultural drift whose mechanisms remain unspecified. For such an enterprise seeks to explain culture without explaining cultures. Why should a specific array of central features be held in common? Why should societies differ in their choice of components? Clearly many factors are involved. It would be wrong to neglect those that link cooking terms to the lexicography of a particular speech community – or even more generally, to other 'cultural' items. But the tendency of much phonologically – based analysis is to seek for logical universals and to underestimate the interplay between social processes and linguistic forms. In contrast Lehrer concludes by acknowledging that the similarities and differences in cooking terms may be related to basic human activities in the sphere of production and reproduction; at the simplest level, 'cooking terms usually presuppose certain utensils such as pots and ovens' (p. 166). And, since the basic category cuts in a set are no longer seen as either universal or arbitrary but, as Rosch puts it, 'follow the structure of co-occurrence of attributes in the real world' (1976: 4), these factors should be embodied in the vocabulary.

Notes to the text

1. INTENTIONS AND REMARKS

1. By 'polemical' I refer to the attempt to reorient the direction of enquiry in a particular academic setting by means of all-embracing slogans.
2. See the informative article by E. Gellner, 'The Soviet and the savage', *Times Literary Supplement*, Oct. 1974, as well as Pierre Bonte's introduction to 'Ethnologie et Marxisme', *La Pensée*, no. 171 (1973). On the other hand Y. Bromley has redefined the work of ethnologists in the Soviet Union as concerned with 'ethnos' (Bromley 1977), a concept not dissimilar to that of 'culture' or even of Durkheim's 'conscience collective' (Bohannan 1960).
3. It is Sahlins (1976) that refers to these as 'the two structuralisms'.
4. In the discussion of *verstehen* and ethnomethodology.
5. In the discussion of the concepts of class as against stratification, summarised by the Indian social scientist André Beteille (1969).

2. STATE OF PLAY

1. See the controversy that followed the publication of Arens's book, *The Man-Eating Myth* (1979).
2. See the volume *Destins de Cannibalisme, Nouvelle Revue de Psychoanalyse* (1972), especially the contribution by Jean Pouillon.
3. Similar matrices using +/− are employed by Lévi-Strauss for a whole range of analytic purposes, see for example, *Anthropologie structurale deux* (1973), pp. 230, 244, 308 and 350.
4. I am indebted to Geoffrey Hawthorn for this comment:

> The theory is in one respect classically functionalist: it assumes that societies (including their 'cultures') are systems (sets of inter-related elements in which a change in one element would bring about a change in the others, even if, as in his case, the elements are defined not by their separable characters but by their relations with other elements); and it assumes that the systems serve the end (need?) of circulation, i.e. of system maintenance (maintenance of the system *as* a system). It's different from the coherence implied in the neo-Wittgenstinian approach to social relations through language (the coherence that Ernest Gellner exposed and criticised in an essay on Peter Winch): in itself and in the function given to language (for Lévi-Strauss a marker, for Wittgenstein something much stronger, indeed *constitutive*).

5. See also the essays of E.A. Hammel, 'Sexual symbolism in flatware', *Papers of the Kroeber Anthropological Society*, 37 (1967), 23–30, and *The Myth of Structural Analysis: Lévi-Strauss and the Three Bears* (Addison-Wesley Module in Anthropology, 1972). Outside the sphere of cooking the well-known essay by Lévi-Strauss on the story of Asdiwal has been parodied by an ethnographer of the North-West, Hélène Codère, in her article 'La Geste du chien d'Asdiwal: the story of Mac' (1974). On a comparable treatment of a possible Chomskian approach, see Oliver Ramburger, 'The deep grammar of haute cuisine', *Linguistics*, 17 (1979), 169–72.

6. For a more detailed discussion, see Goody 1974.

7. For some churches a 'real' transformation takes place; for others the act is 'symbolic'.

8. 1922. But see especially Srinivas' development of this procedure in analysing the rituals of the Coorgs (1952).

9. e.g. E. Goody, *Contexts of Kinship* (Cambridge, 1973).

10. e.g. in the analysis of Shakespeare's work undertaken by Caroline Spurgeon, S. Wilson Knight and L.C. Knights, among many others.

11. See Dunn 1978 (1980).

12. See Evans-Pritchard (1961) and much subsequent discussion, e.g. Schapera (1962), I.M. Lewis (1968). In linguistics, see of course de Saussure (1916 [1966]). For a general comment, see Parain (1967).

13. The story of a Chinese origin is denied by Root (1971: 369) on the authority of the Spaghetti Historical Museum at Pontedassio in Liguria. Written documentation is said to begin from the thirteenth century and includes papal bulls fixing standards of quality, though the words *pasta* and *spago* are fourteenth century. There may have been a common origin in central Asia (Anderson, E. and M. 1977: 338).

14. A selection of the work of the *Annales* school on food and drink has been made available in English by R. Forster and O. Ranum (1979). See also E. and R. Forster (1976) for further examples of historical research on the subject. Braudel's *Les Structures du quotidien* (Paris, 1979) is largely a repetition of his earlier work (1967).

15. Here I use the term 'reproduction' in the more specific meaning rather than in the wider sense of societal reproduction. See Balibar's discussion of reproduction in Althusser *et al.*, 1966.

16. 'But if the social values and nutritional dogmas shape a people's food habits, it is their economic institutions that enable them to produce their supplies' (Richards 1939: 8).

3. PRODUCTION AND CONSUMPTION IN NORTHERN GHANA

1. The 'actual practice' may include verbal elements, of course; I prefer the distinction to that between 'ideal' and 'actual' because the characteristic of verbal behaviour lies in the way that it can elaborate notions, descriptions etc., in the absence of the activity itself. The same is true of painting and the graphic arts, as well as of dance and gesture, but to a much lesser degree; language promotes the creation of 'norms', of 'ideals', of dreams and visions.

2. See Macfarlane 1978.

3. Wrigley 1957.
4. URADEP or the Upper Region Agricultural Development Project, partly financed by the World Bank and the British Government.
5. For a highly 'formal' analysis, which reduces or elevates the study of the state to that of the firm, see Hopkins 1973.
6. In fact some of the gunmen (*mbongwura*) in the Gonja army were from Akan groups who fled before the arrival of the Ashanti.
7. The Konkomba for example now occupy 'Grunshi Zongo', a former slave settlement a few miles to the south of Salaga.
8. The sale of firewood also brings in a few cowries for the owners. Slaves are only employed, so to speak, to fetch the wood. One load sells at 500 cowries. But above all it is water that provides an income for the inhabitants of Salaga during the dry season. Although the village is riddled with holes like a skimming ladle and you can find more than two hundred wells scattered among its houses, pathways, open places and approaches, water becomes very scarce towards the end of December, and the owners of wells sell an eight litre pot for 100 to 150 cowries...

   From the 1st of February the wells are dry. At this time, all the women and all the children with sufficient strength start off at five o'clock in the morning to fetch water for the house and for sale. (Binger 1892: ii, 99).
9. The LoDagaa had a few guns; the late chief Gandaa acquired several for hunting; other are used in funeral ceremonies. How long this has been the case I do not know. The only bows and arrows I have seen among the Gonja, on the other hand, are those carried by the Chief Archer of Bole (the Nangbewura) at the great Damba festival.
10. Financed before Independence by the Colonial Development Corporation.
11. When I first worked in Birifu (1949), the plough farming that had been encouraged by the local agricultural station had virtually stopped. Today three farmers use ploughs, all ex-soldiers, and this form of farming, encouraged by a German agricultural mission and Christian groups, is on the increase.
12. The 'hungry period' was characteristic of much seasonal agriculture. Of medieval England the author of *Piers Plowman* writes:

   > By then harvest was nighing, new corn came to market,
   > And folks were fain of it and fed hunger with the best.
   > No beggar would eat bread if beans were in the baking,
   > Only if it were morning white of the finest flour.
   >
   > (1949: 42)

The last sentence indicates the persistently high valuation given to white as distinct from brown bread, from Roman times onwards, except of course in Germany and some of the northern countries of Europe where rye persisted. On the other hand there is no evidence of any overall nutritional advantage of one type of wheat loaf over another, contrary to much popular thinking (McCance and Widdowson 1956; Forster and Ranum 1979: x).
13. Salt formed a main feature of the trans-Saharan trade but it was also a key

feature of commerce in China and in medieval Europe. Of Europe Duby writes that this

> prime necessity... probably constituted the principal item of long-distance trade, in weight if not in value... nearly all the traffic between Bavaria and Slav countries was based on this commodity, and we may guess that the production and carriage of salt destined for Lombardy lay at the source of early capital accumulation in Venice and Comacchio. (1974: 105)

14. R. Austin Freeman, 1898; Goody, 1964.
15. In essence land is still *extra commercium* in northern Ghana but it has become subject to monetary transfer in the cocoa-growing areas of the south.
16. The term 'agro-town' has been applied to the large pre-colonial towns of the Yoruba in Nigeria. In England well into the fifteenth century the leading citizens of the capital still owned land around the city walls, grazed their animals on the town common and shut up their shops to go harvesting; 'the preference for self-sufficiency died hard' (Davis 1966: 40–1).
17. As Binger remarks: 'Certes, les nègres mangent des mets simples, mais leur préparation n'est pas moins très longs' (1906: 27).
18. For an indigenous description of the process see Goody (1972a). For a recent study of beer in a neighbouring group, see Hagaman 1977. The Myth of the Bagre devotes a great deal of attention to the preparation of beer, and indeed to women's tasks generally. The trade was governed partly by people's preferences for one brewer as against another and partly by the multiplex ties of village life. In late medieval England the brewing of beer, which was largely in the hands of women, 'was one of the most casual and unorganized of medieval trades' (Davis 1966: 12). Nevertheless the nature of city life (in 1309 there were 1,300 brewers in the City of London for a population of well under 50,000), led to the appointment of official ale-tasters; like bread it was subject to price control.
19. Lines 2399–2436 of the version of the Bagre published (1981) with French and English translations as *Une Récitation du Bagré* (Classiques africains, Paris), which is a version of the Black Bagre recorded at the Chief's house, Birifu, in 1969.
20. For a colourful representation, see Bowdich 1819.
21. *The Myth of the Bagre* (1972), p. 132.
22. *ibid.* p. 136.
23. Lines 1025–1049 of the version of the White Bagre recited by Sielo at Bagre Bells, held at Marba, Birifu, December 1976. Recorded by K. Gandah and J. Goody and available on microfiche from the Department of Social Anthropology, University of Cambridge.
24. In this context I use the word 'peasant' to denote a cultivator who farms fields that he may 'own', rent or hold under some other form of tenure, who produces not only for subsistence but also for selling in the market, for paying the rent or for acquitting his labour services. Hence there can be no such thing as a peasant society, or even a peasant 'mode of production', since peasants form part of a society differentiated into town and country, practising a specialist division of labour and differentiated from the

standpoint of access to resources, even at the village level. That is to say, landlordism will be present (though not everyone is necessarily a tenant), holdings will be differentiated and of varying size, and the population will include the landless as well as landowners and tenantry. In recent years attempts have been made to define further features of 'peasantry', in relation to household size and so forth, the definition becoming weighed down with a whole array of auxiliary characteristics which should be the subject of empirical investigation rather than definitional attributes. With such a definition it is not difficult to show that any particular society does not conform to every feature of the composite picture, as Macfarlane has done in the case of England. But while his demonstration is just in many respects, the same criticism applies to 'peasants' other than the English, who thereby lose their uniqueness in the face, for example, of French experience (Duby 1974).

25. Segalen (1980) notes that eating together was the practice in most parts of rural France.

26. I should add that my friend and former student, archaeologist Dr Roland Fletcher, spent some time during 1970 in the Chorobang section of the town, where he claims to have observed a group of men eating together. It is just possible that he may have observed an instance of what I failed to see, but it seems more likely that this was an irregular occasion, such as the consumption of a sacrifice. Esther Goody also reports that in 1976 the heads of two large compounds of weavers in Daboya claimed that until the previous year they ate together in the mosque; meanwhile the other male members of each compound (about 20 in all) ate in two groups, one of elders and one of the other married men, the food being provided by the individual wives whose turn it is to cook. Clearly this is not a subject on which one can be dogmatic; consumption groups of males are sometimes larger than the groups that produce the food. But statements about past practices should be treated with great caution for the reasons that I have stated; it is easy to confuse metaphor with practice.

27. On order of segmentation, see Fortes 1949a. It is often difficult to distinguish when one is dealing with conjugal families, households, minimal lineages or larger descent groups, a fact that is of considerable importance in examining some aspects of social organisation. For example, in analysing the operation of cross-cousin marriage as an exchange system, it is critical to examine the nature of the exchanging units in terms of size, order of segmentation and similar features.

28. See E. Goody 1973: 66.

4. THE HIGH AND THE LOW

1. Freeman speaks of the Sung city-dwellers as being 'the best-fed mass population in world history to that time' (1977: 143) due to the twin revolutions in agriculture and commerce.

2. Murray 1963: 56; the references are to M. Murray, *Saqqara Mastabas*, i, 32–40. For a complete meal from the 1st dynasty at Saqqara, see W.B. Emery, *A Funerary Repast*, Scholae Adriani de Buck Memoriae Dicatae, i.

See also the discussion on grains and breads in Darby *et al.*, *Food: the Gift of Osiris*, 1977: 501ff.

3. 'The peasant was content with bread and onions, some cheese and fish, and his drink was water' (Murray 1963: 87).

4. For an early recipe, see Goody 1977a: 139.

5. *The Deipnosophists* (trans. C.D. Yonge), 3 vols. (London, 1854), II, 437.

6. J.I. Miller, *The Spice Trade of the Roman Empire* (Oxford, 1969).

7. Quoting Richard Hughes, 'A toast to monkey head' in *Far Eastern Economic Review*, 29 April 1972, pp. 27–8.

8. The Andersons also note that most Asians cannot digest raw milk except when they are children because the lactose enzyme stops being produced in the gut at about six years of age; hence those dependent upon dairy products treat the milk with bacteria such as *Lactobacillus* to break down the lactose. The technology was too closely identified with northern 'barbarians' for it to spread in China, although similar bacilli are used to make soy sauce and other ferments. Since soya beans are rather indigestible if they are only boiled, they have to be processed into bean curd and other products (Anderson 1977: 341).

9. Marco Polo, *The Travels* (trans. R. Latham) (London, 1958), p. 215. In Arabia too there were 'men of wealth and consequence, who eat foods of better quality' (p. 311). 'They eat all sorts of flesh, including that of dogs and other brute beasts and animals of every kind which Christians would not touch for anything in the world' (p. 220).

10. Jacques Gernet, *Daily Life in China on the Eve of the Mongol Invasion, 1250–1276* (London, 1962), p. 136.

11. *Ch'ing-ming shang-ho t'u*, published in reproduction by the Wen Wu Press in Peking. See Roderick Whitfield, 'Chang Tse-Tuan's Ch'ing-ming Shang-ho T'u', Ph.D. thesis, Princeton University, 1965. I am indebted to Dr. Whitfield for these references. This scroll known as *Spring Festival on the River* is also used to introduce Michael Freeman's account of Sung cooking (1977: 143).

12. Gernet, *Daily Life in China*, p. 50.

13. The Chinese appear to have developed noodles (*mien*) during the Han period but only after the adoption of techniques for large-scale milling of flour from the West; wheat flour seems to have been made in the first century B.C. (Yü 1977: 81).

14. Gernet, *Daily Life in China*, pp. 133ff.

15. In the early Ming period, a number of hereditary occupations were established under northern influence, but, according to Mote (1977: 211), these 'did not fit the realities of Chinese society' and were abandoned.

16. In the north of China during the T'ang period, cooking was essentially a male art, but in the south a different attitude prevailed (Schafer 1977: 129). In Hangchow of the later period there was a tradition of female chefs (Freeman 1977: 157).

17. Eating together seems to be more a town than a village custom. The Hsus report that men and women sat separately although the wife of the most

senior male sometimes ate at the men's table. In towns men and women might eat together (1977: 304).

18. Arthur Waley, *More Translations from the Chinese* (New York, 1919, pp. 13–14. I owe this reference to J. Finkel, 'King Mutton, a curious Egyptian tale of the Mamlūk period', *Zeitschrift für Semitistik*, 8(1932), 122–48.

19. This idea has been recorded for many societies in Africa and an animal version of this relationship occurs in the Bagre myth of the LoDagaa (J. Goody, *The Myth of the Bagre* (Oxford, 1972), p. 131). Asking for some of her mate's food, the female fruit bat says 'Give me yours and I'll give you mine.'

20. For India, see Dumont 1970: 137ff.

21. Om Prakash, *Food and Drinks in Ancient India* (Delhi, 1961), p. xx.

22. M. Srinivas (*Religion and Society among the Coorgs of South India*, Oxford, 1952), writes: 'The adoption of vegetarianism, teetotalism, and Sanskritization enables a low caste to rise in status in course of time' (p. 226).

23. Prakash, *Food and Drinks*, p. xxiii.

24. *ibid.* pp. 29, 30.

25. *ibid.* p. 100.

26. *ibid.* p. 120.

27. *Manu* III, 118.

28. *Pakka* food is defined by Pocock as made from sugar and milk and cooked in *ghī* as opposed to *kacha*, fried or boiled food (1972: 45). For a more extended discussion of this distinction, as well as of the nature of the food hierarchy, see Miller 1975: 69ff., and the treatment in Khare's two studies.

29. Khare elsewhere speaks of the 'important differences that emerge either due to an incomplete knowledge of orthodoxy or because of poor logistic support' (1976a: 156).

30. A distinction is made in Gujerati between boiled (*bhāt*) and uncooked (*chokar*) rice.

31. The exchange rate was fifteen to the pound. The date of the *puja* was 26 January 1977.

32. For the literature on the left hand, see Hertz (1960) and Needham (1973).

33. Of the Yogi of Maabar Marco Polo writes:

They do not eat out of platters or on trenchers: but they take their food on the leaves of apples of paradise or other big leaves not green leaves, but dried ones; for they say that the green leaves have souls, so that this would be a sin' (1958: 279).

34. See Claudia Roden, *A Book of Middle Eastern Food*, (London, 1968), and A. Christensen, *L'Iran sous les Sassanides*, (Copenhagen, 1936), pp. 447–79, where he gives details of the 'king's dish', the 'Khorassanian dish' and the 'Greek dish', derived from Ta'ālibī, *Histoire des rois de Perse* (trans. H. Kotenberg) (Paris, 1900). 'Only costly delicacies such as Indian olives, edible earth from Khorosan, pistachio-nut, sugarcane washed with rose-water, quince from Balkh and apple from Syria were acceptable to the higher

circles' (Mez 1937: 397); meanwhile, 'pomegranates, figs, water-melons, being much too cheap were left to the common folk'.

35. *Le Livre des Avares de Jāhiz* (Paris, 1951) (trans. C. Pellat), p. 15
36. An Egyptian manual quoted by Rodinson (1949: 108–9) who gives a similar example from a cookbook written by a Turkish woman.
37. See the seventeenth century work of Hājjī Khalīfa; for the classical forebears see Bilabel on Kochbücher and Orth on Kochkunst in Pauly-Wissowa, *Real Encyclopädie*, pp. 932–82.
38. From Mas'udi's 'Meadows of Gold' (trans. A.J. Arberry) in 'A Baghdad Cookery Book', *Islamic Culture*, 1939.
39. Freeman (1977: 144) claims that development occurred in the Sung period.
40. For the slaughter of the pig in cooking, see the recent example from Minot in Burgundy (Verdier 1979); for recipes from the Dordogne, see Guinaudeau-Franc (1980).
41. W. Carew Hazlitt, *Old Cookery Books and Ancient Cuisine*, (London 1886), pp. 18, 53. The well-known French works, *Le Viandier* by Taillevent, and *Le Ménagier de Paris,* are of the fourteenth century.
42. Walter Scott, *Ivanhoe: A Romance* (1830 edn), pp. 13–14. The earliest comment on this state of affairs seems to be in the seventeenth-century work by J. Wallis, *Grammatica Linguae Anglicanae*, (Oxford, 1653). According to Wright (1862: 348), refinement in cookery came with the Normans.
43. For an earlier form see Caxton's printing of John Lydgate's poem 'The Hors the Shepe and the Ghoos' (approx. 1478). For earlier MS versions see Hodgkin 1911: 52. The list reproduced here comes from the 1508 edn.
44. *New vermehrtes Trincier-büchlein* (Rintelen, 1650), quoted by Elias 1978: 119.
45. Elias 1978: 118, quoting L. Sahler, *Montbéliard à table. Mémoires de la Société d'Emulation de Montbéliard* (Montbéliard, 1907, vol. 34, p. 156), adding clerics to the list.
46. 'Pur ceo qe par trop outraiouses et desmesurables services de mes et viandes qe les grantz seignures de nostre reaume einz ces houres unt fet et uses de fere, et uncore fount et usent en lur hostel, e de ce qe autres meindre gentz de mesme le realme, a queus teles choses ne appent pas de enprendre, se aforcent de countre faire les graunts en fesauns teles utrages, outre ce qe lur estat demaunde' (Ordonance of Edward II, 6 August 1316, *Annales Londonienses*, 238).
47. The most famous is *Liber Niger Domus Regis Angliae*, the Black Book of the Household of the King of England, compiled in the reign of Edward IV. Another is *The Northumberland Household Book* of 1512.
48. See Fynes Moryson's observations on the differences at a Scottish knight's house in 1598 (*An Itinerary written by Fynes Morison Gent.*, London, 1617).
49. Colin Clair, *Kitchen and Table* (New York, 1964), p. 58.
50. For a late French example, see Rose's *School of Instructions for the Officers of the Mouth*, 1682, a result of the revival of class cuisine after the restoration of the English monarchy in 1660. For the running of a noble establishment earlier that century, see Braithwaite's 'Rules and Orders for the Government of the House of an Earl' (c. 1617).
51. We could describe this as the equation of totemism and incest. To do so

would be to fall into two of the traps which, in their search for wideranging 'truths', anthropologists are only too likely to encounter. The first is the over-simple use of the = sign (equating x with y), the second is the use of heavily laden concepts (e.g. totemism, incest) as all-embracing terms of art. Analysis does not flourish under such conditions.

52. 'New Year's festivals... gave ecclesiastical sanctions as well as public structure to excess' (Cosman 1976: 37). Such occasions were justified not only as celebrating God's plenty; they also had both the political and the moral function of reaffirming 'the boundaries of control'.

53. M. Gluckman, *Custom and Conflict in Africa*, (Oxford, 1955).

54. M. Djilas, *Conversations with Stalin* (London, 1962), pp. 73, 137.

55. *Time*, 12.12.1969.

56. For the medieval equivalent see the section by Cosman (1976: 109) on 'food and sex' as well as a more general account of the *Consuming Passions* of the English by P. Pullar (1970).

57. Report from *Le Monde*.

58. Smout 1972: 76. One side result may have been an increase in infanticide because of the greater shame of bastardy; there may also have been an increase in homosexuality (Smout 1972: 77; Flandrin, 1972).

5. INDUSTRIAL FOOD

1. For an example of an attempt to 'improve' the diet of the urban proletariat the reader is referred to the booklet of Charles Elmé Francatelli, late maître d'hôtel and chief cook to Her Majesty the Queen, entitled 'A Plain Cookery Book for the Working Classes' (1852, reprinted by the Scolar Press, London, 1977). The first entry, Boiled Beef, is described as 'an economical dinner, especially where there are many mouths to feed', and, 'as children do not require much meat when they have pudding' there should be 'enough left to help out the next day's dinner, with potatoes'. Such fare contrasts with that of the poorer classes in France and many parts of Europe who 'very seldom taste meat in any form' (p. 47). The staples of later English cuisine are already there: Toad in the Hole, Meat Pie, Sausage Roll, Bread Pudding, Rice Pudding, Cocky Leaky, Irish Stew, Bubble and Squeak, Jugged Hare, Fish Curry, Boiled Bacon and Cabbage, Tapioca Pudding, Brown and Polson Pudding, Blancmange, Stewed Prunes, Welsh Rarebit – the list reads like the roll of honour of school catering, and one is surprised to find it reinforced by a cook in royal employ and with such continental credentials as his name and title imply. However, the working classes are also taught how to bake their own bread, brew their own beer, to cure hams, and to make A Pudding of Small Birds. Their potential benefactors are also instructed on how to prepare 'economical and substantial soup for distribution to the poor'.

2. On the early use of dried food for soldiers and travellers in China, see Yü 1977: 75. Chang points out the many ways in which China made use of preservation techniques, by smoking, salting, sugaring, steeping, pickling, drying, soaking in many kinds of soy sauces, etc. For example, meat (either raw or cooked) was pickled or made into a sauce. It also seems that even

human flesh was pickled and some famous historical personages ended up in the sauce jar (Chang 1977: 34). In Turkey dried meat was used by soldiers in the field (Braudel 1973:134); elsewhere such food was intended for the poor, as with the *carne do sol* of Brazil and the *charque* of Argentina.

3. On the processing of fish see the valuable book, *Fish Saving*, by F.L. Cutting (1955), and for a fascinating catalogue of North Atlantic fish as food, see Alan Davidson's *North Atlantic Seafood* (1979). Both works contain useful bibliographic information.

4. Butter, cheese, cream and, in Asia, yoghurt were ways of preserving milk. Throughout Eurasia, eggs were preserved by a variety of methods. Butter was salted for preservation, not only for internal use but also for sale. At Isigny in Normandy the inhabitants benefited from the right of 'franc salé' which enabled them to set their butter and export it to the capital as early as the twelfth century (Segalen 1980: 88).

5. According to Drummond and Wilbraham (1939). Other authors however are sure that it was Durand's patent that was used by Donkin and Hall. Keevil mentions the figure of £1,000 for the purchase of the invention (1972: 6) and Durand is even referred to as the 'father of the tin can'. However iron containers coated with tin were already used by the Dutch to preserve salmon, a forerunner of the sardine process (Cutting 1955: 86). Appert himself visited London in 1814 to try and place orders for his bottled goods, and found the English industry more advanced in certain ways.

6. The contribution of canned goods to the running of the colonial regime, or rather to the maintenance of the metropolitican cuisine in foreign parts, is illustrated by Mrs Boyle's account of her journey to Wenchi in the interior of the Gold Coast in the middle of the First World War. She remarks that a large number of the boxes that had to be headloaded from railhead at Kumasi contained 'food supplies of all kinds, provided in those days for so many Colonial officers by Fortnum & Mason, and ranging from soap and candles to tinned peaches, butter, sausages and so on – in fact enough to stock a District Officer's house for at least nine or ten months.' (1968: 3).

7. Despite early contributions to the technology of canning, the British industry remained small untill the 1930s. Quantities of canned food were imported before the First World War, mainly from America; even in the field of canned vegetables, the share of the home market in 1924 was only 5.1% (Johnston 1976: 173).

8. See Doudiet (1975) on coastal Maine cooking from 1760.

9. Drummond and Wilbraham report the case of a London fishmonger who 'as early as 1820' used ice to bring Scotch salmon to London (1957: 308–9).

10. On the making and storing of ice among wealthy families in the Indian city of Lucknow, see Sharar 1975:168.

11. See L.A. Coser, 'Domestic Servants: the obsolescence of an occupational role' in *Greedy Institutions* (New York, 1974). According to Hobsbawm (1968: 131), the figure rose to 1.4 million by 1871, of which 90,000 were female cooks and not many more were housemaids. See also Keevil's remark on the growth of the firm of Fitch Lovell:

Prosperity, high wages and inflation have also had their effect on the food trade. The well-off can no longer obtain domestic servants to cook for them. Attracted by high wages more and more women take jobs outside their homes, so a demand has been created for convenience foods and labour-saving gadgets. Nowadays the typical domestic servant is in a factory making washing machines, the typical shop assistant working in a cannery. A whole new food manufacturing industry has sprung up. (1972: 9).

12. Indicative of this change, Collins points out, was the change of names. Post Toasties was formerly 'Elijah's Manna', and the Kellogg Co. was the 'Sanitas Nut Food Company'. 'Most breakfast cereals were originally marketed as "natural", "biologic" or, in the case of Grape Nuts, "brain" foods' (1976: 41).
13. See Anderson 1977: 338; but also Root 1971.
14. A London regulation, revoked in the fourteenth century, ran 'Let no baker sell bread in his own house or before his own oven, but let him have a basket with his bread in the King's market' (Davis 1966: 24).
15. See for example the entries from the Chester Mayors' Books reprinted by Furnivall (1897: lxiii).
16. In Chester in 1591 the oath was taken by 33 Butchers and 30 Bakers. The Butchers' oath included the statement that 'all such your victuall that yow shall utter and sell, to poore and Riche, at reasonable prices' (Furnivall 1897: 153).
17. In German they were originally *Kolonialwarenhändler* (dealers in colonial produce).
18. On the impact of multiples on the retail trade itself, see Keevil's account of the growth of Fitch Lovell:

Already by 1900 the growth of multiple shops was well under way and in the 1930s great integrated companies like Allied Suppliers, and Unigate began to appear. These companies expanded rapidly, as did multiple shops in every field, helped by the low value of property and low rents. The standardisation of packaging made possible mass advertising of branded food, selling it long before it reached the shop. Traditional wholesaling was becoming an expensive luxury and far-sighted firms like Fitch Lovell diversified out of it as quickly as possible. (1972: 8)

19. McCance and Widdowson note that the distinction between brown and white breads goes back at least to Roman times when 'white bread...was certainly one of the class distinctions' (1956: 6). Indeed in eighteenth-century France white bread was customarily offered to the master and brown to the servants, even when eating at the same table (Flandrin 1979: 105). But the milling and preparation of bread was another, perhaps more basic ground, for class distinction, since both water and wind mills were at first the property of the manor or of the monastery. In Norman times and later, the miller rented the mill, and the other tenants were expected to bring their grain to be ground. Such relations lasted well into the seventeenth century. Like the mill, the bakehouse was also the property of the lord; serfs were compelled to bring their meal or dough to be baked there for a fixed charge, an imposition that they tried to avoid whenever possible for there was never

the same need to use the bakehouse as the mill (McCance and Widdowson 1956: 13–14). All monasteries had their own bakehouses until the dissolution under Henry VIII. This basic food of the mass of the British population has shifted from domestic production in the early Middle Ages, to the lord's bakehouse under feudalism, to the local bakery under early capitalism, to the concentration of production in a few firms – four controlling about 70 per cent of bread production, according to Collins (1976:18) – and its distribution through that contemporary descendant of the grocer's shop, the supermarket.

The Chinese preference for the less beneficial white rice is also associated with status, partly because the milling was more expensive and partly because it stored better (Anderson 1977: 345). The same preference is found in India and the Middle East.

20. See Vehling 1936: 33 for a comment on Roman adulteration of food.

6. THE IMPACT OF THE WORLD SYSTEM

1. This point, like many others, was made to me by Esther Goody, with whom numerous of the domestic observations were shared and from whom some of the comments are undoubtedly 'borrowed'.
2. On the underlying reasons for the failure of this enterprise, see Hart 1979.
3. On the development of the Nigerian bread industry, see Kilby 1965.
4. However a Gonja woman was manageress of the State-owned bakery in Tamale in 1978–9.
5. This differentiation already existed but only for 'mother's brother' and 'father's sister', i.e. for one's parents' siblings of opposite sex; the new terms are English ones substituting for local usage and employed by the elite of all ethnic groups.
6. In the contemporary West African sense ('grand' in French).
7. In this section particularly the ideas are Esther Goody's more than mine.
8. for the Middle East and Eastern Europe, see Inalcik 1975; for Egypt, see Irwin and Schwartz 1967; for China, see Marco Polo 1968; for East Africa, see Harrison 1968, Pearson 1976; for North Africa, see Chaudhuri 1965; for West Africa, see Blake 1942.
9. Esther Goody was the source of this information.

7. COOKING AND THE DOMESTIC ECONOMY

1. Of people, yes; Bowdich records the claim of the king of Ashanti to have 3,333 wives (1819: 289), and he was followed by 'a hundred negroes of different colors' (p. 292). The food provided daily consisted of 'twenty pots of white soup, and twenty pots of black'.
2. The 'exorbitantly large' households of the aristocracy in medieval England were almost entirely male; the Northumberland household consisted of 9 women and 166 men (Girouard 1978: 15, 27).
3. 'La cuisine procède de deux sources: une source populaire et une source savante, celle-ci nécessairement située dans les classes riches de toutes les époques. Il existe au fil de l'histoire une cuisine paysanne (ou marinière) et une cuisine de cour; une cuisine plébéienne et une cuisine familiale exécutée

par la mère de famille-ou l'humble cuisinière domestique – et une cuisine de professionels que seuls des chefs fanatisés, entièrement voués à la practique, ont le temps et la science d'exécuter'. (Jean-François Revel, *Un Festin en paroles*, 1979: 28)

4. See E.N. Goody's account of the Gonja (1973).
5. R.E.F. Smith writes of the Russian system of shifting agriculture (*zalezh'*) where the hoe is 'a normal implement of recent slash and burn farmers' (1959: 50). But he notes that unlike the heavy plough, the scratch plough (either the forked *sokha* or the *ralo*, ard) could also be used in slash and burn farming providing there was sufficient land.
6. On the other hand, many African farmers keep large domestic animals for 'their own sake', not as draught animals but as suppliers of protein (usually for sacrifice), for reasons of prestige, storage of wealth or 'capital increase'. So the use of such livestock for ploughing is not entirely an additional cost but rather an additional function.
7. M.M. Ali, *A Manual of Hadith* (Lahore, 1951), p. 303. See also al-Bukhāri (El Bokhari), *L'Authentique tradition musulmane, choix de h'adiths* (trans. by G.-H. Bousquet, 1964), cited by Tillion.
8. Such redistributive systems are of great analytic interest and are also reported for pre-revolutionary Russia (Male 1971: 56–65), Palestine (Granott 1952) and for parts of India (Barth 1959: 64–5; Aberle 1978). They are the counterpart of differentiation, characteristic of advanced not simple agriculture.
9. Northern Ghana provides a remarkable example of the speed with which such differentiation occurs, in this case largely based on the tractor. Large acreages have been taken over by individuals since the area cultivated is a function of the energy available (plus the availability of land, access to markets and the workload of the farmer).
10. In West Algeria there is often a *dot* (*un mobilier*) at marriage, later deducted from the inheritance, as well as a dower (*douaire*) from the husband. As Tillion notes, this latter may degenerate into a symbolic payment or even be kept by the father.
11. *Wat* spices, for example, consist of ginger, onions, cardamom, black and white 'asmud', cloves, 'kmoon', cinnamon and 'lewoas giwoas'.
12. For Ghana, see Sylvia Eshun, *Popular Ghanaian Dishes* (Ghana Publishing Corporation, Tema, 1977).
13. L. van der Post has elaborated his views in *First Catch Your Eland* (London, 1977).
14. In earlier attempts to characterise systems of stratification in Africa, I spoke of 'estates', e.g. in Gonja. I would want to distinguish the social strata of hieratic systems from the castes of India and the 'orders' of feudal societies.
15. Contrary to O'Laughlin's interpretation of my approach (1975: 355).

APPENDIX

1. For a Périgordian recipe for 'Soupe de la nuit de noce', see *Cuisine de France, Périgord, Quercy, Bordelais* (Paris, 1970).

Bibliography

d' Abbadie, A. (1868). *Douze ans de séjour dans la Haute-Éthiopie*. Paris

Aberle, K. Gough (1978). *Dravidian Kinship and Modes of Production* (Irawati Karve Memorial Lecture). Delhi: Indian Social Science Research Council

Addo, N.O. and Goody, J.R. (1974). *Siblings in Ghana*. Accra

Ahsan, M.M. (1979). *Social Life under the Abbasids*. London

Ali, M.M. (ed.) (1951). *A Manual of Hadith (Sahiḥ Bukhārī)* Lahore (The Ahmadiyya Anjuman Ishaat Islam)

Allen, D.E. (1968). *British Tastes: an Enquiry into the Likes and Dislikes of the Regional Consumer*. London

Althusser, L. *et al.* (1966). *Lire le Capital*. Paris

Anderson. E.N. Jnr, and M.L. (1977). 'Modern China: South', in Chang, K.C. (ed.), *Food in Chinese Culture*. New York

Anon. (1945). *The Empress Menon School Cook Book*. Addis Ababa

Anon. (1970). *Cuisine de France, Périgord. Quercy. Bordelais*. Paris

Arens, W. (1979). *The Man-Eating Myth*. New York

Arhin, K. (1968). 'Status differentiation in Ashanti in the nineteenth century: a preliminary study'. *Research Review. Institute of African Studies*, Legon, Ghana, 4: 34–52

Athenaeus (1854). *The Deipnosophists* (trans. C.D. Yonge). London

Augé, M. (1978). 'Vers un refus de l'alternatives sens-fonction', *L'Homme*, 18:139–54

  et al. (1974). *La Construction du monde: religion, représentations, idéologie*. Paris

Austin, T. (ed.) (1888). *Two Fifteenth Century Cookery Books*. London (Early English Text Society, no. 91)

Barclay, G.W. (1954). *Colonial Development and Population in Taiwan*. Princeton

Barth, F. (1959). *Political Leadership among Swat Pathans*. London

Barthélémy, J.J. (1824). *Voyage du jeune Anacharsis en Grèce vers le milieu du quatrième siècle avant l'ére vulgaire*. Paris

Barthes, R. (1979) [1961]. 'Toward a psychology of contemporary food consumption', in Forster, R. and Ranum, O. (eds.), *Food and Drink in History: Selections from the Annales, Economies, Sociétés, Civilisations*. Baltimore

Beck, B. (1969). 'Colour and heat in south Indian ritual', *Man*, 4: 553–72

Bede (1972). *Ecclesiastical History of the English People* (eds. B. Colgrave and R.A.B. Mynors). Oxford

Berlin, B. and Kay, P. (1969). *Basic Color Terms*. Berkeley

Bibliography

Beteille, A. (1969). *Social Inequality*. Harmondsworth

Binger, Le Capitaine (1892). *Du Niger au Golfe de Guinée*. Paris

Bitting, A.W. and K.G. (1916). *Canning and How to Use Canned Foods*. Washington D.C.

Bitting, A.W. (1937). *Appertizing; or, the art of canning; its history and development*. San Francisco

Bitting, K.G. (1920). Introduction to Appert, N., *The Book for All Households* (trans. K.G. Bitting). Chicago

Blackman, J. (1976). 'The Corner Shop: the development of the grocery trade and general provisions trade', in Oddy, D. and Miller, D. (eds.), *The Making of the Modern British Diet*. London

Blake, J.W. (1942). *Europeans in West Africa. 1450–1560*, 2 vols. London

Bohannon, P. (1960). 'Conscience collective and culture', in Wolff, K.H. (ed.), *Emile Durkheim (1858–1917)*. Ohio

Bonte, P. (1973). 'Pourquoi ce numéro "Spécial Ethnologie"?' *La Pensée*, 171: 3–9

Boserup, E. (1970) *Women's Role in Economic Development*. London

Bosman, W. (1967) [1705]. *A New and Accurate Description of the Coast of Guinea, divided into the Gold, the Slave, and the Ivory Coasts*. London

Bossard, J.H.S. and Boll, E.S. (1950). *Rituals in Family Living*. Philadelphia

Bowdich, T.E. (1819). *Mission from Cape Coast Castle to Ashantee*. London

Boyle, L. (1968). *Diary of a Colonial Officer's Wife*. Oxford

Braudel, F. (1973). *Capitalism and Material Life, 1400–1800*. London (French edn. 1967)

(1979). *Les Structures du quotidien: le possible et l'impossible*. Paris

Bromley, Y.V. (1976). *Soviet Ethnography: Main Trends*. Moscow

Burnett, J. (1966). *Plenty and Want: A social history of diet in England from 1815 to the present day*. London

Butterick (1925). *The Story of the Pantry Shelf, an outline of grocery specialites*. New York

Chang, K.C. (ed.) (1977). *Food in Chinese Culture: anthropological and historical perspectives*. New Haven

Chaudhuri, K.N. (1965). *The English East India Company*. London

Christensen, A. (1936). *L'Iran sous les Sassanides*. Copenhagen

Clair, C. (1964). *Kitchen and Table*. New York

Clancy, M.T. (1979). *From Memory to Written Record: England 1066–1307*. London

Clignet, R. (1970). *Many Wives. Many Powers*. Evanston

Codère, Hélène (1974). 'La Geste du chien d'Asdiwal: the story of Mac', *American Anthropologist*, 76: 42–7

Collins, E.J.T. (1976). 'The "consumer revolution" and the growth of factory foods: changing patterns of bread and cereal-eating in Britain in the twentieth century', in Oddy, D.J. and Miller, D. (eds.), *The Making of the Modern British Diet*. London

Condominas, G. (1957). *Nous avons mangé la forêt*. Paris

Corley, T.A.B. (1976). 'Nutrition, technology and the growth of the British biscuit industry, 1820–1900', in Oddy, D.J. and Miller, D. (eds.), *The Making of the Modern British Diet*. London

Bibliography

Coser, L.A. (1974). *Greedy Institutions*. New York

Cosman, M.P. (1976). *Fabulous Feasts. Medieval Cookery and Ceremony*. New York

Crawley, E.A. (1927) [1902]. *The Mystic Rose: A Study of Primitive Marriage and of Primitive Thought in its Bearing on Marriage*, revised and greatly enlarged by Theodore Besterman. London

(1929). *Studies of Savages and Sex*. London

(1931). *Dress. Drinks. and Drums: Further Studies of Savages and Sex*. London

Crellin, H.G. (1979). 'Commercial Yam Farming among the Konkomba of Northern Ghana'. M. Litt. thesis, University of Cambridge

Cummings, R.O. (1941). *The American and his Food*. Chicago (2nd edn.)

Cutting, C.L. (1955). *Fish Saving: a History of Fish Processing from Ancient to Modern Times*. London.

Dahrendorf, R. (1959). *Class and Conflict in Industrial Society*. London

Danilova, L.V. (1971) [1968]. 'Controversial problems of the theory of pre-capitalist societies', *Soviet Anthropology and Archaeology*, 9: 269–328

Davidson, A. (1979). *North Atlantic Seafood*. London

Davis, D., (1966). *Fairs. Shops and Supermarkets: a History of English Shopping*. Toronto

de Heusch, L. (1971). *Pourquoi l'épouser?* Paris

Detienne, M. (1972). *Les Jardins d'Adonis*. Paris

Deutch, R.M. (1961). *The Nuts among the Berries*. New York

Djilas, M. (1962). *Conversations with Stalin*. London

Douglas, M. (1966). *Purity and Danger*. London

(1971). 'Deciphering a meal', in Geertz, C. (ed.), *Myth, Symbol and Culture*. New York

and Isherwood, B. (1979). *The World of Goods*. London

Doudiet, E.W. (1975). 'Coastal Maine cooking: foods and equipment from 1970', in Arnott, M.L. (ed.), *Gastronomy the Anthropology of Food and Food Habits*. The Hague

Drummond, J.C. and Wilbraham, A (1939). *The Englishman's Food: A History of Five Centuries of English Diet*. London (rev. ed. 1957)

Duby, G. (1974). *The Early Growth of the European Economy: warriors and peasants from the seventh to the twelfth century*. London

Dumont, L. (1966). 'A fundamental problem in the sociology of caste', *Contributions to Indian Sociology*, 9: 17–32

(1970). *Homo Hierachicus: the caste system and its implications*. London (French ed. 1966)

Dunn, J.M. and Roertson, A.F. (1973). *Dependence and Opportunity: political change in Ahafo*. Cambridge

Elias, N. (1978). *The Civilizing Process*. Oxford

Emery, W.B. (1962). *A Funerary Repast in an Egyptian Tomb of the Archaic Period*. Scholae Adriani de Buck Memoriae Dicatae, i. Leiden

Eshun, S. (1977). *Popular Ghanaian Dishes*. Tema

Event-Pritchard, E. (1940) *The Nuer: a description of the modes of livelihood and political institutions of a Nilotic people*. Oxford

(1961). *Anthropology and History*. Manchester

Bibliography

Farley, J. (1783). *The London Art of Cookery* (3rd ed.). London

Fiéloux M. (1980). *Les Sentiers de la nuit. Les migrations rurales lobi de la Haute-Volta vers la Côte d'Ivoire.* Paris

Finkel, J. (1932). 'King Mutton, a curious Egyptian tale of the Mamlūk period', *Zeitschrift für Semitistik*, 8: 122–48; 9 (1933–4): 1–18

Firth, R.W. (ed.) (1957). *Man and Culture*. London

Flandrin, J-L. (1972). 'Mariage tardif et vie sexuelle – discussions et hypothèses de recherche', *Annales E.S.C.*, 1351–78

(1979). *Families in Former Times: Kinship, Household and Sexuality.* Cambridge (French edn. 1976)

Forbes, R.J. (1954). 'Chemical, culinary and cosmetic arts', in Singer, C. *et al.* (eds.), *A History of Technology*, vol. I: *From Early Times to Fall of Ancient Empires.* Oxford

Forster, E. and R. (eds.) (1975). *European Diet from Pre-Industrial to Modern Times.* New York

Forster, R. and Ranum, O. (eds.) (1979). *Food and Drink in History: Selections from the Annales, Economies, Sociétés, Civilisations.* Baltimore

Fortes, M (1949a). *The Web of Kinship among the Tallensi.* London

(1949b). 'Time and social structure: an Ashanti case study', in Fortes, M. (ed.), *Social Structure.* Oxford

(1954). 'A demographic field study in Ashanti', in Lorimer, F. (ed.), *Culture and Human Fertility.* Paris

(1959). *Oedipus and Job in West African Religion.* Cambridge

(1961). 'Pietas in ancestor worship'. *Journal of the Royal Anthropological Institute*, 91: 166–81

(1962). 'Ritual and office in tribal society', in Gluckman, M. (ed.), *Essays on the Ritual of Social Relations.* Manchester

(1967). 'Totem and taboo', *Proceedings of the Royal Anthropological Institute*, 1966: 5–22

(1974). 'The first born', *Journal of Child Psychology and Psychiatry*, 15: 81–104

(1980). 'Anthropology and the psychological disciplines', in Gellner, E. (ed.), *Soviet and Western Anthropology.* London

and Fortes, S.L. (1936). 'Food in the domestic economy of the Tallensi', *Africa*, 9: 237–76

Fortune, R. (1857). *A Residence Among the Chinese: Inland, on the Coast, and at Sea.* London

Francatelli, C.E. (1852). *A Plain Cookery Book for the Working Classes.* London (reissued 1977)

Frazer, J.G. (1890). *The Golden Bough.* London

(1907). *Questions on the Customs, Beliefs and Languages of Savages.* Cambridge

Freeman, M. (1977). 'Sung', in Chang, K.C. (ed.), *Food in Chinese Culture.* New York

Freeman, R.A. (1898). *Travels and Life in Ashanti and Jaman.* London

Freud, S. (1913). *Totem und Taboo.* Vienna (Eng. trans. J. Strachey, London, 1950)

Furnivall, F.J. (1868). *Early English Meals and Manners.* London (Early English Text Society, no. 32)

Bibliography

(1897). *Child-marriages, Divorces, and Ratifications, etc. in the Diocese of Chester, A.D. 1561–6: depositions in trials in the Bishop's Court, Chester...also Entries from the Mayors' Books, Chester, A.D. 1558–1600.* London (Early English Text Society, no. 108)

Gardiner, A.H. (1947). *Ancient Egyptian Onomastica.* London

Gellner, E. (1974). 'The Soviet and the savage', *Times Literary Supplement,* 1166–8, reprinted *Current Anthropology* (1975), 16: 595–601

Gennep, A. Van (1943). *Manuel de folklore français contemporain.* Paris

Gernet, J. (1962) [1959]. *Daily Life in China on the Eve of the Mongol Invasion, 1250–1276.* London

Gibbal, J.N. (1971). 'Stratégie matrimoniale en milieu urbain abidjannais', *Cah. O.R.S.T.R.O.M.,* sér. sci. hum., 8: 187–99

Girouard, M. (1978). *Life in the English Country House: a Social and Architectural History.* Yale

Gluckman, M. (1955). *Custom and Conflict in Africa.* Oxford

(ed.) (1962). *Essays on the Ritual of Social Relations.* Manchester

Goody, E. (1973). *Contexts of Kinship.* Cambridge

(1981). *Parenthood and Social Reproduction.* Cambridge

Goody, J. (1954). *The Ethnography of the Northern Territories of the Gold Coast, West of the White Volta.* Colonial Office, London (mimeo)

(1956). *The Social Organization of the LoWiili.* London: HMSO

(ed.) (1958). *The Developmental Cycle in Domestic Groups.* Cambridge

(1959) 1969]. 'The mother's brother and the sister's son in West Africa', *Journal of the Royal Anthropological Institute,* 89: 61–88, reprinted in J. Goody, *Comparative Studies in Kinship.* London

(1961). 'Religion and ritual: the definitional problem', *British Journal of Sociology,* 12: 142–64

(1962). *Death, Property and the Ancestors.* Stanford

(1964). 'The Mande and the Akan Hinterland', in Vansina, J. (ed.), *The Historian in Tropical Africa.* Oxford

(1968). *Tradition, Technology and the State in Africa.* London

(1969). 'Marriage policy and incorporation in northern Ghana', in Cohen, R. and Middleton, J.F. (eds.), *From Tribe to Nation in Africa: studies in incorporation processes.* San Francisco

(1972a). *The Myth of the Bagre.* Oxford

(1972b). *Domestic Groups.* Reading, Mass.

(1972c). 'The evolution of the family', in Laslett, P. (ed.), *Household and Family in Past Time.* Cambridge

(1974). 'Polygyny, economy and the role of women', in Goody, J. (ed.), *The Character of Kinship.* Cambridge

(ed.) (1974). *The Character of Kinship.* Cambridge

(1974). 'British functionalism', in Naroll, R. (ed.), *Main Currents in Ethnological Theory.* New York

(1976). *Production and Reproduction.* Cambridge

(1977a). *The Domestication of the Savage Mind.* Cambridge

(1977b). 'Against "ritual": loosely structured thoughts on a loosely defined topic', in Falk-Moore, S. and Mayerhof, B. (eds.), *Secular Rituals*. Amsterdam

(1978). 'Population and polity in the Voltaic region', in Friedman, J. and Rowlands, M. (eds.), *The Evolution of Social Systems*. London

(1980). 'Rice-burning and the Green Revolution in Northern Ghana' *Journal of Development Studies*, 16: 136–55

(1981). 'Sacrifice among the LoDagaa and elsewheree: a comparative comment on implicit questions and explicit rejection', *Systemès de pensée en Afrique noire: le sàcrifice* iv. C.N.R.S. Ivry.

and Goody, E. (1967). 'The circulation of women and children in northern Ghana', *Man* (N.S.), 2: 226–48

Goody, J. *et al.* (1977). *Ses Preference, Resources and Population*. Revised report of a research project sponsored by the Rockefeller and Ford Foundations, New York, and the Ministry of Overseas Development, London. Cambridge, mimeo

et al. (1981a). 'On the absence of implicit sex-preference in Ghana', *Journal of Biosocial Sciences*, 13: 87–96

et al. (1981b). 'Implicit sex preference: a comparative study', *Journal of Biosocial Sciences*, 13: 455–66

Granott, A. (1952). *The Land System in Palestine: history and structure*. London

Guinaudeau-Franc, Z. (1980). *Les Secrets des fermes en Périgord noir*. Paris

Hagaman, B.L. (1977). 'Beer and Matriliny: the Power of Women in a West African Society'. Ph. D. thesis, Northeastern University

Halliday, M.A.K. (1961). 'Categories of the theory of grammar', *Word*, 17: 241–91

Hammel, E.A. (1967). 'Sexual symbolism in flatware', *Papers of the Kroeber Anthropological Society*, 37: 23–30

(1972). *The Myth of Structural Analysis: Lévi-Strauss and the Three Bears*. Addison-Wesley Module in Anthropology. Reading, Mass.

Harrell-Bond, B.E. (1975). *Modern Marriage in Sierra Leone: a study of the professional group*. The Hague

Harrison, J.B. (1968). 'Colonial development and international rivalries outside Europe 2. Asia and Africa', *New Cambridge Modern History*, 3: 532–58. Cambridge

Hart, K. (1979). 'The Development of Commercial Agriculture in West Africa'. Discussion paper prepared for the United States Agency for International Development.

Hassall, A.H. (1855). *Food and its Adulteration*. London

Haudricourt, A.G. and Granai, G. (1955), 'Linguistique et sociologie', *Cahiers internationaux de Sociologie*, 19: 114–29

Hazlitt, W.C. (1886). *Old Cookery Books and Ancient Cuisine*. London

Hémardinquer, J-J. (1979). 'The family pig of the Ancien Régime: myth or fact?' in Forster, R. and Ranum, O. (eds.), *Food and Drink in History: Selections from the Annales*. London

Hertz, R. (1960). 'The Pre-Eminence of the Right hand: A Study in Religious Polarity', in *Death and the Right Hand*, pp. 89–113 (trans. R. and C.

Bibliography

Needham), Glencoe, Illinois (trans. of 'La préeminence de la main droite: étude sur la polarité religieuse', *Revue philosophique*, 58 (1909): 553–80)

Heseltine, M. (trans.) (1969). *Petronius* (rev. edn.). Cambridge, Mass.

Hobsbawm, E.J. (1968). *Industry and Empire*. New York

Hodgkin, J. (1911–14). 'The Proper Terms II. Tearmes of a Keruer', *Transactions of the Philological Society*, 1911–16. Part ɪ, 52–94, Part ɪɪ, 123–37

Hopkins, A.G. (1973). *An Economic History of West Africa*. London

Hsu, F. (1949). *Under the Ancestors' Shadow*. London

Hsu, V.Y.N. and F.L.K. (1977). 'Modern China: North', in Chang, K.C. (ed.), *Food in Chinese Culture*. New York

Inalcik, H. (1975). *The Ottoman Empire*. London

Irwin, J. and Schwartz, P. (1967). *Studies in Indo-European Textile History*. Calico Museum of Textiles, Ahmedabad

Issawi, C. (1950). *An Arab Philosophy of History: selections from the Prolegomena of Ibn Khaldun of Tunis (1332–1406)*. London

al-Jāḥīz (1951). *Le Livres des Avares de Jāḥiz* (trans. C. Pellat). Paris

Jefferys, J.B. (1954). *Retail Trading in Britain 1880–1950*. London

Jesperson, O. (1943). *Growth and Structure of the English Language*. (9th edn). Oxford

John, E. (1960). *Land Tenure in Early England*. Leicester

Johnston, J.P. (1976). 'The development of the food-canning industry in Britain during the inter-war period', in Oddy, D.J. and Miller, D. (eds.), *The Making of the Modern British Diet*. London

Jolly, J. (1928). *Hindu Law and Customs* (trans. B. Ghosh). Calcutta Greater Indian Society Publication, no. 2

Jorn, A. and Arnaud, N. (1968). *La Langue verte et la cuite: étude gastrophonique sur la marmythologie musiculinaire*. Paris

Katz, J.J. and Fodor, J.A. (1963). 'The structure of a semantic theory,' *Language*, 39:170–210

Keevil, A. (1972). *The Story of Fitch-Lovell, 1784–1970*. London

Khare, R.S. (1976a). *The Hindu Hearth and Home*. Delhi

(1976b). *Culture and Reality*. Simla

Kilby, P. (1965). *African Enterprise: the Nigerian Bread Industry*. Stanford

Kramer, S.N. (1956). *From the Tablets of Sumer*. Indian Hills, Colorado

Kuhn, T. (1962). *The Structure of Scientific Revolutions*. Chicago

Lane, M. (ed.) (1970). *Structuralism: a Reader*. London

Latraverse, F. (1975). 'La binarisme en phonologie', *L'Arc*, 60: 38–44

Leach, E.R. (1954). *Political Systems of Highland Burma*. London

Legge, J. (1879–91). *The Sacred Books of China*, 6 vols. Oxford

Lehrer, A. (1969). 'Semantic cuisine', *Journal of Linguistics*, 5: 39–56

(1972). 'Cooking vocabularies and the culinary triangle of Lévi-Strauss', *Anthropological Linguistics*, 14: 155–71

(1974). *Semantic Fields and Lexical Structure*. Amsterdam

Lévi-Strauss, C. (1945) [1958]. 'L'Analyse structurale en linguistique et en anthropologie', *Word*, ɪ (2): 1–21, reprinted in *Anthropologie structurale*. Paris

(1949). *Les Structures élémentaires de la parenté*. Paris (Eng. trans. Bell, J.H. and

Bibliography

von sturmer, J.R., *The Elementary Structures of Kinship*, London 1969)

(1958). *Anthropologie structurale*. Paris (Eng. trans. *Structural Anthropology*, London, 1963)

(1962). *La Pensée sauvage*. Paris (Eng. trans. *The Savage Mind*. London, 1966)

(1964). *Le Cru et le cuit*. Paris (Eng. trans. Weightman, J. and D. *The Raw and the Cooked*, London, 1970)

(1965). 'Le triangle culinaire', *L'Arc*, 26: 19–29 (Eng. trans. Brooks P., *Partisan Review*, 33 (1966), 586–95

(1966). *Du Miel aux cendres*. Paris (Eng. trans. Weightman, J. and D., *From Honey to Ashes*, London, 1973)

(1968). *L'Origine des manières de table*. Paris (Eng. trans. *The Origin of Table Manners*, London, 1978)

(1971). *L'Homme nu*. Paris

Levine, D.N. (1965). *Wax and Gold*. Chicago

Lewis, I.M. (ed.) (1968). *History and Social Anthropology* (A.S.A. Monographs, no. 7). London

Lovejoy, P.E. (1973). 'The Hausa Kola Trade (1700–1900): A Commercial System in the Continental Exchange of West Africa. Ph.D. thesis, University of Wisconsin

Lyons, J. (1963). *Structural Semantics*. Oxford

McCance, R.A. and Widdowson, E.M. (1956). *Breads Brown and White*. London

Macfarlane, A. (1978). *The Origins of English Individualism*. Oxford

Male, D.J. (1971). *Russian Peasant Organisation before Collectivisation*. Cambridge

Malinowski, B. (1927). *Sex and Repression in Savage Society*. London

(1929). *The Sexual Life of Savages*. London

(1935). *Coral Gardens and Their Magic*. London

Maquet, J.J. (1961). *The Premise of Inequality in Ruanda*. London

Marx, K. (1967) [1867]. *Capital*. New York

Mas'udi (1939). 'Meadows of Gold', trans. Arberry, A.J., in 'A Bagdad Cookery Book', *Islamic Culture*, pp. 21–47

Mathias, P. (1959). *The Brewing Industry in England 1700–1830*. Cambridge

Mead, W.E. (1931). *The English Medieval Feast*. London

Meillassoux, C. (1975). *Femmes, greniers et capitaux*. Paris

Mencius (1970). *Mencius* (trans. D.C. Lau). London

Merton, R.K. (1949). *Social Theory and Social Structure*. Glencoe, Illinois

Mez, A. (1937). *The Renaissance of Islam* (trans. from German). London

Miller, D.B. (1975). *From Hierarchy to Stratification: changing patterns of social inequality in a North Indian village*. Delhi

Miller, J. (1969). *The Spice Trade of the Roman Empire*. Oxford

Mintz, S. (1979). 'Time, sugar and sweetness', *Marxist Perspectives*, 2: 56–73

Moryson, F. (1617). *An Intinerary written by Fynes Moryson Gent*. London

Mote, F.W. (1977). 'Yuan and Ming', in Chang, K.C. (ed.), *Food in Chinese Culture*. New York

Murray, M. (1905). *Saqqara Mastabas*, I. London

(1963). *The Splendour that was Egypt* (rev. edn). New York

Needham, R. (ed.) (1973). *Right and Left: Essays on Dual Symbolic Classification*. Chicago

Bibliography

O'Laughlin, B. (1975). 'Marxist approaches in anthropology', *Annual Review of Anthropology*, 4: 341–70

Oppong C. (1974). *Marriage among a Matrilineal Elite*. Cambridge

Parain, C. (1967). 'Structuralisme et histoire', *La Pensée*, 135: 38–52

Pearson, M.N. (1976). *Merchants and Rulers in Gujarat*. Berkeley

Piers Plowman (1949). *Visions from Piers Plowman* (trans. N. Coghill). London

'Platine' (1978a). 'Cuisine médiévale', *L'Histoire*, 4 (Sept.): 96–8

   (1978b). 'Variations franco-britanniques', *L'Histoire*, 5 (Oct.): 102–03

   (1978c), 'L'Huitre et la truffe', *L'Histoire*, 5 (Oct.): 102–4

Pocock, D.S. (1972). *Kanbi and Patidar*. Oxford

   (1957). '"Difference" in East Africa: a study of caste and religion in modern Indian society', *South-Western Journal of Anthropology*, 13: 289–300

Polanyi, K. *et al.* (1957). *Trade and Market in the Early Empires*. Glencoe, Ill.

Polo, Marco (1958). *The Travels* (trans. R. Latham). London

Porphyry (1965). *On Abstinence from Animal Food* (trans. T. Taylor). London

Pouillon, J. (1972). 'Manière de table, manière de lit, manière de langage', *Destins de Cannibalisme, Nouvelle Revue de Psychoanalyse*, 6: 9–25

Power, E. (trans.) (1928). *The Goodman of Paris* (Le Ménagier de Paris). London

Prakash, O. (1961). *Food and Drinks in Ancient India*. Delhi

Prentice, E.P. (1950). *Progress: An Episode in the History of Hunger?* New York (privately printed)

Pryor, F.L. (1977). *The Origins of the Economy: a comparative study of distribution in primitive and peasant economies*. New York

Pullar, P. (1970). *Consuming Passions: being an historical enquiry into certain English appetites*. Boston

Radcliffe-Brown, A.R. (1922). *The Andaman Islanders*. Cambridge

Ramburger, O. (1979). 'The deep grammar of haute cuisine', *Linguistics*, 17: 169–72

Revel, J.-F. (1979). *Un Festin en paroles*. Paris

Richards, A.I. (1932). *Hunger and Work in a Savage Tribe*. London

   (1937). *The Food and Nutrition of African Natives*. Memorandum 13, International Institute of African Languages and Cultures

   (1939). *Land, Labour and Diet in Northern Rhodesia*. London

   and Widdowson, E.M. (1936). 'A dietary study in Northeastern Rhodesia', *Africa*, 9: 166–96

Rivière, G.H. (1950). 'Presents et ages de la vie', *Offrandes et Cadeaux. L'Amour de l'Art*, pp. 46–51

Robaglia, S. (1935). *Magaridou: journal et recettes d'une cuisinière au pays d'Auvergne*. Nonette

Roden, C. (1970). *A Book of Middle East Food*. London (1st edn 1968)

Rodinson, M. (1949). 'Recherches sur les documents arabes relatifs à la cuisine', *Revue études islamiques*, pp. 95–106

Rolland, J.-F.(1976). *La grande capitaine*. Paris

Root, W. (1971). *The Food of Italy*. New York

Rosch, E. (1976). 'Human categorization', in Warren, N. (ed.), *Advances in Cross-Cultural Psychology* (vol. 1). London

Sahlins, M. (1976). *Culture and Practical Reason*. Chicago

Bibliography

Saussure, F. de (1966). *Course in General Linguistics.* New York (French edn, 1916)

Schafer, E.F. (1963). *The Golden Peaches of Samarkand.* Berkeley.

(1977). 'T'ang.' in Chang, K.C. (ed.), *Food in Chinese Culture.* New York

Schapera, I. (1962). 'Should anthropologists be historians'? *Journal of the Royal Arthropological Institute,* 92: 143–56

Schildkrout, E. (1978). 'Roles of children in urban Kano', in La Fontaine, J.S (ed.), *Sex and Age as Principles of Social Differentiation* (A.S.A. monograph, no. 17). London

Segalen, M. (1980). *Mari et femme dans la société paysanne.* Paris

Sharar, A.H. (1975). *Lucknow: the Last Phase of an Oriental Culture.* London

Simoons, F.J. (1967). *Eat Not This Flesh.* Wisconsin

Smith, R.E.F. (1959). *The Origins of Farming in Russia.* Paris

(1977). *Peasant Farming in Muscovy.* Cambridge

Smith, W. Robertson (1889). *The Religion of the Semites.* Edinburgh

Smout, T.C. (1972). *A History of the Scottish People.* London

Spence, J. (1977). 'Ch'ing', in Chang, K.C. (ed.), *Food in Chinese Culture.* New York

Srinivas, M.N. (1952). *Religion and Society among the Coorgs of South India.* Oxford

Steensgaard, N. (1974). *The Asian Trade Revolution of the Seventeenth Century.* Chicago

Stevenson, H.N.C. (1954). 'Status evaluation in the Hindu caste system', *Journal of the Royal Anthropological Institute* 84: 45–65

Stouff, L. (1970). *Ravitaillement et alimentation en Provence aux XIVe et XVe siècles.* Paris

Teuteberg, H.J. (1975). 'The general relationship between diet and industrialization', in Forster, E. and R. (eds.), *European diet from Pre-Industrial to Modern Times.* New York

Thomas, L.L., Kronenfeld, J.Z. and D.B. (1976). 'Asdiwal crumbles: a critique of Lévi-Straussian myth analysis', *American Ethnologist,* 3: 147–73

Thomas, L.V. (1960). 'Essai d'analyse structurale appliquée à la cuisine diola', *Bulletin de l'Institute française d'Afrique Noire,* 22: 328–45

Thompson, A.H. (1913). *English Monasteries.* Cambridge

Tillion, G. (1966). *Le Harem et les cousins.* Paris

Van de Post, L. (1977). *First Catch your Eland.* London

Vehling, J.D. (trans.) (1977). *Apicius: Cooking and Dining in Imperial Rome.* New York

Verdier, Y. (1979). *Façons de dire, façons de faire: la laveuse, la couturière, la cuisinière.* Paris

Verney, F.P. and M.M. (eds.) (1925). *Memoirs of the Verney Family during the Seventeenth Century.* London

Waley, A. (1919). *More Translations from the Chinese.* New York

Wallis, J. (1653). *Grammatica Linguae Anglicanae.* Oxford

Warner, R. (1791). *Antiquitates Culinariae.* London

Weiskel, T.C. (1980). *French Colonial Rule and the Baule Peoples: Resistance and Collaboration, 1889–1911.* Oxford

Bibliography

Whitfield, R. (1965). 'Chang Tse-Tuan's Ch'ing-ming Shang-ho T'u.' Ph. D. thesis, Princeton University

Whyte, M.K. (1978). *The Status of Women in Pre-industrial Societies.* Princeton

Wilson, C.A. (1973). *Food and Drink in Britain.* Harmondsworth

Wolf, E. (1966). *Peasants.* Englewood Cliffs, New Jersey

Worsley, P.M. (1956). 'The kinship system of the Tallensi: a revaluation', *Journal of the Royal Anthropological Institute,* 86: 37–75

Wright, L. (1975). *The Road from Aston Cross: an industrial history, 1875–1975.* Leamington Spa (Smedley–HP Foods Ltd)

Wright, T. (1862). *A History of Domestic Manners and Sentiments in England during the Middle Ages.* London

Wrigley, C.C (1957). 'Buganda: an outline economic history', *Economic History Review,* 10: 69–80

Yalman, N. (1963). 'On the purity of women in the castes of Ceylon and Malabar', *Journal of the Royal Anthropological Institute,* 93 (part 1): 25–58

Yü Y-s (1977). 'Han', in Chang, K.C. (ed.), *Food in Chinese Culture.* New York

Zahan, D. (1969). *La Viande et la graine.* Paris (Presence africain)

ADDITIONAL ITEMS

The reference include books that provide completer bibliographies. I give below some additions plus a selection of books that may interest the reader, to which should be added many of the fine collection of cookbooks published by Penguin Books.

Ashley, W. (1928). *The Bread of our Forefathers.* Oxford

Battisti, C. and Alessio, G. (eds.) (1957). *Dizionario Etimologico Italiano.* Florence

Blainey, G. (1966). *The Tyranny of Distance: how distance shaped Australia's history.* Melbourne

Bourdeau, L. (1894). *Études d'histoire générale: Histoire de l'alimentation.* Paris

Brillat-Savarin, A. (1975 [1826]). *Physiologie du goût, avec une lecture de Roland Barthes.* Paris

Catelot, A. (1972). *L'Histoire à table.* Paris

Cohen, M.N. (1977). *The Food Crisis in Prehistory: overpopulation and the origins of agriculture.* New Haven

David, E. (1954). *Italian Food.* London

(1977). *English Bread and Yeast.* London

Dion, R. (1959). *Histoire de la vigne et du vin en France.* Paris

Dizionario Enciclopedico Italiano. (1960). ed. Instituto della Enciclopedia Italiana. Rome

Fischler, C. (ed) (1979). 'La Nourriture: pour une anthropologie bioculturelle de l'alimentation', *Communications,* 31

Gollan, A. (1978). *The Tradition of Australian Cooking.* Canberra

Gonon, M. (1961) *La Vie familiale en Forez au XIVe siècle et son vocabulaire d'après les testaments.* Paris

Grass, G. (1978). *The Flounder: a celebration of life, food and sex.* London

Bibliography

Guiral, P. and Thuillier, G. (1978). *La Vie quotidienne des domestiques en France au XIXe siècle.* Paris

Guy, C. (1971). *La Vie quotidienne de la société gourmande en France au XIXe siècle.* Paris

Harris, M. (1975). *Cows, Pigs, Wars and Witches.* London

Hartley, D. (1954). *Food in England.* London

Lichtenfelt, D. (1913). *Die Geschichte der Ernährung.* Berlin

Merlin, A. and Beaujour, A.Y. (1978). *Les Mangeurs de Rouergue: cuisine paysanne contre gastronomie.* Paris.

Rees, J.A. (1932). *The Grocery Trade: its history and romance.* London

Renfrew, J. (1973). *Paleoethnobotany: the prehistoric food plants of the Near East and Europe.* New York

Renner, H. (1946). *The Origin of Food Habits.* London

Rorabaugh, W.J. (1979). *The Alcoholic Republic: an American tradition.* New York

Sass, L. (1976). *To the King's Taste: Richard II's book of feasts and recipes.* London
(1977). *To the Queen's Taste: Elizabethan feasts and recipes.* London

Tannahill, R. (1973). *Food in History.* London

Wolff, P. (1954). *Commerces et marchands de Toulouse vers 1350–1450.* Paris

Index

247

Index

Index

Index

BY THE SAME AUTHOR

The Social Organisation of the LoWiili, 1956, reprinted Oxford University Press, 1966

Death, Property and the Ancestors, Stanford University Press, 1962

Comparative Studies in Kinship, Routledge and Kegan Paul, 1969

Technology, Tradition and the State in Africa, Oxford University Press, 1971

The Myth of the Bagre, Clarendon Press, 1972

Production and Reproduction, Cambridge University Press, 1977

The Domestication of the Savage Mind, Cambridge University Press, 1977

The Récitation du Bagré, Armund Colin, 1981 (with S.W.D.K. Bandah)

EDITED BY J.R. GOODY

The Developmental Cycle in Domestic Groups, Cambridge University Press, 1958

Succession to High Office, Cambridge University Press, 1966

Salaga: the Struggle for Power (with J.A. Braimah), Longmans, 1967

Literacy in Traditional Societies, Cambridge University Press, 1968

Bridewealth and Dowry (with S.J. Tambiah), Cambridge University Press, 1973

The Character of Kinship, Cambridge University Press, 1974

Changing Social Structure in Ghana, International African Institute, 1975

Family and Inheritance: rural society in Western Europe, 1200–1800 (with J. Thirsk and E.P. Thompson), Cambridge University Press, 1976